Analyst–Patient Interaction

AF849636

Collected Papers on Technique

Michael Fordham
Edited by Sonu Shamdasani

Routledge
Taylor & Francis Group
LONDON AND NEW YORK

First published 1996
by Routledge
2 Park Square, Milton Park, Abingdon, Oxfordshire OX14 4RN

Simultaneously published in the USA and Canada
by Routledge
711 Third Avenue, New York, NY 10017

First issued in paperback 2014

Routledge is an imprint of the Taylor and Francis Group, an informa business

Typeset in Times by LaserScript, Mitcham, Surrey

British Library Cataloguing in Publication Data
A catalogue record for this book is available from the British Library

Library of Congress Cataloguing in Publication Data
A catalogue record for this book has been requested

ISBN 13: 978-1-138-87202-8 (pbk)
ISBN 13: 978-0-415-12184-2 (hbk)

Contents

Introduction 1
Sonu Shamdasani

1 **Notes on the transference (1957)** 12
2 **Counter-transference (1960)** 41
3 **Suggestions towards a theory of supervision (1961)** 49
4 **Reply to Dr Edinger (1961)** 57
5 **A comment on James Hillman's papers (1962)** 59
6 **Problems of a training analyst (undated)** 62
7 **Reflections on training analysis (1968)** 73
8 **Technique and counter-transference (1969)** 85
9 **Reply to Plaut's 'Comment' (1970)** 106
10 **The interrelation between patient and therapist (1972)** 110
11 **Jung's conception of transference (1974)** 114
12 **Defences of the self (1974)** 139
13 **Analyst–patient interaction (1975)** 147
14 **Discussion of Thomas B. Kirsch, 'The practice of multiple analysis in analytical psychology' (1976)** 157
15 **Analytical psychology and counter-transference (1979)** 161
16 **Contribution to symposium 'How do I assess progress in supervision?' (1982)** 177
17 **How I do analysis (1988)** 180
18 **Fordham's rejoinder to Spiegelman's comments (1988)** 186
19 **The supposed limits of interpretation (1991)** 188
20 **Rejoinder to Nathan Schwartz-Salant (1991)** 197
21 **On not knowing beforehand (1993)** 199

Sources 208
Bibliography 210
Index 215

Introduction

Sonu Shamdasani

It would not surprise many people if the *Collected Papers on Technique* of an analyst who started practising in the days before established training might have little interest today, in an age of increasing professionalisation and state legitimation. For those contemporary clinicians for whom the invention of new conceptual nomenclature spells more than the history of the field, such a volume might simply seem to indicate developmental positions that have long been superseded. That such is not the case stems not only from the significance of the transformation of practice and the new lines of theoretical articulations that these papers opened, but also from the clearsighted way in which they raise controversial issues and problematics that are by no means stilled. All the less reason, then, to be assured that one can skip over these papers in the belief that what is of value in them has already been assimilated and augmented in subsequent work by others. The controversies that still surround Michael Fordham's writings on technique attest to their significance. What makes them essential reading, irrespective of whether one agrees with their conclusions – and anyone who knows him will be familiar with the way he continually questions and reworks his previous conclusions – is that they have staked out inescapable markers in this field.

The papers themselves provide their best introduction and overview, particularly as the recapitulation of his previous views on topics to set the contours of new problematics is a rhetorical form that Fordham favours. Given this, I will leave my remarks here to marginal comments – rather than give a schematic account which is in some respects superfluous, and which would be hard placed to do justice to the careful and intricate elucidation, which is their strength.

Jung's work left an ambiguous legacy for his followers. Amongst the problematic issues that he raised for the 'practice of psychotherapy', to use the title of the relevant volume of his *Collected Works*, are the following: the relations between culture and therapy, between technique and spontaneity in practice, between 'reductive' and 'synthetic' methods in analysis; issues concerning individuation and the ends of analysis, democratic and aristocratic views of the suitability of different types of analysis; questions on the very possibility of technique, clinical theory, and the validity of diagnosis; theses on the merits of the use of the 'chair' as opposed to the 'couch'; the differences between free association, types of interpretation and active imagination – and all these shot through with an unabated mimetic rivalry in relation to Freud and psychoanalysis. It is important to note that one of the main areas of contention between Jung and Freud was the question of technique: for the theoretical modifications that Jung was introducing were leading to a changed conception of analytic technique. At the same time classical psychoanalytic technique was not simply rejected by Jung, but pragmatically relativised within a more pluralistic conception of therapy.

Jung was always interested in cases that were at the borders of what was considered analysable, as witnessed, for instance, by his early work with schizophrenia. His technical modifications may be seen to stem from problems posed by cases traditionally regarded as recalcitrant to what was being formulated as classical psychoanalytic technique – such as, 'psychotic', 'borderline' and elderly patients. For instance, in 1926 in 'The relations between the ego and the unconscious' (Jung, 1928, p. 130) Jung claimed that classical psychoanalytic technique was completely at a loss when it came to dealing with the problems posed by what he termed the archetypal transference – when larger than life images, such as that of saviours and devils, are projected onto the analyst. This was because for Jung such images did not have an 'origin' in a parental prototype, to which they could be traced back. He claimed that this explained numerous failures and relapses in psychoanalysis. His formulation of supplementary techniques, such as the synthetic method of interpretation, amplification and active imagination, were attempts to deal with such instances.

It was primarily Fordham who inherited and took on these aspects of Jung's estate, and who attempted to evaluate the clinical relevance of these technical innovations. This aspect of the transmission of the responsibility for clinical research is movingly brought out in one of Jung's letters to Fordham, on the topic of children's dreams, on which Jung lectured to his seminar group (Jung, 1987). Jung wrote:

> As I told you I know that it is a pity that I never found the time to do more work on children's 'great' dreams, but I'm afraid that if I should tackle such a job I would have to do it in a thorough way and for that purpose I would have to elaborate on a much bigger material. This task is definitely too much for me. I cannot think of beginning anything of such a kind as long as I'm not through with the work in hand, namely the Mysterium Coniunctionis. And what with my correspondence and all sorts of urgent things cropping up continually I just cannot see my way to anything so ambitious as a book about children's dreams. This would really be your province and I should like to persuade you to try your hand on such material. You are welcome to my material and I think you are in a position to add more to it. If you try it you will see that it is no easy thing, but tremendously interesting. For a time I was utterly fascinated by the beauty and profundity of such early childhood dreams. There I observed some

of the best examples of autochthonous reconstructions of archetypal ideas. Through your careful investigations of my books you have acquired enough orientation over the already existing material that could assist you in a thorough examination of children's dreams. For most of their collective symbolism you would have the amplifying material ready-made. I'm now at an age when it becomes unwise to continue the great adventure of pioneering research. I must leave the joy and the despair of it to younger forces.

(Jung to Fordham, February 22nd, 1952, private possession, Michael Fordham)[1]

When Fordham wrote his first papers on technique, it was not only the positions he took that aroused controversy in the Jungian world, but also whether technique was a subject that could be studied. In his Bailey Island seminar in 1936, whilst discussing the reasons why he felt that it was important for an individual to have an analyst of both sexes, Jung said:

but these are technical problems. I could give you a whole book about these peculiar technical secrets, but I cannot go into all that.

(Jung, 1936, p. 156)

For the classical school of Jungian analysis, these lacunae were made into a virtue. What Jung had not formulated was regarded as unformulatable. Further, it was claimed that the effects of formulations of technique would restrict the essential uniqueness of the analytic encounter. Fordham contested the representation of Jung's position that was used to support these claims. He further felt that this tendency had resulted in making analytical psychology into a quasi-religious cult, which he found unacceptable. He writes that his book *The Objective Psyche* (1958) was in part written to combat this tendency (Fordham, 1985, p. 2). Furthermore, he was critical of the standards of practice that at times such positions led to.

In his autobiography, Fordham assesses and discusses in detail his classical analyses with H. G. Baynes and with Hilda Kirsch. Whilst appreciative of them in many respects, Fordham suggests that it was particularly the problematic remainders of these analyses which guided his subsequent research interests. The difficulties that Fordham encountered were not wholly atypical of how classical Jungian analysis was then practised. In this respect, Fordham's work was a reformation. It is by and large the papers that follow that have significantly reorientated the practice of Jungian analysis since. Of his analyses Fordham wrote:

There were some consequences of my work with Baynes and Hilda Kirsch which were to prove important in directing my researches afterwards: neither analyst seemed to know how to analyse my childhood, nor did they understand about transference. I made both these fields of study my particular concern. Another effect was that I never used amplification as Baynes had done with me, and indeed largely eliminated it from my practice. Finally there was the

> influence of being published as a case: nearly all the case material I published was material collected from children – they could not be identified as I could be in Baynes book, *Mythology of the Soul*. I think that I did not publish much material from my adult cases because of this, although I think this was mistaken.
>
> (Fordham, 1993, p. 74)

Baynes had published Fordham's material in his *Mythology of the Soul*. This contains no statements concerning the transference, and Fordham's material veritably drowns in the midst of the endless mythological parallels. This, then, was a telling and instructive counter-examplar for Fordham.

Most of these papers were written when Fordham was in the process of editing the *Collected Works* of Jung and, in the process, helping to shape what has come to be the 'English Jung'. (Much of the editorial work and selection of volumes was not only carried over into the translations of Jung into other languages, but was also carried over into the 'original' German edition.) They were the first to embark on an elucidation of Jung's writings on the practice of therapy. Fordham's paper on Jung's concept of the transference still remains the most lucid exposition of the subject to date. This elucidation was by no means a subject that was dealt with once and for all, but is a continual preoccupation of Fordham's work. Hence in one of his recent papers, Fordham returns to some of Jung's cases, to study how he proceeded in practice (Fordham, 1989).

Fordham's strategy in relation to Jung's theory and practice of therapy is threefold. First, by means of personal contact, and a gathering of anecdotes of Jung's practice, Fordham extrapolates Jung's mode of proceeding in varied situations, particularly in therapeutic consultations, which forms a counterpoint to his writings on the subject. (Fordham, 1975, 1978, ch. 11). Second, Fordham elucidates Jung's complex theoretical models of the transference, and his various, and at times contradictory, views of its significance, and directions as to its handling. And third, Fordham subjects both of these to a clinical appraisal in the light of his own practice, and comparatively in relation to current views of practice.

This threefold strategy forms a model of what may be described as a clinical-historical approach; and this intertwining of the clinical and historical is distinctive throughout these papers, and clearly distinguishes them from the prevailing ahistoricism of the clinical field. Fordham likens this situation to 'giving our attention to the end branches of a tree without looking at its trunk, let alone its roots' (Fordham, 1989, p. 213). Psychoanalysis and analytical psychology as theories and practices stand in a special relation to their forebears – and for Fordham, a neglecting of this dimension forsakes the specificity of the field.

In his laudatory introduction to Fordham's collection of papers, *New Developments in Analytical Psychology*, Jung wrote of Fordham's papers that:

> every single one of them is so carefully thought out that the reader can hardly avoid holding a conversation with it. I do not mean in a polemical sense, but

> rather in the sense of affirmation and in the desire to carry the objective discussion a stage further and collaborate on the solution of the problems involved.
>
> (Jung in Fordham, 1957, p. xi)

Jung's dialogical reading trope is significant, as he especially singled out Fordham's 'Notes on transference' for special merit:

> The paper on transference merits attentive reading. Dr Fordham guides his reader through the multifarious aspects of this 'problem with horns' – to use an expression of Nietzsche's – with circumspection, insight and caution, as befits this in every respect delicate theme. The problem of the transference occupies a central position in the dialectical process of analytical psychology and therefore merits quite special interest. . . . The author takes full account of the overriding importance of this phenomenon and accordingly devotes to it a particularly attentive and careful exposition. The practising psychologist would be very wrong if he thought he could dismiss general considerations of this kind based on broader principles, and dispense with all deeper reflection.
>
> (ibid., p. xii)

Fordham's paper leads Jung to some of his last reflections on the problemata of the handling of the transference, and its relation to authority, technique, individuation and healing. These reflections indicate the reciprocality, and far reaching mutuality of the dialogue between Jung and Fordham on the issue of the transference.

For Fordham, clarification of Jung's ideas on the practice of psychotherapy was urgently required due to the poor quality of the reading of Jung that was taking place, as much within as outside of analytical psychology. Within analytical psychology, Fordham claimed that 'Jung's statements had become erroneously generalized and even dogmatized without justification' (this volume, p. 28). This clarification of Jung's ideas should be of more interest than simply that of an intradisciplinary affair within analytical psychology. Through complex political and institutional processes that have yet to be adequately recognised, let alone mapped, the reading of Jung by psychoanalysts, which is still largely regarded as being off limits, has often been conducted in secrecy. The significance of Jung's ideas for the general psychotherapeutic field has by and large been denied; their precedence has been unacknowledged through being unrealised, as well as through straightforward plagiarism. Fordham's clarification of Jung's ideas on therapy thus has a great significance for a general psychotherapeutic audience today, as he claims that many of Jung's seminal insights concerning the analytic encounter have subsequently been developed by psychoanalysts, without any reference to Jung. In his review of Robert Langs' *The Therapeutic Interaction*, Fordham listed six instances of this:

1 The concept of analysis as a dialectical procedure.
2 That the analysis is as much in the analyst as the patient.

3 That for changes to take place in a patient, an analyst may need to change as well.
4 That resistances in the patient can be created by the analyst.
5 That the analyst introjects the patient's psychopathology.
6 The personal influence of the analyst in producing therapeutic effects

(Fordham, 1978a, pp. 195–6)

Whether or not this situation continues and, by corollary, whether Fordham's work will gain the recognition it surely deserves in the field of analytic psychotherapy as a theoretician on technique of the first rank, consists in whether those in the field are content simply to inherit and reduplicate the pernicious politics of its history.

The question of transference and countertransference was a central research topic in the early days of the Society of Analytical Psychology. This was the specific focus of what was known as the transference groups. In his chairman's address at the society's AGM in July 1954, Fordham noted:

> A new sign of activity within the society has been the continued interest in the transference, round which is circulating some of the conflicts within the society. If my reading of these conflicts is correct, they turn on the question, not of the existence of transference phenomena, but upon the desirability, or otherwise, of interpreting some of them in personal terms, and on the ways of handling and reacting to transpersonal contents. These I believe to be fruitful conflicts because they are ones capable of conceptual and methodological solution. The transference groups are, however, not just composed of persons interested in a topic; they are the equivalent of the growing vitality of committee members.
>
> (Fordham, 1954, p. 3)

The minutes in Fordham's possession cover sixteen meetings from October 1953 to February 1954. The members of this group were Hella Adler, Frieda Fordham, Michael Fordham, Alfred Plaut, Gordon Stuart Prince, Mary Stein, Ruth Strauss and Mary Williams. These minutes, which were written in rotation by the members, give an unparalleled glimpse of the creative and dialogical way that research into the transference was conducted on a group level, as well as making for entertaining and often humorous reading.

The symposium on training in 1961–2 was the first held on this topic in analytical psychology. The debates originally raised there in the form of 'Zürich vs London' remain at issue currently in the different training groups and their relation to other organizations. In her editorial introduction to the symposium on supervision in the *Journal of Analytical Psychology* in 1982, Judith Hubback wrote in relation to the earlier symposium:

> Over twenty years have passed since that discussion, and experience has accumulated; yet many of the issues raised then in respect of the general subject of training are very much alive.
>
> (Hubback, 1982, p. 103)

The significant way that changed conceptions of technique led to the adoption of different procedures of training is described in the papers included here on training and supervision.

Fordham's papers, with their microscopic accounts of the analyst–patient interaction, were not without very large political and institutional effects, which form their backdrop. In the history of the Jungian movement, London has been the home of not only the debate and the question of technique, but also of the *multiplicatio* of institutions, with currently four internationally recognised training societies, each with different training policies. Fordham provides his own account of this (Fordham, 1979, pp. 50–3). The history of these institutional splits has yet to be written. It is clear, though, that issues around technique played, and still play, a major role. Such a history would no doubt shed an interesting light on the complex interrelations of technique, transference and institutional politics.

That technique should be one of the main research areas in the early days of the Society of Analytical Psychology is due to the fact that the issue of how training was to be conducted is inseparable from the question of the possibility of technique, which underlies the possibility of transmissibility. Fordham states 'the issue centred on whether the practice of therapy can be taught'. Fordham conceives of their linkage in the following manner:

> Technique, it will be conceded, involves reliable knowledge that can be communicated to candidates who under optimal conditions acquire it. As our knowledge of technique progresses and as we know more and more about the dynamics of the analytical situation, so our training improves and trainees start off from a better position as analysts.
>
> (this volume, p. 92)

Thus questions of supervision, training and technique are inextricably interlinked. A crucial question running throughout all of this is the question of the relation between analytical psychology and psychoanalysis. Is there a specificity to analytical psychology, such that it requires a different form of training from psychoanalysis? What relevance to the question of training do differing views of the psyche have? These issues are debated in these papers. One of the upshots of this was the rejection by the Society of Analytical Psychology of training procedures that were being adopted at that time in the Jung Institute in Zürich, such as the practice of multiple analysis, the use of an academic curriculum with examinations, and the lack of a distinction between analysis and supervision. For Fordham, analytical psychology, which was in many ways defining itself negatively against psychoanalysis, was falling prey to precisely those aspects of the institutional politics of psychoanalysis that Jung had critiqued. Fordham pointed out that:

> ironically there has grown up a very strong tendency to develop the very dogmatism amongst analytical psychologists against which he [Jung] took such a strong stand.
>
> (this volume, p. 87)

In his obituary of Jung, Fordham wrote that:

> His name is still almost automatically linked with that of Freud as most nearly Freud's equal, and if his main life's work was in the end to be founded on a personal and scientific incompatibility with Freud, there are those who believe, like myself, that this was a disaster, and in part an illusion, from which we suffer and will continue to do so until we have repaired the damage.
>
> (Fordham, 1961, p. 167)

This was a brave statement to make, and context in which to make it. As a consequence of this stance, Fordham has at times met with a great deal of enmity in the Jungian world, leading Carl Meier to describe him as being the person who had carried the Jungian shadow for forty years. In moving much closer to the procedures of training and modes of practice concurrent in psychoanalysis, a significant shift in the mimetic relation of analytical psychology to psychoanalysis was made and, in particular, the oppositional logic by which analytical psychologists defined themselves in relation to psychoanalysts was breached. In rejecting the specific training procedures adopted in Zürich, it could be argued that what were also being rejected were attempts to establish a specificity for analytical psychology by means of constructing the identity of a closed field, that was not sufficiently open to dialogue and interchange with its others, in this case primarily psychoanalysis. However, such a move on the part of analytical psychologists is not without attendant dangers, theoretically and institutionally, of an erasure of difference, and a homogenisation, which at times has been motivated by issues of prestige and acceptance in the predominately psychoanalytic orientation of the psychotherapeutic field. Might such a situation result in the history of analytical psychology ending up as a curious, supplemental chapter in the history of psychoanalysis? Work needs to be done on the relation of how the policies and issues discussed here were related to the institutional history of psychoanalysis. Plaut recalls the early days of the Society of Analytical Psychology as follows:

> We would constantly ask, 'What does the Institute of Psychoanalysis say or do in this matter?' . . . they were clearly the administrative and ideological model for the Society for a very long time and I don't think it's quite over yet.
>
> (Samuels, 1989, p. 170)

Psychoanalytic institutes have at times furnished Jungian institutes as the ideal exemplars and counterexemplars. The resultant double binds have not been without effects. Theoretically, this is also at stake in the issue of inter-theory translation. It was Fordham who in many ways enabled analytical psychologists to have access to the developments of psychoanalysis, and provided a glossary for terminological translations. Some of this work is distilled in a list of correspondences between Jung and Klein, in Fordham's paper 'Some historical reflections' (Fordham, 1989). He wrote:

The following is a list of correspondences between the formulations of Jung and Klein. I have no intention of suggesting that the comparisons are more than indicative.

JUNG	KLEIN
Archetypes	Unconscious fantasy
Primitive identity	Paranoid-schizoid position
Empathy and alchemy	Projective identification
Concept building etc.	Epistemophilic instinct
Inner world primary datum	Inner world primary
Symbol-making basic	Symbol-making essential to thought
The two mothers	Good and bad mothers (breasts)
Heroic feats	Manic defence
Separation, individuation	Depressive position
Self and opposites	Operation of love and hate

(Fordham, 1989, pp. 223–4)

Fordham further reflects on these parallels in his unpublished paper 'The Jung–Klein hybrid' (Fordham, 1990). These conceptual bridges made possible positions of hybridity for analytical psychologists, both theoretically and on the level of identity. This is illustrated by the way that some in the United States now term themselves 'Jungian psychoanalysts'. At the same time, Fordham is aware of some of the dangers of this situation. Concerning self psychology he wrote:

> The recent studies of narcissistic disorders by psychoanalysts with the introduction of self theory has some striking similarities with my own conclusions studying the same field, but I would not have thought of the conditions described as being primarily narcissistic. In so far as many of the features are evidently narcissistic – the grandiose self and the mirror transference as described by Kohut – I would agree, but I would be disposed to interpret the narcissism as a manifestation of an introversion neurosis and to conclude that the narcissism comes about through identification with the often exalted images derived from the archetypes of the collective unconscious. I do not want to argue again the long contested question about the nature of the libido, but only wish to point out that psychoanalysts can use the extended theory of narcissism because of the sexual theory of the libido. Consequently any inturning libido is automatically narcissistic. For Jung the libido was not exclusively sexual and so narcissism cannot be used in the same extended sense.
>
> (Fordham, 1985, p. 95)

Fordham's distinction between narcissistic features and conditions is an attempt to distinguish between similarity on a descriptive level and concomitant theoretical commitments, which are often collapsed. The issues here discussed in terms of the 'Jung and Klein' and 'Jung and Kohut' have ramifications beyond purely the issue of the relative merits of these linkages, and concern the problematics of inter-theory translation in general.

Fordham's work on technique, when coupled with his pioneering work on childhood and child analysis, made possible one of his most important institutional achievements: the founding of the Child Analytic Training at the Society of Analytical Psychology. This was the first of its kind in analytical psychology. An account of its early history is given by Dorothy Davidson in the issue of the *Journal of Analytical Psychology* devoted to Fordham and his work (Davidson, 1986). Fordham gives a moving account of the antagonisms on the part of his colleagues that he had to contend with in this area (Fordham, M. 1976). The reciprocal interrelation of Fordham's work in this area, and his work on technique, is borne out by the impact of the Child Analytic Training infant observations seminars on him, and how these have led him in turn to revise his understanding of development and, following from this, the handling of regressed states in analysis.

A difficulty in the selection of articles for this collection is that in a way all of Fordham's works are about analytic technique, understood in a broad sense, or have crucial implications for it. Moreover, given Fordham's views on the significance of childhood development, and the increasing part that this has played in his changing conceptions of analytic technique, his writings in these areas can hardly be overlooked if one is to form an adequate apprehension of his views on technique. Thus the selection has been governed by the criteria of the overt thematisation of issues related to technique. The collection provides markers for the progression of Fordham's writings in this area. However, the framing effect of this collection has dangers if it is seen as a closed and well-sealed vessel, containing the essential on the subject. The one exception to this policy is that material has not been reproduced from Fordham's *Jungian Psychotherapy*, as this is still in print, and inclusion would have entailed incorporating the bulk of the volume. May it suffice to indicate that it contains crucial material on technique, as well as being one of the best introductions to psychotherapy as a whole.

These papers set a standard and a model of clarity for clinical writing in their taut, austere and classical composition. This clarity does not imply simplicity. The complexity and continual refinement of Fordham's thought may be seen in the subtle shifts of emphasis and redefinitions as one reads through this collection. The apparent similarity of theme and subject matter often cloaks radical new departures and shifts of emphasis. Fordham's early work on training and technique has a certain ideality in tone, which reflects the struggle towards first formulations; this gives way in his later work to a more nuanced sense of formulating problematics as they arise in the actualities of the clinical situation, through which many of his earlier formulations are realigned. The lack of fanfare that accompanies these papers perhaps in some measure accounts for the fact that they have yet to receive the recognition they deserve. Thus, for example, Fordham's elucidation of the notion of the pathological nexus between therapist and patient in 'Reflections on training analysis', which is important in understanding the iatrogenic effects of analysis, pressingly calls for further research. The material reproduced from the different versions of 'Analytical psychology and countertransference' indicates the understated way in which Fordham has introduced major shifts in orientation, which those who take their point of departure from his work have not always realised. Hence, for example, the continued currency of Fordham's concept of the syntonic counter-transference, long after he had abandoned its use. This paper also highlights how Fordham's work provides a critical evaluation of the current state of psychotherapy. In 1979, in the face of the veritable rage and overextension of the use of the term counter-transference, Fordham argued that it had outgrown its usefulness, and urged its restriction. Fordham claimed that it had served its purpose:

> I believe the theory of counter-transference has performed its main function. It has had the desirable effect of taking analysts out of their ivory tower, making it possible for them to compare notes on what they actually do during analytic psychotherapy.
>
> (this volume, p. 171)

By underscoring the therapeutic value and strategic usefulness of a 'discarded' theory to analysts as a whole, Fordham does for the history of analytic technique what the theory of counter-transference had originally done for practice – in recuperating the use-value in what would previously have been simply discarded as error.

At the time of writing, Fordham is enjoying a vigorous old age – in his own view, practising better than ever, writing, receiving numerous visitors, committed as much as ever to the research and spirit of investigation that have guided his life work. The themes of these papers are continually being reworked, and prevailing therapeutic opinions revoked. This ceaseless sifting, and refinement of listening, is perhaps their greatest gift.

Sonu Shamdasani

NOTE

1 I thank the Erbengemeinschaft C. G. Jung for permission to quote this letter.

POSTSCRIPT, 1995

Whilst this work was in press, Michael Fordham died in his sleep at the age of 89 after a brief hospitalisation. He had continued practising, writing and receiving visitors until then.

Chapter 1

Notes on the transference (1957)

PART 1. INTRODUCTION

In his foreword to 'Psychology of the transference' Jung says: 'The reader will not find an account of the clinical phenomena of the transference in this book. It is not intended for the beginner, who would first have to be instructed in such matters, but is addressed exclusively to those who have already gained sufficient experience in their own practice' (Jung, 1946, p. 165).

It is nothing short of astonishing to find how little has been published in the past about the clinical transference experiences that Jung presupposes in his essay. There is no reference to the subject in the index of Baynes' comprehensive series of case studies, *Mythology of the Soul*, nor does Frances G. Wickes make specific reference to it in her book, *The Inner World of Man*, while J. Jacobi devotes to it only a cursory discussion in her authoritative work, *The Psychology of C. G. Jung*. Recently, however, papers by Gerhard Adler, Henderson, Moody, Plaut, L. Stein and myself (1957b) have appeared, and these have begun the filling-in of Jung's outline, which this essay continues. Here I shall discuss those aspects of the transference that have struck me as especially significant because they have given rise to discussion among trainee analysts and colleagues. I have not attempted to define the term in detail, since this has been done already by Stein (1955a), and it is only necessary to state that it will be used here in a wide sense to cover the contents of the analytic relationship.

Jung, in his writings upon the transference, lays special emphasis upon the part played by the personality of the analyst in any analysis. This was first expressed when he was a psychoanalyst; he then proposed that all analysts should undergo a training analysis, and he has since stressed it over and over again. His view appears to have stemmed from the association experiments, for Baynes, who should be in a good position to know, says (1950, p. 108):

> Jung discovered the unavoidable influence of this personal factor when experimenting with word association tests. He found that the personality and sex of the experimenter introduced an incalculable factor of variation. . . . Jung realized that it was quite impossible to exclude the personal equation in any psychological work. He accordingly decided to take it fully into account.

Much of Jung's behaviour arises out of this 'discovery': the relatively informal setting, the use of two chairs with the analyst sitting in front of the patient (since modified) and the axiom that the analyst is just as much in the analysis as the patient, lead inevitably, in any thorough analysis, to his divesting himself of his persona; he is enjoined to react with his personality as a whole to the patients in analysis. It is manifest that only those with a differentiated personality can do this without making nonsense of the whole procedure, for an analyst's attitude and behaviour need to accord with what he says and, since he will be drawn into the state of primitive identity with his patient, it is essential for him to be conscious of his primitive reactions. It is this that makes a long and thorough personal analysis an absolute prerequisite for all analytical psychologists who wish to become practising analysts.

It is Jung's thesis that there is a therapeutic content in the analyst's personality. This cannot be just his consciousness; indeed, it is the unconscious that is far the more important in this respect, and so his theory of transpersonal archetypes may be expected to orientate us here. With it we can explain why the patient apparently calls out suitable or adapted therapeutic reactions in the analyst which, together with the unadapted ones of the patient, form the main substance of all intense transferences. It is, further, the analyst's archetypal reactions that form the basis of his technique, which without them must lack all true effectiveness. Thus Jung's theory has deepened our understanding of the 'incalculable factor' to which Baynes referred, converting it into a definable class of personal and transpersonal functions whose further investigation is thus made possible.

The distinction between the personal and the transpersonal unconscious, made by Jung in order to demarcate his investigations from those of Freud, is extremely subtle, and it is impossible to agree to the setting up of clear dividing line between the two, for many personal relationships, particularly those of transference type, express archetypal forms, and *vice versa*. Consequently, though the distinction is useful in other fields of study, I have found it better, in describing the transference, to conceive of a single unity that appears in consciousness in either personal or transpersonal form, or in both. The objective quality of experience, described as part of the numinous archetypal images, cannot be overlooked in any of the transference manifestations, and this is true in whichever form they appear. It is this that makes the study of the analyst–patient relationship so fascinating and rewarding.

From this complex relationship it results that both analyst and patient are laying the foundations of an increase in consciousness of all the innumerable psychic experiences that emerge out of the unconscious within the transference. By being analysed, all the patient's personal relationships are affected, particularly his capacity to handle interpersonal affects more fruitfully, by distinguishing between what is within and what is beyond the powers of his ego to control and manipulate.

Those outside the control of the ego comprise the contents of the transpersonal or objective transference that forms the subject-matter of Jung's essay on the transference in the individuation process. Yet even though they may be recognized as transpersonal they frequently, indeed more often than not, are first experienced personally.

The recent renewal of interest in the transference among analytical psychologists has given rise to uncertainty as to its place and importance in the analytical process. This would appear to centre on whether there are psychotherapeutic methods in which it does not occur.

Studying Jung's ideas on this topic makes it clear that he believes the bulk of psychotherapeutic procedures do not involve transference analysis, and in many of his essays the argument does not take the transference much into account.

He divides treatment up in various ways and specifies his own contribution in a variety of styles, but he is constant in holding that methods and techniques such as confession, suggestion, advice, elucidation, and education all aim at making the patient more normal, and he links this up with the needs of the majority of patients and particularly those in the first half of life. These, if they need analytic treatment, should be treated by the methods of psychoanalysis, which is classed a method of elucidation or interpretation of the unconscious process, based on a general theoretical outlook, or individual psychology, essentially an educational procedure aiming to socialize the individual.

But those methods are not valid with the class of patients to whom normality is meaningless and of whom individual development is, so to say, demanded. With these patients all methods must be abandoned 'since individuality . . . is absolutely unique, unpredictable and uninterpretable, in these cases the therapist must abandon all his preconceptions and techniques and confine himself to a purely dialectical procedure, adopting the attitude that shuns all methods' (1935, pp. 7, 8). Then the patient's psychical system becomes 'geared to mine [Jung's] and acts upon it; my reaction is only thing with which I as an individual can confront my patient' (*Ibid.*, p. 5).

For a long time Jung found great difficulty in describing what happened when the patient's and the analyst's psyches were geared together. In 1931 he wrote (p. 51): 'Although I travelled this path with individual patients many times, I have never yet succeeded in making all the details of the process clear enough for publication. So far this has been fragmentary only'. Later on this gap was filled in to some extent by 'Psychology of the transference'.

I surmise that Jung's difficulty arose from emphasizing the highly individual nature of the process; indeed, if the individuality is 'unique, unpredictable and uninterpretable' it is also indescribable in general terms. When, therefore, Jung wrote an essay on the transference in individuation, using alchemical myths to do so, he must have decided that it was possible to generalize. His decision can be understood only by realizing that as the result of abandoning preconceptions and setting the individual in the centre of consciousness a very general process begins to operate, as indeed the theory of compensation postulates. It is the general processes that he describes.

In various places Jung recognizes that the transference can become a central feature in any analysis, for instance in his qualified agreement with Freud that the transference 'was the alpha and omega of the analytic method' (1946, p. 172), but he came to regard the transference in psychoanalysis as different from that which developed in the individuation process because of the different attitude of the analyst towards the patient.

The value of Jung's differentiation between patients who require treatments that aim at normality and those who seek individuation is useful, but has its limitations. It could blind us to realizing that in the first class of case individual characteristics cannot be lacking, and that the individuating case not infrequently shows signs of needing to be more normal. My analytic studies of children forced me to see this in a surprising way, for I found that the attitude that Jung defined as correct for patients embarking on individuation was just the attitude that led to developments in the ego in children. A direct relation between analyst and child was indeed essential. This consideration first based on individual analysis of children, was then supported by an opportunity provided during the last war when hostels were organized for difficult children. There I was fortunate enough to observe the remarkable work of one matron whose capacity for establishing a direct therapeutic relation with the children in her care rendered it possible for her to relax imposed discipline to a far greater extent than would otherwise have been possible. She became a 'fellow passenger in the process of individual development' that occurred in each child.

These observations naturally surprised me, but then I began to see that there was something essentially the same in all my analytic procedure. I had basic 'belief' in the individual of whatever age, and began to criticize the attitudes described by Jung as methods or techniques of interpretation and education because they seemed to be imposed on patients. I came to consider that it was not necessary to impose adaptation on a younger personality or an unadapted one, because the aim of the young individual or the unadapted person was in any case to do what other people did, i.e. his natural aim was to become normal or adapted.

Later I came to see that the archetypes have a special relation to ego development (1957b), and this led me to examine closely the significance of archetypal forms in the interpersonal transference relationship formed by younger people. I soon realized with particular force that archetypal activity in a young patient took on a more personal form than in the second half of life, and that in consequence it was to be found in the transference projected on to the analyst. These projections call forth a response in the analyst that leads to the condition of primitive identity with the patient, out of which a stronger ego can develop (*ibid.*, p. 108). This conclusion led to my giving more emphasis to the value of analysis in the first half of life than is generally current in analytical psychology.

The position would seem to differ where individuation in its proper sense begins, for this process presupposes that the problem is not one of developing the ego but of differentiating it from and bringing it into relation with the unconscious out of which the self appears as an experience apart from the ego. It presupposes that the patient has reached the stage at which his vocational aims are satisfied and spiritual problems are pressing to the fore (cf. Henderson, 1955).

In these circumstances the transference can take on the more obscure, less intense, more collective, transpersonal, even social form. But even here the reactions of the analyst, while they are different because inevitably orientated in the direction of individuation, are no less important.

It appears to me consistent with Jung's position to state the basis for my own analytic work by asserting that 'I believe in the individual'. This gives me a certain detachment from my belief and makes it possible to develop it into a theory and then proceed to investigate the transference in the light of it. For if my theory be correct, then absence of manifest transference in younger people must be due to insufficient appreciation by the analyst in the first place and later by the patient of what he is doing.

That the transference develops under special circumstances will be generally agreed. In this paper these will be considered first, before the content of the relationship between analyst and patient is gone into. Though I recognize that there is no clear line of demarcation between the formal setting of analysis and its content, and that the two interact, yet this distinction is useful. Thus the frequency of interviews, the naturalness or artificiality of the situation, the way in which the patient's libido is deployed (discussed below under the heading 'Energy distribution') all depend upon the transference of the patient and the reactions of the analyst, to be discussed under the heading of 'Counter-transference'. None the less I have designed this paper with the contrast in mind, as the reader will find if he follows the headings of the sections into which the text is divided.

PART II. GENERAL CONSIDERATIONS

The analytic interview

Analytic interviews consist in the regular meeting of two people for an agreed period, it being assumed that one of them, the patient, wants to come enough to repeat his visit, while the other, the analyst, agrees to put himself, his experience, his knowledge, and all his attention at the patient's disposal for this agreed period. The analyst was once himself a patient; he has been analysed as part of his training experience, and through this experience he knows what it is like to be on the other side of the bargain. He also has knowledge, acquired during his training, and techniques that are going to be useful in what follows. It can be assumed that his training will have made it possible for him not to use his techniques to interfere in the 'alchemical' process that will gradually involve patient and analyst more and more. The analyst will know that every single statement he makes is an account of the state of his psyche, whether it be a fragment of understanding, an emotion, or an intellectual insight; all techniques and all learning how to analyse are built on this principle. It is thus part of the analyst's training experience to realize that he is going to learn, sometimes more, sometimes less, from each patient, and that in consequence he himself is going to change (cf. Jung 1931a).

The patient's position is in many respects similar to the analyst's, for everything he says will be treated as an expression of his psyche; he also will be using techniques, though less refined ones; he also will be using his understanding and employing his insight, in relation not only to himself but also to his analyst. The essential difference between patient and analyst is to be sought not in these spheres, but in the patient's greater distress, his lesser awareness, and his greater need to increase his consciousness so as to change himself and his way of life. It is not to be sought in the absence of involvement in the process on the part of the analyst. Analytical psychologists all follow Jung in rejecting the idea that the analyst can possibly act only as a projection screen.

Though the analysis starts on a simple basis, the interviews soon become filled with the complexities that form the subject of the bulk of this paper. Here it need only be said that the complexity is brought about by the specific aim of investigating the unconscious. This conscious aim has archetypal roots and so has a long historical background, originating in the earliest initiation ceremonies and proceeding through religion, mysticism and alchemy to their more scientific, analytic equivalent. It is, however, important to keep firmly in mind the simple basis of the interview and to maintain it by such arrangements as keeping the time and frequency of interviews relatively stable. The stable form then becomes an expression of the analyst's reliability when all else is in a state of flux. The simple outline gives a frame of reference to which fantasies, projections and speculations can be referred.

'Naturalness' versus 'artificiality' of the transference

The definable basis of the analytic interview may be seen as embodying the naturalness with which the analyst meets the patient, but the recurrent discussion of whether the transference is natural or artificial covers a wider field. The constant preoccupation of analysts with 'naturalness' springs from the ascetic nature of analysis. Analysts are subject to the reproach of unnaturalness because of the sexual tensions aroused in the patient, who reproaches the analyst for his 'unnatural behaviour'. This reproach, however, usually springs from a projection of incest fantasies, which the patient misunderstands and wishes to act out. The antithesis could be stated in another way by considering how far the analyst's technique induces the transference and how far it is the inevitable consequence of two people meeting together under the conditions just described. Since the meaning of technique will only appear later the vaguer definition of the issue will here be adhered to.

In the essay already referred to, Jung makes it clear that he regards the transference as a 'natural' phenomenon, by which he means that it is not peculiar to the analytic relationship, but can be clearly observed in all social life. Jung's view is without doubt supported by many observations and by comparison with other relationships all confirming the application of his theory of archetypes to the transference: since archetypes occur within the transference and in many spheres of life, so that they are general phenomena, the transference must partake in this general phenomenon. Yet in regarding analysis as the equivalent of these social situations, it must at the same time not be overlooked that in none of them is so much attention given to the psyche of two persons under relatively standard conditions, and in none of them is so much effort expended in undoing resistances. Furthermore, in other personal relations and social situations little effort is devoted to finding out what is going on in them, and so the main bulk of the energy bound up in them remains unconscious. In this sense the word 'artificial' might be appropriate, but only with the qualification that the patient comes because of the distortion of his personality, which has been induced by failures in his development. It is this 'artificial' distortion that analysis of the transference seeks to correct, and therefore what is 'artificial' in the analysis is more than matched by what is distorted in the patient, particularly at the beginning of any analysis; but the distortions progressively lessen as the analysis proceeds, until at its ideal termination all residues of frustration will be dissolved by the patient leaving his analyst. Then the simple basis of the whole process from which the analysis began can once again be clearly envisaged by the patient.

Analysis and life

Closely related to the discussion of whether the transference is 'natural' or 'artificial' is the question of how it is related to something broadly termed 'life', by which is usually meant all the patient's everyday activities, other than his analysis, which get related to what is 'natural'.

Henderson (op. cit.) implies that almost the whole psyche of a patient becomes concentrated in analysis, so that 'life' would theoretically almost cease while the personality is being transformed. Because of this he finds it necessary to posit a post-analysis period in which a new adaptation to life by the new personality is achieved.

My experience does not accord with this view. It is true that if a satisfactory result is to be achieved, many changes in the life of the individual are inevitable; but these take place step by step during the analysis rather than after it, and life continues, reflecting the changes that are continuously taking place within the analytic transference. The type and degree of change vary according to the subject's character; the outward changes are likely to be greater in younger persons and in the more severely neurotic or psychotic patients, whose aim, as Henderson has pointed out, is vocational rather than spiritual. It is in the patients for whom individuation or the formation of a philosophy of life is the main issue that outward changes tend to be less in evidence.

There are two basic considerations that need to be taken into account.

1 The patient comes with a presenting symptom for which he seeks a solution. It is the aim of the analyst to elucidate this, and one of the results of this process is the development of a transference in which the energy previously directly into the symptom is now transferred to the person of the analyst.
2 The problem then is how to handle and ultimately resolve the transference.

As we shall later detail, most of the material revealed in the transference is not of a kind that could lead to satisfactory living, for otherwise it would not have given rise to the symptoms, but rather is made up of just those parts of the personality that are unadapted to life. Therefore when Jacobi (1951, p. 85) states that Jung 'holds an "attachment" to a third person, for example, in the form of a "love affair", to be quite a suitable basis for the analytical solution of neurosis' she appears to misunderstand the nature and importance of transference and its relation to 'life'. In general, if a patient is capable of sustaining a satisfying 'love affair', then the libido invested in it is not of the kind that needs development through transference analysis. Over and over again patients come for analysis just because their erotic experiences do not produce a solution of their neuroses, and only when the illusions contained in these 'affairs' are lived through in the transference, and nowhere else, can a solution be found.

I have taken up the supposed dichotomy - 'life' and analysis – because it is current among analysts, but it is only a rough distinction, for one of the essential qualities of the transference is its living dynamism. Here the question arises of whether analytic phenomena are induced or released. My contention is that they are released, and upon this view my thinking about transference is largely based.

Energy distributions

A study of the distribution of manifest energy released by analysis in relation to the interview bears upon such questions as interview frequency, fantasy, and active imagination, all of which are particularly relevant to analytical psychologists, if only because they have no prescribed standard of interview frequency but rather relate it to the varying needs of patients under different circumstances.

My usual practice is to start with three interviews a week increasing or reducing the number as occasion requires. Jung has prescribed specific frequencies for his individuating cases, whom he aims at putting in a position to conduct their own analyses under his supervision. This subject will be taken up later, though his definite statement that he aims at reducing interviews in his cases has led me to the following considerations.

Let us now consider two extreme cases, one in which the main bulk of the analysis is conducted in the interview, the other in which the interview is supervisory and the main bulk of the manifest activity is expressed in active imagination and dream analysis outside the interview. Since the duration of an analysis can be important, the comparison is useful in seeing that the time available for study of the imaginative and dream products is vastly greater in the second case, and it might be thought that the analysis would be shortened. Since, however, all the time spent on dream and fantasy may depend upon an unrealized projection upon the analyst, and since this drives the patient to produce enough material to fill the interview with reports of dream and fantasy, the duration of the analysis can easily be considerably increased rather than shortened, as is sometimes held by analytical psychologists.

It is the consideration of these defensive uses of dream and fantasy that makes it useful to distinguish between behaviour in the interview and the reporting of what has gone on outside it; this covers all that the patient tells the analyst about himself, his relation to other people in his environment, his dreams, his inner world as exemplified in fantasy, day-dreaming, or active imagination. Using this distinction it is then easier to perceive when the patient is referring to the analyst in talking about somebody else, or when what he tells is conditioned by his attitude to the analyst, so that sometimes the very reporting of material is conditioned solely by the patient's attitude to the analyst.

A young man who was having difficulties in talking during his interviews reported that between them he could converse easily with an imaginary analyst whom he identified with me. In these conversations he would prepare what he was going to say to me in the interview, but when he attempted to put his plan into operation, the thoughts were replaced by various other interests, or there were no thoughts at all. It would seem that most of what is usually called analysis in its positive sense was, in his case, conducted outside the interview, the whole time in the latter being spent in analysing the resistance that conditioned this state of affairs. Since this was very strong no apparent progress was made for a long time.

This example shows clearly how much more energy can be expended outside the interviews than in them, but as the analysis of my patient's resistance progressed the situation began to change so that the imaginary figure became a less prominent feature and it became easier for the patient to talk openly to me. He then spent less time conducting his analysis outside the interviews. This I regarded as a favourable development.

Gerhard Adler, in his paper 'On the archetypal content of transference', describes the phenomena in reverse. He cites a woman patient whose relation to him during interviews could be divided into two parts; the first positive, in which she played the role of a good daughter, the second negative, in which she entered into an aggressively-toned conflict with him. She then went away into the country, and there painted a picture in which a sado-masochistic pattern was depicted; this led on to an animus figure that revealed a vision of the self as a fantasy of the inner cosmos; all these developed away from the interviews. Adler believes that the transference, which continued between interviews, acted as a container (transcendent transpersonal temenos) inside which these events could happen.

Because Adler was aiming to show how the personal was transcended by the archetypal transference and because the case was one in which the individuation process had been constellated there was no necessity to enter into the motives for experiencing fantasies away from the interview. But had an analysis of these been necessary he would have been led to consider the tendency of depressive patients to split their love-hate conflicts so as to internalize the aggressive components that were so manifest in the picture and seemed to have disappeared from the transference. This might very well have proved important in leading to new developments in the transference of his patient, had he wished to investigate them.

It can happen that, if experiences of this type are not considered, the archetypal contents of the transference can dissolve the personal aspect of it, thus leading to depersonalizing defences. This is particularly liable to happen when the unconscious is active enough to give rise to frequent disturbances in consciousness during the patient's life away from the analytic interview. Probably the most important single consideration in avoiding such defences is for the patient to see that the image of the analyst does not disintegrate, melt away, or otherwise become inaccessible between interviews; none of these things appears to have happened in Adler's case or in my own.

To illustrate this depersonalizing defence I may instance a patient who had used active imagination in a previous analysis. She would come to see me with a book in which her dreams and active imaginations were written down, and would read out the experiences she had recorded and the thoughts she had accumulated, thus following a recommendation of Jung's (1931, p. 47f). When I came to make an interpretation I encountered strong defences, and I soon began to suspect that this technique was a means of ensuring that my influence was neutralized. Among the figures with which she conversed was a venerable 'wise old man' who almost invariably supported the patient in her own views and would sometimes tell her that what I had said in the last interview was wrong. It was not this, however, that struck me so much as the nature of the thoughts 'he' produced; they were in no respect unusual, so I asked why she could not think them for herself. My question led the patient to reveal that her 'active imagination' had started from a seminar at which she had been present, in which it had been asserted that active imagination was the be-all and end-all of Jungian analysis. As she had always, from childhood onwards, spent part of her life in an inner world, she took to this technique like a duck to water. She had further gained the impression that all Jungians thought better of people who presented their ideas in this form and that it was easier to contradict the analyst if she got a 'wise old man' to do it, as he would then be more impressed. Once this was revealed she was able to be more open with me, to react more immediately to my interpretations, and to spend her time outside the interviews in more useful occupations than making up fantasies with a view to controlling her analyst.

It will now be clear that, when we draw attention to the distribution of energy released by the analysis in relation to an interview, we are doing so with a view to studying the nature of the transference more carefully. The motives for this distribution are only to be brought to light in the end by realizing the nature of the face-to-face behaviour of analyst and patient in the interview itself; if this is overlooked it is only too easy for an impeccable 'technique' to become a defence against the very aim it was designed to achieve.

The whole trend of my patient's analysis was changed by the revelation of her defensive use of dream and fantasy; it turned into a process of testing what I could love, endure, or hate, while at the same time the trend of her life changed radically and her personal relationships were deepened and extended.

Such experiences have led me to consider all energy distributions and reporting in relation to the transference, and to believe that the omission of motives for telling anything to an analyst may open a rift in the analyst–patient relationship.

'Acting out'

It will now be apparent that the gradual development of an analysis can lead to the analyst's becoming the centre of it, so that the whole patient may become involved in the process of transformation. If, as sometimes happens, this concentration of libido is made into an aim, almost anything, whether adapted or not, that happens outside the transference in the life of the patient is considered undesirable. Those supposedly undesirable activities have come to be termed 'acting out', and this term seems to have received greater prominence than its more vivid equivalent of 'living the shadow'.

The term 'acting out' is borrowed from psychoanalysis, in which it is used to cover the acting of unconscious experience in an appropriate setting; Fenichel (1945, p. 375) says: 'Under the influence of transference, everyone whose infantile conflicts are remobilized by analysis may develop the tendency to repeat past experiences in present reality, or to misunderstand reality as if it were a repetition of the past, rather than to remember the repressed events in their appropriate connection'.

A male patient telephoned to tell me that he was dissatisfied with his analyst and wanted an interview with me for various reasons, which he stated. I replied that I would see him if his analyst agreed. His analyst told me that she was quite prepared for her patient to consult me, but she did not think he really meant what he asked for, because he had not raised the matter with her.

When he arrived at my consulting room he seemed in a somewhat confused state. He repeated what he had said to me over the telephone, and then became relatively incoherent. I gathered, however, that it was his relatives as much as he who wanted the change. So I told him that I thought his relatives had played on some doubts he had about the goodness of his analyst, which he really hoped were not true. At this he became coherent and told me that this was indeed the case, so I went on to tell him that I had no intention of suggesting a change since I thought his doubts were part of his relation to his analyst and needed working through with her. He left my consulting-room, so far as I could see, completely reassured, and I heard later that he returned to his analyst forthwith. In this example the act was not seriously intended.

If the patient means what he does, then it is not acting out, however socially undesirable his act may seem to the analyst or to those in his environment. It would seem probable that the patient cited by Gerhard Adler was acting out, though nothing undesirable in a social sense occurred. If, however, she was acting out, the fantasy that determined the experience, which occurred during the weekend, did not appear. It is not essentially a question of whether the behaviour occurs in the interview or outside it, for many patients - hysterical ones in particular - dramatize their affects in the analytic hour and thus prevent unconscious fantasies or memories from becoming conscious. Acting out is a special form of defensive behaviour wherever it occurs, and is based, as my example indicates, upon a projection to which neither analyst nor patient has been able to gain access. It will have been observed that the contents of the patient's doubts did not come into consciousness at the time he was interviewed by me.

Acting out in the interview has been described by Stein in his article, 'Loathsome women' (Stein, 1955). There he found that two of the patients 'walked round the analyst's chair in a menacing manner. They described increasingly narrow circles, reminiscent of the "hag track" . . . in order to try and stir him up' (pp. 69-70). Stein found that they were aiming at getting him to 'man-handle' them. Here he suggests that a primitive drama is being enacted and thus is not realized at first, either by him or his patients. They are 'living their shadow' which contains an archetypal image.

In using a psychoanalytic term, *acting out*, it is necessary to realize that it is being altered in the process and at the same time extended, to cover and emphasize the purposive aspect of the act in question, i.e., the attitude that Stein emphasizes in using the phrase 'in order to stir him up'.

In psychoanalysis, acting out is a replacement activity and as such needs to be reduced to its source. It is therefore undesirable, inasmuch as it is inadequate as a form of expression.

Living the shadow is likewise considered undesirable in analytical psychology, but for the added reason that it is acting in a primitive manner and is undesirable because it is consequently unadapted. For instance, the aim of getting the analyst stirred up with a view, as Stein remarks, to induce him to 'man-handle' the patients will not succeed, and they do not really want this to happen, for they have come to the analyst just because of the failure of their primitive and guilt-ridden activities to produce adequate satisfaction.

A projection-perception scale

Though transference can only partly be described in terms of projection, yet this mechanism has the advantage of being easily defined, and furthermore it can be analysed, though not thereby necessarily dissolved.

Alongside projections the patient makes observations that turn out to be objective. Both processes are recognized by repeated tests on the part of the patient, who sometimes as if by revelation, sometimes by slow laborious analysis, comes to realize their nature. As the analysis proceeds the patient may be expected to get an increasingly true view of the analyst, so that a progression can be defined from illusion, due to projection, which may very well be creative, to reality based upon perception of the analyst as what Fairbairn (1952) calls a 'differentiated object'.

The patient's perceptions lead, in any thorough analysis, to his becoming aware not only of contents in the analyst of which the analyst may know, but also of those of which he is unconscious. If, under these circumstances, the analysis is to proceed it must be recognized that the patient gets into a position from which he can make the analyst aware of a part of his personality that he himself had either not seen or not been able to integrate with his ego. If the analyst can recognize it and benefit from it, all is well. Analysts find it difficult to do this.

But this is not all: an interesting situation arises when the patient makes a true projection on to the analyst, and again he may be conscious or unconscious of the situation. Where the patient's projection corresponds to an unconscious conflict of the analyst, the analysis may terminate if one or the other does not become aware of it in time; it is not necessarily the analyst who is the first to make the discovery. A patient of mine with a particularly strong father fixation told me she had to wait for two years in order to take up her problem because she saw that I was not ready to handle it. On looking over the period I had to admit that her view had substance, even though the subsequent analysis showed that this waiting was an ego-defence on her part. It is one of the advantages of the analyst's sitting in full view of the patient that these difficulties can be more easily handled than if he is out of sight and uses that position to maintain a supposed anonymity.

I mention these limiting problems because it is necessary to understand that the concept of a projection-perception scale has complications, but they do not invalidate the general idea, which is of value in considering such problems as the relation of active imagination to transference.

Jung has pointed out that the content of some projections can be dissolved, but that finally the projected archetypal images cannot; they only become detached from the person of the analyst. If there appears to have occurred at the same time an increase in positive perceptual awareness of the analyst, then it may be said that the projection has not only been withdrawn, but has become adequately integrated, inasmuch as the ego of the patient has become strengthened. If on the contrary this does not occur, it is almost certain that either the projection is still active or else that it has led to a fascination of the patient in another sphere; either it has been projected on to another person, or it has led to his becoming fascinated by the image in his inner world. In this case nothing has been gained and much may have been lost.

The interrelation of projection and perception is therefore a useful indicator of progression and regression of the ego.

PART III. PARTICULAR TRANSFERENCE MANIFESTATIONS

The dependent transference

The state of dependence arises when repressed infantile contents are released and the analyst seems to fulfil the imagined role of parent. Then projection predominates over objective perception. During this period, in which infantile patterns predominate (they never disappear), the analyst will refrain from compulsive attempts to control the direction the analysis should take, from giving advice, and from behaving too much in the many ways in which parents behave to their children. Unless he does this he will be dramatizing the transference projections and interfering with the aim of analysing them. However attractive this activity on the part of the analyst may be, and however therapeutically exciting and successful over a short term, it endangers the ultimate development of the patient's relation to the analyst. For this reason also social contracts between analyst and patient outside the analysis will be avoided.

The adoption of a parental role takes many subtle forms. It is even hidden in the implications of being analysed, when this means being subjected to a process understood by the analyst but not by the patient. Under this assumption all kinds of aspects of the parent imagos hide, and these have to be unearthed and analysed so as to reveal the true state of affairs.

The withdrawal of projected parent imagos is an essential prerequisite for the emergence of the self and its realization in consciousness. Analyses that give continued space for the emergence of the self are almost invariably long, because of the need for gradual maturation. Indeed I am inclined to believe that length is one of the essential features of radical analyses that lead to self-realization. It is useless to object because an analysis goes on so long, and equally futile to know what is best for these patients who cannot 'live'. They can live only in the transference, and to try to break it by any means only leads to probable disaster.

In an ideal analysis the analyst would not need any defences, nor would he display counter-transference illusions, in the sense to be defined later, but his reactions of whatever sort would be *adapted* to the patient's requirements at every point.

These requirements are manifestly complex, but they may usefully be classed under two headings: (a) those belonging to the transference neurosis and the repetition of infantile patterns of behaviour, termed by Freud the repetition compulsion, and (b) those belonging to the archetypal transference, in which the analyst can become more openly involved with the patient. The dependent transference is caused by the predominance of class (a), and it is often assumed that to interpret it induces an undesirable regression. The disorientation among analytical psychologists in this sphere appears to derive from the neglect of a very useful concept put forward long ago by Jung in 'The theory of psychoanalysis'. In this essay he criticizes psychoanalysts for their too great fascination with infantile sexuality, which came to be investigated in its own right, so that the importance of the present came to be neglected. He introduces the idea of the 'actual situation', which he defines as the cause of neurotic conflict and of regression to infantile patterns; he thus seems to deny the importance of fixation points. In his later writings, however, it is clear that he still adheres to the relative importance of arrested development in the genesis of neurosis, though without relating it to the concept of 'actual situation'.

The important issue that Jung raised has not yet been settled. It is still an open question how to evaluate two evident casual elements: those that lie in the present and those that lie in the past. If, however, the actual situation is defined as the totality of present causes and the conflicts associated with them, then the genetic (historical) causes are brought into the picture, inasmuch as they are still active in the present as contributing to the conflicts there manifested. If we keep to this principle fruitless regression will not occur, because past and present are constantly kept in relation with one another and only those causes that actually operate in the present are taken up by the patient.

Where then does the transference come into the picture? It provides good conditions for investigating this 'actual situation', so long as the essential simplicity and sufficient 'naturalness' of the interview is maintained and the analysis conducted with regard to the true relationship factor as well as to the illusions that appear alongside it. These conditions provide the best chance of induced or artificial regressions being avoided and fixation points, to which little attention has been paid by analytical psychologists being *revealed.* The fixation theory has been overlooked, as has also the contingent problem of the relation of the self to ego development. Far from being only 'biological roots', the zones and fixation points are, in my view (cf. Fordham, 1957a), also centres of developing consciousness round which archetypal motifs, as deintegrates of the self, centre in alluring profusion. The magical sense of the anal zone has recently been interestingly discussed by Whitmont (1957), who has brought the whole problem into closer relation with recent developments in psychoanalysis.

The analysis of the dependent transference, which invariably leads into the infantile relation to the mother, is a lengthy and painstaking procedure. Yet it is essentially constructive since it is the only way in which many individuals can reach the growing points of their ego and so rebuild the previously inadequate structure.

The objective transference

In 1935 Jung wrote that

> All methods of influence, including the analytical, require that the patient be seen as often as possible. I content myself with a maximum of four consultations a week. With the beginning of synthetic treatment it is of advantage to spread out the consultations. I then generally reduce them to one or two hours a week, for the patient must learn to go his own way.
>
> (p. 20)

And again (1935a, pp. 26-7):

> The psychoanalyst thinks he must see his patient an hour a day for months on end; I manage in difficult cases with three or four sittings a week. As a rule I content myself with two, and once the patient has got going, he is reduced to one. In the interim he has to work at himself, but under my control. . . .In addition I break off treatment every ten weeks or so, in order to throw him back on his normal milieu. In this way he is not alienated from his world - for he really suffers from his tendency to live at another's expense.

I now wish to bring these statements into relation with another and later statement (Jung, 1946, p. 71): 'The bond [of the transference] is often of such intensity that we could almost speak of a "combination". When two chemical substances combine both are altered.' The question that must spring to mind is how, if the relationship is so intimate, it can be desirable for meetings to be so infrequent.

There have always been certain implications in Jung's concept of a transpersonal objective psyche, which Robert Moody expresses very clearly in relation to the transference when he says of a case (1955, p. 537): 'Once the animus figure had been formulated by the unconscious, it played the rôle of a function that led the patient step by step, and *often regardless of the analyst* [italics mine], towards the various problems that stood between her and a harmonious relationship to the unconscious.'

If the unconsciousness is transpersonal and operates 'regardless of the analyst' and if the object is to bring the ego into relationship with it, it is clearly sensible to implement this idea by giving it technical application. It is common knowledge that Jung did this, and reference has already been made to it. He enjoined his patients to write down dreams, keep records of them and associations to them in a book, to start painting, drawing, modelling, and extending this to active imagination. All this is based on the empirical evidence that, in suitable cases, it leads to individuation. Once this process is set in motion interviews with the analyst becomes supervisory. The aim of these techniques was defined by Jung in his essay 'The aims of psychotherapy' (1931, pp. 46ff.). There he says: 'My aim is to bring about a psychic state in which my patient begins to experiment with his own nature.' For this is needed 'not only a personal contemporary consciousness, but also a suprapersonal consciousness with a sense of historical continuity.'

Jung frequently states that his patients are of a special kind, i.e., those who have already been analysed and whose special difficulty is expressed in the symptom of a life lacking in meaning, a depressive state to which an individual solution is demanded. He claims that their problem is misunderstood if it is interpreted in terms of genetic psychology or of social adaptation. It is their individuality that needs emphasis, and therefore they may be expected to have an ego strong enough to stand the impact of the unconscious without too intense an 'alchemical' transference. For these already developed personalities the tendency to 'live at the analyst's expense' in a dependent transference must be undesirable because it derives from a misunderstanding of their problem. Breaking off treatment therefore aims at breaking up the dependent transference, which makes no sense. Jung's action therefore corresponds with his view of their problem, and not with the compulsive dramatization of the parent imagos, as is sometimes claimed.

This interpretation of Jung's statements means that there is no justification for erecting them into general rules, but they must rather be viewed as technical recommendations for the treatment of a special kind of case.

When I was learning to become an analyst in 1933, however, little reference to the transference was to be heard, and it seemed to be agreed by implication that if the patient's ego was brought into relation with the objective psyche a solution to his problems would appear and the transference would resolve itself without its being made more than vaguely conscious. Thus, Jung's statements had become erroneously generalized and even dogmatized without justification.

Jung's method must depend upon the patient's ability to introject his projections and 'raise them to the subjective plane'. Out of this grows active imagination, which has become the means by which the ego is brought into a vital relation with the archetypal images. It is under these conditions that it may be assumed that the transference would become less intense; they might even signalize its termination. It is here that Jung gives only general statements such as the one already quoted: 'With the beginning of the synthetic treatment it is of advantage to spread out the consultations. I then generally reduce them to one or two hours a week, for the patient must learn to go his own way' (1935, p. 20), a statement that has been interpreted in various ways, leading to considerable confusion. This I will illustrate by discussing two views on the place of active imagination in analysis.

Gerhard Adler, in his paper 'On the archetypal content of transference' (1955), says of his patient that she 'soon learned to use her fantasy constructively and to practise what analytical psychology calls active imagination' (p. 286). But there is no mention of the transference diminishing in intensity; indeed it would seem to have gone on as before, for he says the patient (*ibid.* p. 288) 'felt her relation- ship to me - i.e. her secure positive transference - as a kind of temenos, of protective magic circle, inside which she was safe enough to endure this intense inner experience'.

Henderson (1955), in a comprehensive review of the subject, takes up quite a different position, from which he states that active imagination occurs after analysis of the transference has been completed. He defines four stages in the development of individuation, which begin only after the dependent infantile transference has been sufficiently analysed.

1 The appearance of the self symbols while the transference is at its height.
2 Resolution of the infantile transference and achievement of what Henderson calls 'symbolic friendship'. This term expresses the condition in which the analyst is built into the psyche of the patient as a permanent internal 'friend'. Because this has happened the patient no longer needs regular interviews with the external analyst.
3 Post-analysis period in which a new adaptation is achieved with or without the analyst's help.
4 Discovery of archetypal symbolism through active imagination, providing a means of self-analysis without the analyst's help.

It is there clear that analysts do not agree as to the place of active imagination in the transference process. The drastic difference in view could spring from a variety of roots.

(a) From differing concepts of active imagination. There is indeed a tendency to regard almost any fantasy as active imagination, a tendency which I have commented upon elsewhere (1956), and I have suggested that the term should be used only when the fantasy takes on an object quality to which the ego consciously relates.
(b) From differences in the transference phenomena due to typological differences between patients.
(c) From differences in analytic procedure arising from differences in the personality structure of the analysts.
(d) From inadequate study of the motives for differing distributions of energy.

The confusion appears to me, however, to stem mainly from differing understandings of when the synthetic process begins, and from misunderstanding of Jung's sharp distinction between methods of rational influence and those in which the dialectical relation applies, i.e. his individuation cases. In the general run it is by no means easy to distinguish this clearly. In all analyses synthetic processes are continuously in evidence and, further, in my experience, an objective transpersonal quality attaches itself to the vast majority of all transference phenomena, even when they are expressed most personally by the patient and whether they are more or less intense. When the former, the alchemical combination takes place. However, there are certainly patients whose capacity for imaginative activity either dissolves or masks the personal aspect of the transference, so that it can only be detected with difficulty. These cases could very well develop into Henderson's fourth stage, which would seem to belong to Jung's special sphere, but they might equally well continue after the pattern of Adler's case. As far as my experience goes, the transference cannot be left out, and it will sooner or later form the central feature of any thorough analysis, and though Jung seemed at one time to believe that this was not so, his later work points in the opposite direction. In 'Psychology of the transference' he expounds his view of the 'alchemical' nature of the transference with the reservation that this need not always occur. In my view it always occurs, only with varying intensity. As we have seen above, an apparently weak transference can be converted into a strong one by analysis. I have given this example because I believe that the indiscriminate application of Jung's thesis has led to strong transferences being too frequently overlooked because they are masked. In this connexion it appears to me that there is a point in Moody's statement that is liable to rather serious misunderstanding. It implies that transferences only occur when the analyst participates in some unstated manner and that they never arise 'quite regardless of the analyst'. This is far from the truth; indeed most transferences have the quality of autonomy sooner or later, and they all occur without anybody's willing them.

It may well be reflected that Jung's aim of getting the patient to experiment with his own nature can occur just as well through his imagination playing on the person of the analyst, who is then the equivalent of the paintings and dreams. This has to me the following advantages: it links the whole process up to a human relationship without divesting it of its transpersonal quality; it also increases the possibilities of sorting out projections and perceptions after the manner described above under the heading of 'Projection-perception scale'. But Jung, as is well known, prefers a mild transference (1946, p. 172), and this may be one of the reasons why he takes steps to prevent a stronger transference where he conceives that the alternative method is just as much in the patient's interest. I cannot believe, however, that preferences of this kind make much difference to the development or non-development of the objective transference, which goes far deeper than conscious feelings.

PART IV. COUNTER-TRANSFERENCE

(a) Use and definition of the term

So far we have concentrated on a number of features of the transference that are displayed by the patient either spontaneously or as the result of techniques used by the analyst. But this is only part of the analytic process, since the analyst soon becomes involved himself.

Because it was originally hoped that the analyst's personality would be eliminated from the analytic process, the counter-transference was the first class of reaction by analysts to be studied. It was soon found that the patient's transference stimulates the analyst's repressed unconscious, which becomes projected on to the patient so as to interfere with the way he conducts the analysis. Efforts were therefore made to eliminate this.

The thesis here put forward postulates that the whole personality of the analyst is inevitably involved in any analysis and so the counter-transference is viewed from a different basis. This must lead to reconsideration of the term. A review of it is especially desirable because it has come, as a consequence of Jung's thesis, to cover more of the analyst's reactions than emanate from the repressed unconscious. Indeed it sometimes covers all the analyst's conduct in his analytic work.

In his interesting paper, 'On the function of counter-transference' (1955a), Robert Moody describes how his unconscious led him to a reaction that seemed exactly adapted to a little girl's need, without his altogether knowing at first what he was doing.

His description, of how erotic instinctive processes were mobilized within him and brought into play, would seem according to the present view, to indicate a good analytic reaction. It arose first out of Moody's unconscious archetypal response, only later to become related consciously to the patient. The idea implied in the original theory of psychoanalysis that the analyst can only safely react to his patient with his ego alone is here shown to be certainly erroneous.

It is here contended that each interpretation or other response, if it is to have validity, needs to be *created on every occasion* out of the unconscious, using material provided by the patient to give the unconscious content adequate form, and this is just what happened in Moody's case. The fact that the analyst's reactions are repeated in a similar enough form, in relation to sufficiently similar behaviour on the part of patients, for them to be called a technique does not invalidate their being created on each occasion, for there are always differences enough to necessitate an individual form for the same familiar themes. The fact of the analyst's reacting to a patient is maintained by Jung to be the essential therapeutic factor in analysis; the reaction differs from the patient's transference in that it has a less compelling character and is capable of integration; in other words, the analyst has a living relation to the unconscious at those points where the patient lacks it. This it is that facilitates the cure. Moody's behaviour was his spontaneous archetypal response to the sexual transference manifested by his child patient. If this is counter-transference, then it could be argued that all analyses are based on counter-transference, and so the term would take on a new and very wide meaning. At first I was inclined to think the extended usage was objectionable, because it blurred its original negative meaning and so opened the door to almost any unconscious behaviour by the analyst. Yet the change in our understanding of transference as a whole is better reflected by the wider usage, for *participation mystique*, projection and introjection can play valuable, even essential, parts in analytic procedures (cf. Money-Kyrle, 1956).

A solution to the quandary is made possible by dividing the general heading into two and referring to counter-transference illusion and counter-transference syntony. This differentiation is especially justified because there is a need to indicate the direction in which to look in order to become conscious. In analysis there are reactions on the part of the analyst that are syntonic and can make the patient more conscious, but these are different from the counter-transference illusion, where the increase in consciousness will come about only if the analyst himself examines his own reaction.

(b) Counter-transference illusion

The use of a recording apparatus reveals very neatly how counter-transference illusion can arise from projection. To be sure, I had found that some patients before ending their analysis would review those parts of it in which they believed I had made mistakes, and I could see that they were often right, but by then details had escaped me. In addition, dreams about the patient give another clue, and it is possible to realize that wrong or mis-timed interpretations spring from a repressed source. However, an accurate verbal record shows up the phenomena far better than anything else, for it can reveal without any shadow of doubt what can happen and how the analyst's own psyche can replace the patient's by projection.

Thus one day I ended a recorded interview with mixed feelings. It seemed on the one hand remarkably successful, but there had been a part early on when I had not succeeded in making progress. The patient was a boy of 11 who had problems over his aggressive feelings. The problems were related to his school work, in which he was not being as successful as his intelligence would warrant. The relevant part of the interview ran as follows:

John: 'Why did they block that door up?' (Referring to an area in the wall of my room where the doorway had been built up.)

M.F.: 'Imagine.' (Long silence, then M.F. continued.) 'I expect to keep somebody out!'

John: 'I don't!' (then, after hesitations and much fidgeting) 'Better to have the door there' (i.e. where it is at present, leading into the passage).

M.F.: 'I suppose you thought my idea wasn't sensible. I think that from the way you went so quiet.'

John: 'They could have easily come that way' (referring to where the door is now).

M.F.: 'I still think I am right in believing you thought your remark was more sensible - you didn't think I would agree - you didn't think I would make *stupid* remarks!'

John: 'Beg pardon' (followed by long silence).

M.F.: (Repeats statement).

John: 'It isn't really stupid. It could have been. It's unlikely.' (After a further silence he went on to talk about electric trains, implying by asking me questions that I was ignorant on this topic.)

M.F.: 'You must think I'm an *awfully ignorant boob* if I have not heard of Meccano, because everybody has.' (And later on I made a more elaborate interpretation in which the phrase occurred.) 'You didn't know you had a secret feeling that *I was a fool and ignorant* and that you were more sensible than I in some respects.'

John went on to talk about Meccano and became technical in his conversation, and gradually I was able to stop over-acting and make interpretations that did not simply increase his resistance; for example:

M.F.: 'I wondered whether your questions were not something of this sort: "Well, here's something I'm likely to know more about than he does"?

Next I began to see that it was better to be even less active and point out that in his silences he was having secret thoughts. Only when I arrived at this formulation could the analysis of the thoughts proceed.

Listening to the recording made clear to me what I had vaguely felt during the interview. My aggression towards this boy had interfered with my getting to understand what was going on in his mind. I had misinterpreted the child's feelings, replacing more subtle ones by a cruder statement, owing to the repression of memories relevant to a particular period of my own childhood. Then I used to attack my mother by calling her 'stupid', a word that I had repeated in my transference interpretations to John. Evidently I had identified with the memory images and John had represented myself as a child while I, ceasing to be the analyst, represented my mother. Only when I had circumvented this reaction could I frame interpretations that brought me into relation with the boy's 'secret thoughts'; only from then onwards was I able to proceed with the analysis, understanding the child well enough for him to go on to reveal himself more and more fully.

It is to this class of phenomena that the term *counter-transference illusion* applies. The example manifested the following characteristics: (1) there was an unconscious, or rather vaguely conscious, reactivation of a past situation that completely replaced my relation to the patient; (2) during that time no analysis of the patient was possible.

If we transpose this concept to the archetypal level, then the events would have to possess the same characteristics, i.e. the archetypal reaction would not be related to the state of the patient and the analysis would stop until the analyst was able to become conscious of the archetype in question. It is not so easy to find an illusory archetypal counter-transference, especially as a syntonic counter-transference is not necessarily positive. In his paper on 'Loathsome women', Stein has given the content of his counter-transference, apparently partly syntonic and partly illusory, based on a negative anima possession, to a type of woman patient. In this paper he formulates his affective attitude, dreams, and some of his personal experiences. In doing so he has contributed towards objectivity concerning the conflicts in which an analyst can become embroiled. In my experience, when the illusion of the analyst does not become conscious for too long, the analysis ends altogether, and the patient becomes acutely aware of what is happening. But when the analyst realizes what is going on, even if he cannot resolve the projection, a more favourable issue may be expected.

A frequent counter-transference manifestation is the tendency of analysts to make personal confessions to patients on unsuitable occasions. When I have objected to this practice or attempted to draw analysts' attention to their motives, I have been asked: 'Why do you find it necessary to withhold information about yourself from the patient?' Assuming that this question is not aimed at what is usually covered by discretion, and has not behind it the naïve belief that personal confessions in answer to questions improve the personal relationship between analyst and patient, which usually they do not, I reply that I do not find it 'necessary', but that I consider it essential to relate the question to another because of the special liability of confessions to cover counter-transference illusions: 'What do you want to give information to your patient for, in view of the fact that in doing so you usually give a report about yourself as you are, or conceive yourself to be, while this is not at all the person he necessarily imagines you to be?' This question often disposes of the first, but leads to another, for it is then said to be only 'human' to make confessions and also to err. The term *human* is contrasted with *divine* and *animal*, and if translated into psychological language refers to the ego.

My answering question now changes to: 'Why do you want to introduce your ego, i.e. personal consciousness?' If the answer is that the patient wants it or needs it, then we can go on to try to define the conditions under which it is desirable: when is it adapted to the patient's requirements and when a projection? I agree that it may be correct procedure, but I must reiterate that confessions by the analyst are far more frequently obstructive than otherwise, not only because they introduce projections but also because the information is only too often liable to drastic elaboration or distortion owing to the activity of fantastic projections arising from archetypal roots. In these circumstances the analyst as a human being (an ego) is of little consequence. It is then that we are exposed to reproaches of inhumanity and the like, but this is not to be dissolved by trying to be human, i.e. by making confessions, etc. Analysts are inhuman because of the transference, and need to know *how* to be inhuman; this is surely one of the main reasons for undergoing an analysis, so that we may understand the patient's need and, at the same time, maintain our humanity.

But as the patient's ego becomes more established, towards the end of the analysis, it is relevant for the analyst to introduce more and more of himself - not only his ego. Then it is possible and satisfying to both parties to conduct conversations, and to interact in a more and more complete and spontaneous fashion.

Though I have never heard it stated, I have certainly thought that the introduction of the analyst's ego, as I maintain often at the wrong time, has the aim of reducing the transference, but it really avoids its transpersonal aspect by pretending that to introduce 'personal and human feeling helps'. Much more effective in reducing the transference is the method of recording dreams and teaching the patients to work them up before coming to the analysis, and getting them to paint and start on active imagination. The danger of this procedure, however, needs to be kept clearly in mind: as we have seen, it is liable to create an illusion that the transference does not exist when it is in reality just as big but is concealed in the method, which does not by any means prevent 'big transferences'. If it is not taken up by the analyst it only too often turns against him or the patient in the environment, or creates a situation for which there is no means of a decent solution.

All this does not overlook the need for the patient as well as the analyst to distinguish between the transpersonal objective transference and the conscious situation. This criticism of many personal confessions made by analysts is based on their ineffectiveness in attaining what they aim at, not to mention exploiting the patient's belief in the truthfulness of the analyst! If, however, a statement that can be checked by direct observation of the patient can be introduced, this is much more likely to continue the analytic aim of strengthening the patient's ego and helping to gain greater control in the transference.

A female patient was attacking and at the same time trying to seduce me because I would not stop 'being an analyst' and live with her so that she could have day-to-day 'ordinary' relations with me. She attacked me as unfeeling, heartless, and indifferent to her distress. It was as fruitless for me to deny this as it would be for me to inaugurate a more personal kind of approach, to meet her outside the analysis, for instance, or to start those personal confessions for which she asked because she was the victim of a projected hermaphrodite figure. It was not until I took the bull by the horns and asserted that she overlooked that my interpretations were an expression of my concern for her condition, since they were attempts to bring her relief from it, that I made any progress. This I regard as an open statement about the main root of my making the interpretations she did not like; she can confirm my motive by numerous observations of my behaviour if she wants to make them. One of these is that I will go on meeting her poisonous attacks in a friendly way and seeing their positive content.

In voicing the attitude that lay behind my interpretations I am also expressing the fact of my being involved. It was only when I had said this that I broke through her defences and was able to press home my interpretations so as to relieve her of some of her anxiety, for she had been convinced that I was using concepts in order to destroy the mature love she felt, as well as to analyse its fantastic and infantile contents.

(c) The syntonic counter-transference

The extension of the term counter-transference seeks to undermine the idea that the transference consists in projections from a patient upon an analyst who never reacts spontaneously but remains as a kind of impervious reflector in which the patient can see his projections. This thesis holds no charms for Jungian analysts, who unanimously reject it. They hold that because of the archetypes the analyst inevitably becomes sooner or later involved with the patient in an unconscious process, which is first experienced as a projection and then further analysed.

Since the aim of analysis is realization of the self by the patient, whether it results in ego development or individuation, and since the analyst aims at performing a mediating rôle in this realization, all his syntonic reactions will ideally relate to the self, i.e. to the essential wholeness of his nature. Yet it is evident that the self as an integrated whole is seldom in the forefront of the analyst's behaviour, which is more often based on other archetypal forms. Yet it may be discerned obscurely by patients in their experience of their analyst as a god of one kind or another. This easily induces resistances in analysts, but it has indeed a basis of truth, since all the analysts' reactions, whether interpretations, questions, comments, or acts, are operations of their own natures.

The danger associated with the emergence of this archetypal form is inflation. But it is not necessary for analysts to feel any particular merit when this comes into the patient's consciousness, since awareness of the self is no individual achievement but a historical process, as Jung has clearly shown in 'Answer to Job'. The objection to being seen as a god is surely as narcissistic and dangerous as being inflated by it; indeed it reveals a negative inflation. Therefore if a patient dreams or feels I am a god, saying that it is ridiculous, I usually ask him: 'How do you know it is?' This question has behind it the idea that the self is the prime mover behind every analytic procedure, and is a recognition that the patient's 'projection' has a basis of truth in it. My question aims at leaving the door open to a wholeness that transcends consciousness and at the same time expresses my transpersonal involvement. It is therefore appropriate or syntonic.

It is commonly believed that consciousness is one of the great aims of analysis, but this is only partly true if the analysis is based on the self. Then consciousness is the instrument we use in the analytic process; it does not embrace the whole of it any more than the self can be identified with consciousness.

As I have suggested elsewhere, the self is a dynamic structure, having two definable functions (cf. Fordham, 1957a); it integrates and deintegrates, and I have shown that this view of it can be used to explain how consciousness is produced and how an ego is formed in early infancy. This concept arose partly from studies in child psychology and partly from reflection upon my behaviour as an analyst. There are two ways of behaving: (1) trying to isolate oneself from the patient by being as 'integrated' as possible; and (2) relinquishing this attitude and simply listening to and watching the patient, to hear and see what comes out of the self in relation to the patient's activities, and then reacting. This would appear to involve deintegrating; it is as if what is put at the disposal of patients are parts of the analyst that are spontaneously responding to the patients in a way that he needs; yet these parts are manifestations of the self. It was this that led me to see that what Jung describes as the dialectical relationship is based upon processes that neither I nor my patient can control consciously, and that analysis depends upon the relatively greater experience of the analyst in deintegrating so as to meet the patient's disintegration. Moody (1955a) describes the feeling accompanying this experience very well when he says (p.54): 'I decided . . . to allow myself to be drawn into whatever kind of relationship I felt her [his child patient] to be silently demanding of me.' When he did this, he remarks: 'I was somewhat at sea as to what was happening, but I realized that some important development had begun to occur from the time when I allowed my . . . reactions to express themselves freely.'

This experience accords with Plaut's view of incarnation. In his paper on 'The transference in analytical psychology' (1956), he asserts that there are two ways in which analysts handle the projected image: 'One', he says 'will deal with it by educative procedure centred on the elucidation and differentiation of archetypal contents', while others 'will accept the projection in a whole-hearted manner making no *direct* attempt to help the patient to sort out what belongs to him, what to the analyst, and what to neither as well as to both. On the contrary they will allow themselves to become this image bodily, to "incarnate" it bodily for the patient.'

It will be observed that the way of incarnating the image leads to what is described as primitive identity, a condition that Jung has called preconscious and which I have incorporated into the theory of the deintegrating function of the self by pointing to primitive identity as the manifestation of deintegration. It follows therefore that if any new consciousness is to arise and to lead to differentiation of the ego, a lowering of the conscious threshold is inevitable and desirable. This leads to a view of archetypal projections somewhat different from that frequently held. In the case of repressed material emerging from the patient there is less difficulty in detecting projections, because they are more immediately related to memory images, but where archetypes become active, giving rise to 'fantastic images', the position is different for, owing to the concurrent primitive identity, the images can be expressed by the analyst or by the patient. This means that it can be just as valid for the analyst to know of the projection through registering its impact upon himself and perceiving it first within himself, as it is by listening to the patient and realizing it as an inference from what the patient says. Thus if a patient presents infantile material to the analyst, the latter can find out the appropriate reaction from himself, i.e. whether it be a mothering or fathering attitude that he can go some way towards meeting and out of which he can make an interpretation when the patient is ready for it.

At this stage in the transference the affective stability of the analyst is crucial; he must be able to rely on the deintegrates knowing that consciousness will inevitably arise from them. It follows that he *will inevitably find* the right form or response so long as counter-transference projections do not obstruct its development.

It is on the basis of 'incarnating' the image, which should obviously be distinguished from acting out, the explanations and interpretations can begin to find their right place, for without them the patient will sooner or later become disorientated. If, however, the analyst keeps himself apart from the patient by adopting an explanatory or superior rôle without incarnating the image, he does nothing but isolate the patient at just the point at which he needs a primitive form of relationship.

Interpretations are therefore to be regarded as an end product of the analyst's syntonic counter-transference. They stand, as it were, on the basis of less definable affective preconscious experiences out of which they are distilled.

Some analysts depreciate the value of interpreting the transference, but in many places Jung emphasizes the importance of making the transference conscious. For instance, in 'Psychology of the transference' (1946) he says (p. 219),

> As this [breaking infantile projections] is the legitimate aim and real meaning of the transference, it inevitably leads, whatever method of rapprochement be used, to discussion and understanding and hence to heightened consciousness, which is a measure of the personality's integration. During this discussion the conventional disguises are dropped and the true man comes to light. He is in very truth reborn from his psychological relationship and his field of consciousness is rounded into a circle.

This clear statement that it is necessary and desirable to bring the transference into consciousness requires amplification. What does this 'discussion and understanding' involve? To some extent this question has already been answered, but the question of interpretation, the most powerful instrument in the hands of the analyst, needs special consideration.

The great majority of the statements made by the patient, including those reported, are made to a projected figure, and it is evident that the analyst needs to be constantly on the look-out to recognize who the figure may be that he incarnates. This constitutes the major problem of transference interpretation for, if it is not defined, all that he says is reinterpreted by the patient in the light of projection, and misunderstandings inevitably arise. It is for this reason that the patient is introduced to the desirability of saying all that he can about his analyst as it occurs to him either outside the analysis or during his sessions. For this reason also the analyst introduces as few complications as possible, for how he behaves is as crucial as what he says. Therefore, in order to follow what he is doing, the advantage of keeping the essential framework of the interview simple is self-evident. The simplicity also facilitates the detection of projections, which can be interpreted when sufficient material has accumulated.

It follows that the interpretation of patients' material must be regarded as incomplete if its transference content is not referred to when it is sufficiently near consciousness. This applies to all reports embodying present or past occurrences, even to such simple phenomena as bits of history revealed by the patient; they all have reference to the 'actual situation', which in the case of analytic interviews is to be found in the transference.

It is sometimes held that no rules can be made as to when an interpretation should or should not be given, but this is not my experience. The following principle can certainly be formulated: when the patient has brought enough material for the analyst to make the interpretations in such terms that the patient can understand them, the interpretations can be given without hesitation. Under these conditions the patient's ego is mobilized, the reality content of the relationship is increased, and so regressive trends are brought more under control by coming into consciousness.

There is this to be said, however, against a rule - it could prevent the interpretation from being a creative act based on the analyst's past experience combined with the new experience he has of his patient; and it could short-cut the analyst's feeling of concern for the patient, the best safeguard against the use of theoretical interpretations as defences against unconscious activity within the analyst. An interpretation that violates the relationship clearly does not subscribe to the above rule, which aims at maintaining and improving the relationship between analyst and patient.

In 'Psychology of the transference' Jung says (p. 178): 'Even the most experienced psychotherapist will discover again and again that he is caught up in a bond, a combination resting on mutual unconsciousness.' It is out of this unconscious bond that, in my view, interpretations best arise, for if they do not they easily become impositions of the analyst upon his patient. But this bond is not stable, because of the 'ever-changing content that possess the patient', which Jung compares to Mercurius who, in uniting all opposites in himself, appears 'like a demon [who] now flits about from patient to doctor, and as the third part in the alliance, continues its game, sometimes impish and teasing, sometimes really diabolical' (*ibid.* p. 188). Whether the 'demon' becomes a source of consciousness or of confusion all depends on how he is handled. One useful means is to try to start every interview as though a new patient were entering the room, for this helps in getting into relation with the patient's mood of the moment.

Amplification

In 'The aims of psychotherapy' (1931), Jung says (p. 45): 'It is particularly important for me to know as much as possible about primitive psychology, mythology, archaeology, and comparative religion because these fields offer me invaluable analogies with which to enrich the associations of my patients.' The necessity for this knowledge is generally agreed, but it needs to be borne in mind that extraneous mythological parallels, however close, can be used to obscure rather than clarify what is going on in the transference. After the myth has been developed within the transference it will naturally give the patient a special interest in the remarkable parallels that will almost inevitably be sought out in books and will be all the more striking because he knows that their substance was first revealed to him spontaneously.

It is quite clear that what I have described is at variance with the notion of introducing intellectual knowledge when the archetypal projections are in full swing, for whether the analyst likes it or not he will inevitably embody the image, as Jung clearly sees when he says (1946, p. 170):

> Practical analysis has shown that unconscious contents are invariably projected at first on to concrete persons and situations. Many projections can ultimately be integrated back into the individual once he has recognized their subjective origin: others resist integration, and although they may be detached from their original objects they thereupon transfer themselves to the doctor.

There is no possibility of explaining or getting rid of them by educative procedures; if this were possible it would only be necessary to give lectures. The ultimate resolution of these projections depends first and foremost on the analyst's behaviour and experience of his own myth. Once the parent imagos are projected they stay projected till the self appears, which initiates the 'stage of transformation' (1931a, p. 69ff.). Here Jung introduces the idea of the self-education of the 'doctor' as part of the analytic process. He does not, however, mean intellectual education but rather the analysis of the analyst as a means of introducing him to the inevitability of transforming himself as his patient also does.

The thesis of this essay is an extension of Jung's. It states that this mutual transformation extends to all the transference; it only becomes more significant in the 'stage of transformation' in which the mutual unconscious bond between analyst and patient becomes increasingly apparent. Amplification is used to elucidate the content of this, and is only valid when based upon the analyst's experience in the transference. That it can be used to support depersonalizing defences, and mask easily verbalized transference relationships when used earlier, has already been shown, and therefore I aim at using the patient's and my own experienced images first. Then if these correspond to known myths the latter can be added; then they do act, as Baynes (1955, p. 424) so vividly asserts, like the stains of a histologist, throwing obscure psychic contents vividly into relief, enriching the transference and leading to clearer definition of its contents.

Conclusion

These attempts to assess some problems presented by transference analysis will, I hope, lead to other reviews of the subject. They are especially important at the present juncture because the realization of transference analysis as a two-way process, in which the personality of the analyst takes an essential part, can lead and has led to abandoning the attempt to define and verbalize what is contained in it, because the whole process seems too individual and subjective. I believe, however, that Jung's thesis can be used to illuminate and describe its contents in a more realistic and scientific way than if the attempt be made to eliminate the analyst as a person and regard him as a projection screen.

I have no reference to such practices as the patient going to two analysts at the same time, or to the important question of whether the sex of the analyst is significant. These issues still appear too complex to formulate. Neither have I considered the different forms of transference due to psycho-pathological considerations, but have rather confined myself to more fundamental clinical problems.

The general trend of my views is that the individuality of the patient cannot be overlooked in any age group, and that the process of analysis and therefore the transference is always basically the same though patients and analysts react to it differently.

In reading Jung's essays assembled in volume sixteen of the *Collected Works* it is impossible to miss the changes that have taken place in the author's views with the passing of time. Jung is continually seeking adequate means of describing the remarkably complex and difficult field covered by psychotherapy. Fundamentally his view is the same, but the changes are often important. His tendency seems to have been to give more and more attention to the transference, and in 1951 he says (p. 116), 'The intelligent psychotherapist has known for years that *any* complicated treatment is an individual dialectical process' (my italics). Since the dialectical process corresponds with what I have defined as transference he would here seem to be in basic agreement with the thesis of my essay.

Chapter 2

Counter-transference (1960)

In getting up to open a symposium that is to continue next month, I am reminded of another one some years ago on archetypes and internal objects.[1] Then it was decided that a psychoanalyst and an analytical psychologist should make parallel statements on each topic without reference to each other, to see what emerged in the discussion.

I do not believe that our committee altogether realized that they had asked the same speakers to begin again and, I believe, in the same order, but here the similarity virtually ends. For my part I could not say that what I said *then* was influenced at all by reading psychoanalytic literature, for everything worthwhile that had been said about archetypes had been written by Jung, and it was quite unclear whether his theory had any relevance to that of internal objects. This time the picture is radically different.

Starting from a critical study of Jung's formulations, attempts have been made and are continuing to be made by several analysts to supplement his conceptions and to describe practice in relation to their thinking. These researches have led to study of the writings of psychoanalysts who have developed concepts much nearer to our own than heretofore, and it has been possible to hold discussions with them. These I take to be one origin of this symposium.

Before enumerating some of the ways in which counter-transference has been thought about, it has become necessary to define a term that is being given several meanings at the present time. A wide definition is required if the findings of analytical psychologists are to be included under it, partly because of the conception that transference and counter-transference are essentially part and parcel of each other, and partly because both processes originate in the unconscious. The term will therefore be used here to cover the unconsciously motivated reactions in the analyst that the patient's transference evokes; I shall maintain that some of these are illusory while others are what I have termed syntonic, sub-divisions that will be defined later on as occasion arises.

When Jung claimed to have been one of the first, if not the very first, to insist that the training of psychoanalysts should include a personal analysis, and later, when he contended that the therapeutic factor in psychotherapy was the personality of the analyst, he must have in mind the problem of what is here called counter-transference. He does not, however, use this term often, either then or later on, and this raises the question of why. The answer is not far to seek if his work since about 1912 be considered, since in it he has been primarily interested in studying the transpersonal unconscious, and so personal relationships featured no so much for their own sake as for vehicles for unconscious activity. In this investigation personal relationships were conceived to benefit because projections can be withdrawn and the contents of them built into a psychic inner world, of which the animus and anima are the representatives, related to, but most distinguished from, the ego. Since the term *counter-transference* was used by Freud in the setting of the personal psychoanalytic relationship, Jung probably felt its use out of place when formulating his conclusions.

He does, however, use the term twice in *The Practice of Psychotherapy* (1954) in which the main body of his contribution to psychotherapeutic techniques since 1928 is collected; both passages are illuminating. One is in a footnote reference to Freud, where he states that counter-transference was discovered by Freud, protests against the idea that transference is the product of psychoanalytic technique, and emphasizes his view that it is a social phenomenon (p. 171). The second occurs in a paper delivered to a Swiss medical society in which he puts forward the concept of 'stages in psychotherapy' (1931a). Here he calls it a symptom 'or', he says, 'better a demon of sickness' – I shall come back to this later; at present I want rather to consider the context in which this reference is set.

It is during the last 'stage of transformation' that he emphasizes the importance of the analyst's psychic states. He compares the analytic relation to chemical interaction, and continues that treatment can 'by no device . . . be anything but the product of mutual influence, in which the whole being of the doctor as well as the patient plays a part' (p. 71). Later he is very emphatic that it is futile for the analyst to erect defences of a professional kind against the influence of the patient, and continues: 'By doing so he only denies himself the use of a highly important organ of information.'

The analogy of 'chemical interaction' is very far-reaching; indeed, because of the considerable fusion of the personalities that occurs, a fact that can only be overlooked to the detriment of both parties, it becomes necessary for the analyst to transform himself, to some extent at least, if his patient is to get well.

In Jung's writings, and till recently in those of other analysts, there is little detailed evidence available to demonstrate how all this appears in practice, since he rather deliberately contented himself with giving his conception in outline, illustrating it in archetypal imagery, and leaving it to the experience of analysts to work out the details as they find them in their own practices. It is clear, however, that he is sure the patient can have very drastic effects on the analyst and that this can induce pathological manifestations in him, particularly when borderline schizophrenic patients are being treated: in one place he instances a physician who came to see him with an induced paranoia, and refers to doctors and nurses who can suffer from 'short psychotic attacks' induced by the patients under their care. Apparently this has also been noticed by psychoanalysts, for Lindner (1955) described how he discovered that as he himself started to introject his patient's psychosis the patient improved. The reverse could clearly occur when an analyst has an unresolved latent psychosis, a rare but not unknown state of affairs. The whole topic has been interestingly discussed recently by Harold Searles (1959) in his paper 'the effort to drive the other person crazy – an element in the aetiology and psychotherapy of schizophrenia'.

The effect of unconscious interchanges between analyst and patient can thus be not only normal and therapeutic but also pathological and therapeutic. In a cogent way Jung refers, as we have seen, to the 'old idea of the demon of sickness', continuing: 'According to this, a sufferer can transmit his disease to a healthy person whose powers then subdue the demon' (1954, p. 72).

From what has been said, it is evident that since Jung's discussion has been couched in terms of archetypal forms in the unconscious, conceived as a continuum with very flexible or non-existent boundaries, the theory of the ego and contiguous boundary concepts has not been developed far. Yet only when these concepts are used or implied is it relevant to speak of transference and counter-transference and so of projection and inrojection, the most frequent but by no means the only mechanisms here brought into operation.

The concept of the contra-sexual components of the psyche, the animus and anima, which are at first projected on to the opposite sex before becoming the representations of the inner world, needs mention in this context because they are conceived as the 'projection-making factors' (cf. Jung, 1959).

Introducing these archetypes is also necessary because they are conceived to have a special attraction for each other, and indeed combine to form a union in the unconscious termed the conjunction (cf. Jung 1954), of which the analyst can be aware only indirectly through his continuing self-analysis.

These end the considerations that I believe lie at the root of all procedures in analytical psychology. They lead to the idea that every activity of the analyst, be it arrangement of interviews, comment, interpretation, tone of voice, inevitably expresses some facet of the analyst's total personality, which will become more and more engaged with his patient as the analysis proceeds. For this reason care needs to be taken in assessing the importance of techniques. It is claimed that those based on ego structures cannot cover the whole analytic procedure because they can or do exclude unconscious effects mediated through the animus or anima as the case may be; the word 'effect' seems to me preferable to influence.

Among Jung's close followers technique has got rather a bad name, for the understandable reason that it can be designed to influence the patient in the interest of theory, and then can become a defensive abstraction that must often, if not always, be classed as counter-transference. The idea can be illustrated by being considered in relation to Jung's view of psychoanalytic theory, for this he regarded as a technique used against the irrationality of the archetypal unconscious. It is not my object to discuss this proposition, nor to claim that Jung's idea is correct now. I believe that it was in the early days, and is still a prominent feature of therapeutic techniques designed to manipulate patients with a view to removing symptoms.

I now want to suggest how the papers published by members of the London Society are related to what has been said. Plaut's idea of the analyst incarnating the archetype for the patient is based on the introjection of an archetype active in relation to the patient; it is the archetypal predisposition in the analyst that makes the 'incarnation' possible (Plaut, 1956). Moody (1955), who related how he 'found himself' reacting to a child in a therapeutic manner, described a procedure dependent upon the same process, while Stein (1955) in his paper on 'Loathsome women' elaborated the subject of the animus–anima conjunction and how it affected him.

It is perhaps not altogether surprising that it should be an analytical psychologist, Kraemer (1958), who published a case illustrating how a psychotherapist could suffer from illusions about a patient by misusing her dreams to justify a counter-transference. Jung's general thesis does, I think, open the door to the development of such illusions, and this may have been apparent to you. This illustrates again the lack of an adequate account of the ego's part in analytical procedures; there is little discussion of the effect of repression.

It is with a view to introducing the repressed parts of the ego that the term illusion has been useful to me.

Illusory counter-transference

It is conceived that illusions spring from projections arising out of the repressed unconscious, the anima, and also indirectly from the animus–anima conjunction. Repressed elements are particularly important in stabilizing the illusions.

The term illusion seems to me better than symptom, though this is what it is, because it gets away from the idea that counter-transference need necessarily be valueless. The illusory form can be a serious and indeed is the worst obstruction to the development of analytic procedures; it can become organized into manipulative techniques aiming to deny what the patient is, with a view to compelling him to change; and he can then be made to conform to a frame of reference quite different from his need at any particular time.

On the other hand an illusion can be corrected if the defences mainly responsible are successfully overcome. A boy aged 8 who talked only to his family, came to see me. I can remember that he looked quite pleased to come with me from the waiting-room where he was with his mother, but when he came into the room he stood bolt upright and looked away from me; he appeared stubborn and resistant and would not use any of the toys available. I concluded that he was angry at coming to see me so I made this interpretation, but with no effect, so I was left in doubt about the accuracy of what I had said. I later discovered from his mother that the boy was indeed angry, but it was because there were three people in the room – I conducted the first interview with a psychiatric social worker present. The illusion I had held was that only two persons were present. But it is evident that the interpretation, part of which was correct, did not operate entirely negatively, for it led to the right answer in the end. I think that a trained analyst may be expected not to entertain illusions that make it impossible for the analysis to proceed. But the kind of illusion that can be modified and can be corrected, as in my example, will occur however well an analyst is trained, and to expect their eradication is idealistic.

Reflecting on possible counter-transference illusions led me to realize that they covered the whole of psychopathology. It also appeared that what was and what was not illusion depended to some extent on the conception of analysis entertained by the analyst, on analytic ideals, and on the concept of reality held by him.

As I am going to comment further on ideals, perhaps this is the place to state that the transpersonal analytic ideal held by analytical psychologists is most often expressed as a personality who does not need to formulate techniques, but who will operate correctly and therapeutically with his patients. This personality does not need rules of procedure, but can use dreams, fantasies, affects, reflexions, etc., with safety because they are integrated into himself and adapted to the patient's needs.

It will be evident that fixed counter-transference illusions must feature most in the training of analysts. In training, analytic ideas are formulated, in relation to the candidate's transference to his analyst and supervisor, and these enter into the trainee's counter-transference to his patient. It is perhaps an indication of the difficulty of our topic that it is not easy to get collaboration between training analysts in attempts to study what goes on in these parts of training. It would be interesting to know whether psychoanalysts have had any more success.

A check on becoming possessed by the personal ideal analyst – made up in candidates mostly from their past experience of parent figures brought into relation with the way their own analysts have conducted, or are believed to have conducted, their analyses – is to observe analytic rules based on theory; theory in turn is based on the transpersonal ideal. The transpersonal ideal, in contrast to the personal one, lies behind the supervisor's aim of showing the trainee where he or she is subject to illusions about a patient's observed material. But the counter-transference illusions of a candidate can also be unconscious: it is not that he wrongly interprets observed material but that the observations have not reached consciousness. They are therefore not accessible to the supervisor and are most likely to become conscious first in the candidate's analysis. That is one reason why analysis of candidates is needed during training.

My main aim in introducing the subject of training is to underline the importance that some analytical psychologists, of whom I am one, attribute to counter-transference illusions and the place they take in analysis. A central feature of training consists in showing the candidate not only that he is liable to illusions, but also the fruitfulness of finding their place in himself by keeping in touch with the unconsciousness processes in himself; how this will continue to happen anyway as a result of his analysis; and how his continuing self-analysis forms one of the bases of learning. I want to suggest that one function of clinical and theoretical discussions and writing papers is to continue the processes that began in training when counter-transference processes were being discovered, often for the first time. This idea introduces the syntonic counter-transference.

Syntonic counter-transference

It is not, I believe, in the sphere of illusion, in the sense in which it is used here, that analytical psychologists have anything of particular interest to say about counter-transference, but rather when it comes to applying the main content of Jung's concept of analysis. I have already referred to the studies made by others, and I now want to develop one of my own, which grows out of the idea that the unconscious acts as an 'organ of information', i.e. a perceptual system, comparable to the receiving set of a wireless.

It would be easy to close this subject by introducing typology and say that I am referring to intuition; this could be done were it not that introjection and other affective states are clearly part of the process of discovery.

Let me start to develop the concept by giving an example of what I mean by thinking there is a counter-transference that can be called syntonic.

A female patient was showing very marked features of projective identification; her interviews became entirely preoccupied with what was going on inside me and her conviction of her accuracy. At the same time she would intersperse her assertions with questions. Now there are many reasons for not answering them, but I found myself refraining from doing so from another motive; indeed there grew up in me a conviction that to do so would be a blunder. I will assume that you think it valid if I say that I was unable to find a source for this affect in myself. I refrained from making any interpretation for several months, until one day she was talking about her father and, in describing her behaviour with him and his with her, it became apparent that she was re-enacting her relationship with him in the transference: a main feature of his behaviour was that he did not answer her questions.

The feature of this incident to which I want to draw attention is that the analyst becomes aware of inner processes for which it is not possible to account completely, but which later become sensible when considered in terms of the patient. I have taken this example because it is rather more easy to describe than others that occur every day. If one waits for a long time and the patient provides the explanation, it is much more convincing than if the whole process occurs quickly and an interpretation is made. I think, however, that this process lies at the basis of many if not all therapeutic interpretations; thus, giving a good interpretation is an expression of a syntonic interchange in which psychic contents pass unconsciously from the patient into the analyst. Intellectual or intuitive interference is only of minor importance because it is the affective process that gives rise to certainty in the analyst; this can then be conveyed to the patient.

I am not sure whether these ideas about counter-transference were influenced by parallel interest amongst psychoanalysts, and perhaps it does not matter very much, but what I had described and formulated as a syntonic counter-transference was based on very similar evidence to that submitted by Paula Heimann (1950), while Money-Kyrle's paper on 'Normal counter-transference' (1956) also develops a comparable idea to mine: there he says that interpretations depend upon very rapid operation of projection–introjection mechanisms, that is upon affective rather than intellectual processes. To relate this theory to that of analytical psychology it is necessary to add that the absolute unconscious in which the boundary concept does not apply and the space–time frame of reference does not operate. Applied to the analytic situation this means there is always an underlying continuum between analyst and patient, which only gets diminished as analysis proceeds; it is never eliminated.

How elements in this continuum become separated out and become conscious is not known, but image formation plays a large part in it, and at this level projection and introjection play an important part.

Now let us return to the example and see whether the episode can be understood in the light of these considerations. There was a period before anything became conscious at all, but the patient and I were behaving according to a prescribed pattern without realizing it. The father archetype was unconscious and there was no boundary between the patient and myself. It can be conceived that, during this period, as the patient's ego defences against realizing the state of affairs were stronger than mine, the archetype had been driven in the direction of my ego and I began to react syntonically to it. The next part of the process was that the patient's affectively charged pattern became introjected by me and began to become conscious, i.e., I was becoming aware that I was reacting on an irrational basis. next, the patient produced the information necessary for me to understand the affective component in why I didn't answer her questions, and then I could project the pattern back into the patient and make an interpretation in relation to her. An adequate one would be, 'Now I see why I don't answer your questions; it is as it was with your father. You made me like your father by the very persistence of your questions, to which you did not expect an answer.' But this disposes only of the personal content, not the archetypal substratum. The interpretation clarified a boundary so that her experience of her father could then be differentiated from my experience of mine. I became orientated and could begin with certainty, a new phase in the analysis; and when I then came up against vigorous resistances these did not shake me in what I was doing.

This formulation helps to make it understandable why analysts need to take notice of their irrational experiences: realization of a syntonic counter-transference can start with a sense that the analyst is doing or feeling something that he cannot at first explain; it will later become understandable when the unconscious content becomes related to the main ego nucleus, which can perceive and moderate its activity.

There is another consideration to which reference must be made before closing. When the analyst's ego is trained to relax its control, then another centre can be sensed and symbolized which Jung has called the self. To it the ego can relate as a part to the whole, which like Clifford Scott's notion of the body scheme (Scott, 1949), is cosmic – the cosmos being the total analytic situation; as part of the whole the ego can allow for the activity of an unconscious that it cannot understand but that is, as it were, understood by the self; and this makes a great deal of difference.

There are some who will regard this as illusion, but analytical psychologists will not agree and though I have added the concept of the self here as if it were a kind of elegant appendage, it controls and has controlled all my thinking about counter-transference (cf. this volume, Chapter 1) The idea was, it will have been noticed, introduced earlier when the whole personality was conceived to become engaged with the patient.

In this paper, it has been my aim to give in outline the kind of framework inside which one analytical psychologist works. Though many of the examples and references are from the writings of others, I have not, I think, said anything that does not relate to my own experience.

NOTE

1 'Discussion on archetypes and internal objects', *British Journal of Medical Psychology*, Vol. XXII, 1949. The contributors were Gerhard Adler, Michael Fordham, Paula Heimann and Clifford Scott (ed).

Chapter 3

Suggestions towards a theory of supervision (1961)[1]

When the Society of Analytical Psychology in London started to frame a programme of training for candidates there were two issues on which agreement was soon reached, the first easily, the second after some hesitation. It was decided, first, that the training should be based on clinical studies, and with this end in view candidates were to take two control cases after two years of preliminary analysis. This was in line with Jung's repeated claim that his researches are based on clinical experience even though he has often chosen, for reasons which we need not go into here, to present his conclusions in terms of mythology.

The second decision, not so easily arrived at, specified that a training analyst was to supervise the candidate's management of his control cases and to teach on such matters as arose out of the material the candidate brought for discussion.

The doubts about the second decision arose from Jung's emphasis on the importance that the analyst's personality inevitably takes in any analysis. This essential feature of his ideas on analytic practice might have led the training analysts to decide that didactic teaching of theory and technique could best be done by the seminar method to trainees as a group, leaving the rest to the candidate's analyst alone. In this way, it might be assumed, the candidate's skills would be more certain to develop out of his personality and there would be less opportunity for him to separate the acquisition of them from his own personal development. The rejection of this policy was based on the belief that it would change the role of the analyst in important respects. He might well be tempted, or even feel under obligation, to act as teacher, in the didactic sense, as well as analyst, and so be unable to give his sole attention and interest to the inner development of the candidate. This was, I think, the main reason in the minds of some training analysts at least, and in my own in particular, for instituting a supervisor who was not the candidate's analyst.

As time has proved, these early reflections were a good example of how valuable it is to consider Jung's thinking with care: from time to time the issue has been raised again and, indeed, will make the basis for much of what will be said here. Another consideration that favoured the institution of a supervisor was not so well founded but has none the less been justified by subsequent experience.

It was feared that if only the analyst knew the candidate well it would put too much responsibility on one person for estimating the candidate's suitability to conduct analyses. It was believed that the supervisor might be expected to act as a check on the analyst's identification with his candidate which might predispose him to support applications to the Society on inadequate grounds. At the present time there is uncertainty as to how often this consideration is justified.

An issue which needs to be raised here is this: in the beginning it was assumed that it was known in what analysis consisted; it has, however, appeared, over the years, that this was only true in a rather limited sense; indeed, critical examination of our practice has shown that what constitutes an analysis is very uncertain and that the term analysis itself was being used in a rather loose way. I have attempted to define it rather more closely elsewhere (cf. Fordham, 1957) and so need not develop the theme here. It is only necessary to note that analysis was and will here be regarded as essentially different from teaching, in that teaching does not involve handling the transference by means of interpretations.

In what follows it is intended to set down some of my own conclusions that have been arrived at on the basis of the early decisions of the training analysts, which have not been altered since training began. It will involve discussing aspects of the relation between the candidate and his patient, his analyst, and his supervisor, starting from two of the questions regarding supervision that were raised at the beginning and again in the course of years in a more developed form.

(i) Should supervision be in the nature of teaching?
(ii) Should it be regarded as a sort of extra analysis?

The answer to (i) has already been decided upon, but the whole subject of (ii) is not so easy and represents the recurrence of the question raised in the early years when regulations were being laid down. For purposes of this discussion (ii) will need formulating differently so as to avoid it being considered an alternative to (i); this it cannot be since (i) is desirable. The second question implies the need for discussion of the role of the candidate's analyst when training starts, and this subject will provide a suitable jumping-off ground.

It will be assumed here, but only for the sake of brevity, that the essential features of ordinary analysis can be maintained within the framework of training, and so the analyst will not need to alter the essentials of his technique. Therefore it is necessary to consider only, whether he is going to come upon special difficulties when training starts, and whether they are of the kind which warrant more analysis by a second analyst in the guise of the supervisor.

That changes occur in the transference relation between the candidate and his analyst when training starts is sufficiently evident, and the problems arising from them may be considered under the general heading of premature dilutions of the transference which are disintegrative; by this is meant that the candidate's transference is rendered less intense because of anxieties arising from the complex relationships set up as the result of an organized training.

1 The analyst may soon realize that a candidate comes to know more about him than before: the candidate will check his inferences about his analyst during analysis against the view of others and, further, will have accumulated more information about his analyst than may be desirable at any particular time. This is undesirable because the matching of projections against direct perception of the analyst's behaviour (cf. Chapter 1, p. 17) becomes more difficult since the candidate's judgement is interfered with by the opinions of other people.
2 The transference can be further diluted by projection into the control cases and then, as the result of the supervision situation, the development of a transference to the supervisor. It is clearly of the first importance how this is handled, as can easily be demonstrated by continuing analysis after supervision has stopped, a common feature of what may be termed post-training analysis. In this period it becomes easier to analyse those aspects of the candidate which had been hidden in the supervision situation.
3 The seminar group will lead to the candidate working or acting out transference conflicts with other members of the group composed of other trainees.

There is only one suggestion I would like to make here towards management of these rather complex features of training: candidates need to be seen often enough for their analysts to circumvent too much defensive dilution of the transference, and it seems to me beneficial if they are seen on the same day after supervision has taken place or, at the latest, on the next day. Then if the supervisor hits on conflict situations in the candidate, he can feel more confident that they will be available for analysis and will not get covered over again.

Turning now to supervision. As already stated, it was originally instituted with a view to avoiding the analyst becoming a teacher and so obstructing the integration of unconscious contents. Only later did the question arise as to what the more detailed position of the supervisor might become.

Developing Plaut's formulation (1961, p. 100): the supervisor is the most important person in initiating the candidate into membership of the Society because he is mainly occupied in developing the conscious skills of the candidate, and functions as a check on the candidate's tendency to act out during regressions, arising either as part of his analysis or as the result of the stress of training. The complex social factors entering into supervision have been considered in some detail by Minna Emch (1955). There she convincingly shows the complex situation to which training gives rise. The possible combinations in a system involving seven elements, assuming one emotional valence, is 126. If emotional ambivalence is taken into account, the figure rises to 1,183. The elements she considers are: a supervisor, a student, a control case, the training analyst, another past or present supervisor, the training committee, and a seminar leader. These figures compel us to reflect that the emotional stresses involved are so complex that they cannot be described, and they show the necessity to simplify by selecting the attitudes and roles that seem of more importance than others in any training programme of an analytic kind; this simplification need not make us overlook the complexities, however, though it may appear to do violence to the subtle and often rapidly changing cross-currents continually met with during training.

As a starting-point, I wish to propose dogmatically that it is the supervisor's role, together with that of the seminar leaders, to treat the candidate actively as a junior colleague, and not as a patient, right from the beginning. By this is meant that the trainee has the free right to draw on all the supervisor's knowledge and experience as he wants it without respect to any deficiencies in the candidate's personality that may become apparent. In return for this the candidate has much to offer in addition to money; in particular, there are the experiences he brings to supervision which will extend the supervisor's experiences and so give him the opportunity to learn and to develop his theories and techniques.

Since the supervisor will be occupied in listening to the case material presented by the candidate and will aim at discussing the cases as a colleague, he need not dilute the transference, and if he keeps this problem clearly in mind he can help the candidate's analysis in ways to be considered later. Discussion during supervision can be conceived as centring on questions of the general management of cases, and the supervisor suggests reading in so far as it is relevant to the technical and theoretical questions that arise out of his teaching on case material. All this involves imparting technical skills such as the interpretation of all kinds of material brought by the control patient, particular attention being paid to the transference of the control case to the candidate. It will evoke a counter-transference from the candidate and so introduces the important but difficult question: is it desirable for the supervisor to show the candidate where his counter-transference lies and how it is either interfering with his relation to the control case or facilitating it? This question is of particular importance because it leads to the possibility of initiating analysis of the candidate by the supervisor. In my view he should point out counter-transference manifestations but without analysing the candidate, only confronting him with them. This is possible for the following reasons. The supervision time is mainly devoted to the presentation and discussion of material brought by the candidate. Since a candidate is asking for supervision, his time is mainly filled up and he will not want to give information about his own personal life. It is of particular importance that the supervisor never tries to elicit any. This procedure is supported by a further consideration. It is one of the unstated assumptions of candidates that supervisors will refrain from analysing them, and the supervisor, realizing this, implicitly agrees. Unless both want consciously to alter the agreement it should be scrupulously kept.

This view of supervision would at first sight seem to exclude analysis from it altogether. Yet if both the analysis and the supervision are being well conducted, it still happens that a candidate occasionally gives clear indications that he wants bits of analysis from his supervisor. I consider that it is in order for the supervisor to give it because there are sufficient checks against it going far. By "clear indications" I mean that the candidate will state that he does not want supervision but wants to talk about himself, and even his transference to his analyst, for the next hour; at best he will ask openly for the supervisor's agreement. The theory of transference as a social phenomenon makes it easy to understand why this happens. When training starts it is manifest that each candidate will need to project the archetypal forms related to supervision into the Society, the committees, the lecturers, and also the supervisor, who will consequently become not only a real person but an ambivalent figure. If it be borne in mind that the supervisor aims to relate and build on the energies available to the candidate's ego, then it can be realized that in doing so he is fulfilling the archetypal role of initiator. As such he will not draw attention to and indeed will resist discussion of the transference processes involved and will, rather, aim at fulfilling the role that may be expected to match the candidate's deliberate aim of acquiring knowledge and skills in contrast to his unconscious ambivalent needs. Inasmuch as it is not possible to do this with complete success all the time, the candidate and also the supervisor may spend sessions in clarifying the affective situation that has arisen between them. This need not go far as long as the supervisor refrains, as I think he can usually do, from interpreting the unconscious motives of the candidate. Clearly, transference interpretations need to be avoided if the policy I am proposing is to be pursued.

Only when the supervisor is led to act so much as an analyst that his role of supervisor is interfered with for long, will he need to inquire what has happened. There are two possibilities:

1 Suppose the supervision has been correctly conducted along the lines so far defined, then the candidate's transference to his analyst must have run into difficulties; either it is not being taken up by the analyst because the candidate is not being seen sufficiently often by him to allow this, or else the candidate has run into a very strong resistance and needs to use supervision as part of his defence system. In these circumstances I do not believe that the supervisor need do anything but continue supervising as much as possible. It can, however, happen, in spite of the supervisor's efforts, that this state of affairs develops so that a candidate wants analysis from his supervisor in place of his first analyst; by "wanting a change" is meant that he will ask for it from his supervisor after going into the matter with his analyst. Then the change can be openly made. Such a change need not reflect on the candidate so long as the clear need for it comes from him and he gets it recognized as desirable by his analyst as well as his supervisor.
2 The second possible cause for supervision breaking down is that it has been so conducted as to induce a transference neurosis to the supervisor in contrast to the archetypal transference held to be inevitable, and the trainee can then want a change of analyst on neurotic grounds. This will happen when the supervisor's counter-transference to the trainee is not recognized. The change will not take place if his analysis is being well conducted, but angry conflicts

> between supervisor and analyst can result and the candidate will justifiably want to change his supervisor. If the supervisor has induced a neurotic transference, the desire for a change can appear as a neurotic manifestation. This has occurred in the London Society, but it was understood that a change needed to be made, and the candidate went on to become a member of the Society.

The most frequent source for the difficulties just enumerated lies in that part of supervision which consists in showing the candidate where his countertransference to his control case lies. In the process of doing so the candidate's failings inevitably become particularly apparent to the supervisor whose aim, indeed, is to highlight them. But the candidate can then begin to show neurotic phenomena so that the supervisor may get presented, almost on a plate, with the candidate's whole residual neurosis; this is one situation in which the supervisor, who may after all have induced this state, can wrongly believe that the analyst is at fault. It is worth underlining that the manifestations will not lead the candidate to asking for analysis from the supervisor because he will want to take them back to the analyst if all is going well; this formulation holds only when the supervisor neither denies nor manipulates the situation but only sustains it (by sustaining is meant realizing it without doing anything). In this connection, I believe that if the supervisor tells the candidate to disclose to his analyst what has been found in supervision this needs to be classed an a manipulation which interferes with and does not facilitate the candidate's analysis and, if done clumsily, endangers the supervision relationship.

In my opinion the following criterion for giving interpretations holds in supervision: they should not be given unless the candidate offers sufficient personal information to make it quite clear that he wants the interpretation to be given. It is because of the nature of good supervision, whereby information of this kind will not be available most of the time, that only bits of analysis can take place.

To summarize: a supervisor may point out and discuss the candidate's countertransference to his control case and confront him with it, but will avoid making analytic observations or interpretations except under exceptional conditions.

In all this the question of the relation between analyst and supervisor is implied. It seems to me that the analytic methods pursued by each should be reasonably close, at least in the first year of training. When there are considerably different, it can be serious; and the seriousness of it tends to get rationalized and so glossed over.

If the supervisor disagrees too widely with the analyst or if he is convinced the analyst's analyses are not adequate, he will be under considerable strain. He cannot supervise without showing the candidate how to conduct the analysis of his control case according to his own view, but in doing so he knows that the candidate will inevitably compare what he is taught with how his own analysis has been conducted. The risk of seriously diluting the transference is then considerable. This became a very difficult problem for me at one time when I was developing ideas about the transference not held by some other training analysts; also supervision of candidates in analysis with me obstructed their analysis because the supervisor exploited the candidate's bit of transference to him by using a combination of analytic and manipulative techniques. I gained the quite clear impression through the candidate that the supervisor thought my analysis grossly defective and that he tried to complement it. This, however, only led to a preponderantly negative transference to the supervisor and fixed the projections made by the candidate on to him; they could be defined but not reduced. As the candidate continued analysis after supervision, it became clear how damaging the experience had been to the candidate's training, even though he became reasonably clear about what was happening at the time. During this period of conflict over the meaning of analysis within the society, my supervision increased a candidate's wish for analysis of the kind I was showing him how to conduct. I believe it was because I had been conducting supervision in the way here described that the change of analysts was brought about with the conscious agreement of all parties.

The point that has interested me, as an analyst in contrast to being a supervisor, has been that supervisors only take up or try to analyse points that have already come into the candidate's analysis, but were not ready to be resolved. This is of interest because the supervisor could be under the impression that this was not the case.

Bearing these considerations in mind, and also that supervisors often think analysts are not analysing properly when they discover the candidate's residual neurosis, it is manifestly advisable that analyst and supervisor should be selected from amongst analysts who can communicate and map out their points of agreement and their differences, which should not be too great. I do not think it is necessary for the two to meet for discussion of the candidate, but it can be valuable for them to discuss their ideas about analytic practice. I have with few exceptions refrained from discussions with analysts when supervising, and vice versa, and it has worked out well enough in the end as far as I know. I do not think that discussions benefited the candidate, though they have been quite illuminating in terms of the triangular situation which is manifestly at work and is important; the most prominent feature in this appears to be the tendency for rivalry to develop between analyst and supervisor. In view of this eventuality, it follows that when this situation is well handled it leads to a good training, but if it is not then the candidates can be made the instrument of a conflict of two contending parental figures, to his detriment. Whereas some candidates can survive this, others with a less favourable background are liable to become casualties. As in families, this is particularly damaging if the conflict is unconscious.

There is one further function of the supervisor not so far mentioned. It is the function of the supervisor, and not the analyst, to exert control over the trainee's application for membership of the Society. It is of advantage if he makes clear to the candidate his opinion of the candidate's suitability to analyse patients. This grows inevitably out of his aim of treating the candidate as a colleague.

In conclusion, it will be evident that in all training we need to remember this: candidates are put under greater stress than is any trained analyst and so we need to find out how to diminish it. One way to do this is for analyst and supervisor to be clear about what they are doing as part of the training set-up.

NOTE

1 This and the following two papers were part of the "Symposium on Training" (*Journal of Analytic Psychology*, 6,2, 1961 and 7,1, 1962). Fordham also contributed an editorial introduction. The contributors in part I were Michael Fordham, Kathleen Newton and Alfred Plaut, followed by a comment by Edward Edinger and a reply by Fordham (see following). The contributor in part II was James Hillman, followed with responses from Fordham (see following) and Plaut and a reply by Hillman (ed.).

Chapter 4

Reply to Dr Edinger (1961)[1]

Dr Edinger takes issue with the London Society's policy of instituting a supervisor who is not the analyst on the grounds that it splits the candidate in two, and believes that dilution of the transference is indicated in that it helps in its resolution. These ideas require some reply, for, if true, they would certainly be a serious matter for the training in London. I believe, however, that there is room for discussion of Dr Edinger formulation.

The fact that a candidate goes to an analyst and to a supervisor cannot, itself, mean that he himself is split any more than the existence of friends, relatives, and colleagues in work indicates a split in any particular person. It is not, therefore, logical to assume that the candidate is split because he has an analyst and a supervisor. There are, however, conditions under which a candidate's splitting processes can be facilitated and it is these which I attempted to define, if only partly, under the heading of "dilution in the transference". I contend, further, that there are definable conditions which make splitting less likely and that they do not correspond to the conditions obtaining when the analyst becomes the supervisor or when two analysts are analysing one candidate. The understanding of why this is so turns on whether skills can be taught or not, and on the theory of transference adopted; it is evident to me that skills are wanted and can be acquired by candidates. It follows that teaching how to analyse patients is valuable so long as the candidate is sufficiently aware of the relation of the skills he acquires to his personality as a whole. It is the aim of the analysis to produce this consciousness, and it should and indeed seems to be the best way of doing so.

I am glad that Edinger has raised the subject of two analysts and hope that one day this matter will be further argued and documented. Until satisfactory evidence is brought, there seems to me no reason for departing from the reliable procedure of one analyst conducting the analysis of one patient or candidate. These issues, as well as that of transference dilution, confessions by the analyst, and the analyst's influence as a whole, turn on the complex method of transference management into which it is clearly impossible to enter here. I can do no more than indicate that I think clarification is needed in this area; discussion of the subject would lead much further than space would allow. However, I would like to make it quite clear that dilution and resolution of the transference are, in my view, radically different events.

NOTE

1 In his response to Fordham's piece, Edinger argues that the rigid splitting of analysis and supervision in turn leads to undesirable splitting in the candidate. He claims that analysis and supervision are best performed in a single relationship. In addition he expresses his belief in the candidate's need to have experience with more than one analyst (ed.).

Chapter 5

A comment on James Hillman's papers (1962)[1]

There will be agreement with much of what Hillman says in his paper. That analysis is the central feature of training, that candidates must take cases under supervision, and that Jung's works should be closely studied can all be considered as of the first importance. Likewise, the value of group life is well recognized and is being made the subject of searching inquiry in many quarters. I should, however, be giving a false impression if, in saying this, I did not add that I think that some of the agreement, will be based on inadequate grounds. All points of agreement. with the exception of reading Jung's works, need to be kept under constant review, and the basic assumptions clarified and if necessary revised in the light of experience based on experiments. Hillman states, almost apologetically, that the Institute's work is experimental, inferring that this is owing to the lack of adequate tradition. For my part, I think it will be a sad day if tradition ever replaces experiment combined with reflection on the ideas which have made experiments possible.

There is one other general criticism which I should like to make. In my view, the training problems raised by Hillman are overweighted on the side of impressive activities. They seem to leave the trainee out of account for too much, especially with regard to an aspect of training which is opened up if we ask the question: How can a training organization provide conditions under which the candidate will arrive at a good assessment of his own capacity to analyse others? This question, to my mind, is central if the concept of the self is going to percolate all spheres of training and ensure that the analysis is thorough. I am unable to see that the Zürich practice of multiplying lectures and holding examinations helps in this respect – particularly examinations, since the judgement does not lie in the candidate's hands. In other words, I believe that training institutes might well make it their aim to guide the candidate's own judgement of himself. I am glad that we do not have either many lectures or examinations in London. Likewise, I think it is an advantage that our trainees are not dispersed over the face of the globe, since what has been done, for good or ill, cannot be avoided and can be learnt from.

In highlighting the position of the analyst in training Hillman has done us a service, but I think it is worthwhile asking the following question: if the analysis is well conducted, is it possible for the remaining training procedures to be anything but secondary in importance? My own answer to this is that, whatever other people may think, or within very wide limits do, there is no chance that analysis will in reality become subsidiary. This conclusion is based on the experience, in apparent contradistinction to Hillman, that training deepens the analysis and makes it more, not less, transforming. I should like to suggest a reason for the difference in view. Though it inevitably depends upon a number of factors, how the transference is handled is more important than anything else. Therefore, I am not at all happy about Hillman's rather cavalier treatment of this subject: indeed, he gives an account (Hillman, 1962a p. 20) of how transference is "augmented", presumably by using frequent interviews and by interpreting, which bears no relation to any procedure that I have ever heard of. Further, the multi-analyst approach is extremely unconvincing to me and always has been.

In this connection there are several points of detail on which I want to comment, because Hillman seems to have distorted, overlooked, or altered the sense of what I mean.

1 I do not think that his quotations from my writings on transference are altogether fair. In saying that the analyst becomes the centre of the analysis I meant just that, not that everything gets concentrated in the analysis. Further, when I said that the "concentration of libido is made into an aim", I regarded this as a mistaken attitude arising from a fear of "acting out". I cannot see that what I wrote could be used as I understand Hillman to use it, because the rest of the section in my book is directed to show that it is an absurd aim. I did this by defining the meaning of "acting out" or "living one's shadow". I myself regard the above aim as delusional in that it cannot be implemented, and I thoroughly agree with what Hillman says about the ubiquity of projections (1962a, p. 20). His description corresponds exactly with usual expectations; it therefore seems that at least two training and analytic procedures produce the same effect in one sphere.
2 My observations on dilution of the transference were based on empirical observation within a defined training procedure. If these phenomena cannot be observed in Zürich training, then there are two alternatives: either they have not been looked for or else they do not appear because the procedure is different. There is no need to introduce philosophy.
3 My quotation from Emch was given simply as a reminder of the numerous conflict patterns which training evoked.
4 Hillman believes that my proposal that the supervisor should exert control over the candidate's final application (not his acceptance or rejection) is an illustration of the way in which the analyst's position is diminished. This I believe to be an error, which I can illustrate as follows:

The supervisor is inevitably in the best position to judge the standard of the candidate's analytic work with patients. If, therefore, he considers the candidate competent, then the candidate's suitability can be considered further by the

Society as represented by its committees with the training analyst present. This does not jeopardize the position of the training analyst in any way, so long as his analysis of the candidate is good and so long as he does not collude in the illusion of his omnipotence or omniscience. Another advantage of asking the supervisor to act in this way is that it reduces the reality load on the candidate's illusions about his analyst's parental authority.

Tempting as it may be to discuss the many interesting points raised by Hillman, I shall refrain from doing so for a specific reason. I do not believe that it would be profitable until the analysts in the Institute have made it more clear why they have adopted the multi-analyst procedure and made it a rule that two (or more?) analysts are necessary[2].

NOTES

1 In his papers "Training and the C. G. Jung Institute, Zürich" and "A note on multiple analysis and emotional climate at training Institutes" (Hillman, 1962, 1962a), Hillman describes and gives the rationale for the training programme at the C.G. Jung Institute, Zürich, with emphasis on the examination requirements and the practice of multiple analysis as befitting the specificity of analytical psychology, compared to psychoanalysis. In the second piece Hillman critiques Fordham's 'Notes on transference' (Chapter 1, this volume) as advocating procedures that would induce transference, which would distort the natural flow of the libido, as well as the candidate's religious life (ed.).

2 In his reply, Hillman accepts Fordham's clarification of his views and further elaborates on the need for a comprehensive study programme. Hillman agrees with Fordham and Plaut on the need for more material to be published on the practice of multiple analysis (ed.).

Chapter 6

Problems of a training analyst (undated)[1]

My introductory paragraph today was written after the bulk of this paper had been completed. By that time I knew that the training analyst's conflict centred on his relation to the Society much more than on his candidate's who all the same focused them. Consequently I shall leave the actual training analysis to the end where I shall only discuss it briefly: mostly we shall occupy ourselves with the relation between the training analyst and the Society, represented by the professional committee, as it exists now or has functioned in the past. It has, I think, been largely due to the behaviour of the training analysts that more rigorous methods of selection have had to be introduced. They have resulted from a prolonged dialectic that has gone on in the professional committee and, since the policy of the Society is being made there, I think it will be of interest if I put down what I think one training analyst could contribute to policy and method, both of which are the concern of the Society as a whole.

We shall do well to begin by clarifying the training analyst's position vis-à-vis his analysand and show wherein this is different from that in other analyses.

There are six headings under which we can consider the matter; they all relate to the special situation in which the training analyst finds himself as a member of the Society to whom the candidate seeks admission. The candidate believes that the analyst will have most influence in achieving this aim and this is sometimes, though not always, true. Here are the headings:

1 The beginning of a training analysis.
2 The application of the candidate to be considered for training.
3 Situations deriving from the candidate attending seminars and taking cases under supervision.
4 The application for associate membership.
5 The continuation of analysis after training has finished.
6 The relation between the training analyst and the new member of the society.

Not all these headings will be given the same weight, indeed we shall pay most attention to the second heading: the analyst's situation when the candidate applies for training. Under present circumstances, and as far as I personally am implicated, the candidate's application is by far the most important. After this it is only just too gross an exaggeration to say that all is gained or lost in relation to the candidate's analysis.

1 The beginning of the analysis is influenced by the analysand's belief that he wants to be an analyst. The implication here is that this is his true aim and the analysis is being undertaken with a view to implementing his intention.

So stated the analyst can suspend judgement and await events. He will consider the candidate's assertion as one symptom amongst others though it may turn out to be a special and rather crucial one for the development of the analysis.

Though the training analyst suspends judgement he is at once brought up against the conditions laid down for training: the candidate expects to be in analysis for four years at least and he knows that he is required to attend for analysis three times a week. Both these factors exercise restraint in two directions: on the candidate because there is plenty of time; on the analyst because he can get into difficulties over interview frequency. If he thinks it desirable for the candidate to come more often, his authority may meet that of the Society's rules and regulations. Similarly if he thinks that three times a week is excessive or unnecessary he will run the risk of jeopardizing the candidate's acceptance when he applies for formal training. Both these restraints can act as symptoms and be analyzed as such, but their reality has to be taken into account as well. If, in short, the analyst deviates from the Society's requirements he is liable to come under fire first from the candidate and later from the Society and he may be tempted to exploit the transference in what he believes to be the candidate's interest of his own conscience. It also means that if a departure such as an increase or diminution in interview frequency is desirable the reasons for it will have to be made clear to the candidate. I should state here that in my view a training analyst ought to involve the candidate so that more than three times a week becomes a manifest necessity.

A word here about regulations: it can only be to everybody's advantage if the basic rules for training are explicitly stated and scrupulously enforced since only then can both candidate and analyst know where each stands vis-à-vis the Society. I say this even though in more than one case I wanted to start four times a week but had to give in and wait till this became an obvious necessity. It is sometimes thought that clear cut conditions mean closure in the sense that rules are unalterable, but if good reason for a change becomes apparent then rules can surely be altered. Here I would like to interpolate a reflection about changing them; what about occasions when an analyst deviates from the rules? It might help him if it became current practice for him to inform the committee and if necessary justify briefly his reasons for the variations and ask the members what they think. This would keep the committee informed of current practices and so facilitate progressive learning about training. It might also help to keep regulations up to date. For instance it is becoming rather more common for analysts to consider three times a week inadequate. How often is this happening and why?

2 Now we come to the second heading. After a nominal two years, the candidate is formally eligible for training and can apply to the Society to be accepted as a trainee of the Society.

By this time the analyst may be expected to have formed a judgement as to the candidate's suitability or otherwise and express it to the professional committee. When he meets the committee he will be in a strong position: he has far more information at his disposal than any committee member and more than either of the two interviewers who will have seen the candidate only for about fifty minutes each. Now it seems to me desirable for his meeting to result in a discussion rather than the committee scrutinizing the analyst's report as tends to happen. The difficulty in initiating such a discussion in this: the analyst will have so much information that it will take him a great deal of time to organize what he knows if wants to make it intelligible to the committee with a view of getting his information discussed. It is my impression that whether he succeeds or not depends just as much upon how he presents his information and his conclusion than on the committee itself. If it could be understood that the situation can be thought of as a learning situation on both sides it would be good. The committee need to learn from the analyst what sort of candidate is being considered; for his part the analyst needs to learn how effective and valid his conclusion is by its effect on the committee members, who represent both their own ideas and the Society's policy at any particular time.

What is the training analyst to sort out for special mention? Before the professional committee had drawn up a list of matters considered important, it was very difficult indeed to know how much to contribute and it was tempting for the analyst to confine himself to praise of the candidate. This procedure has been rejected but it took quite a long time to realize how necessary it was to do so. In spite of this, there is still a very real difficulty here which can be shown up if we make a list of headings to indicate what confronts the training analyst. The following is an attempt to outline what is necessary if he were to present a good and relatively complete picture to the committee. He would have to describe:

1 The structure of the candidate's character covering his inner resources (inner life), range of interests and commitments, personal, scientific, aesthetic, etc.
2 The origins of the cross section picture given under 1. This would mean a detailed history insofar as it has been obtained and reconstructed. It would entail an account of the gaps in the history of where and why they occur.
3 The course of the analysis. In this the nature and vicissitudes of the transference (ambivalent or pre-ambivalent) must feature prominently as well as the degree of insight into the transference data exhibited by the candidate.
4 An account of how much his analysis means to the candidate and in particular has it led or is he likely to pursue it so as to lead, to a really transforming experience. To put this differently, what are the candidate's potentialities and what are the possibilities of his realizing them and what would his doing so entail?
5 What in all this makes the analyst think that the candidate is going to use his abilities in the analysis of others?
6 What makes the analyst consider that the candidate is now in a position to make good use of the training provided by the Society?

It is, I think, rather clear that if these headings were gone into in detail, committee meetings would be lengthened unbearably and I think uselessly. The analyst must therefore only use these headings (of which 1, 2 and 3 have been elaborated very helpfully by the professional committee) so that his idea can be presented in disciplined form. His hope must be to get from the committee help in assessing whether his tentative or convinced conclusions are right or wrong in relation to current Society policy and the policy–making function of the committee. In all this the interviewer's function will be in a good position to ask pertinent questions and assess or reassess their observations in the light of what the analyst can say. At its best the whole process would thus be a dialectic process. It would be ideally best if the analyst never made up his mind about the candidate before the meeting but I fear that this is out of the question.

By now you will be well on the way to understanding my main thesis: at the present time acceptance or rejection of a candidate for training depends 80 per cent upon the analyst's view and this is where his main conflict lies. Thereafter the analyst will be able to share responsibility increasingly as others gain more and more knowledge of the candidate, but before this has happened the main responsibility must be his. There would be advantages to be gained by trying to develop techniques whereby so much responsibility was not vested in the training analyst because of his relation to his candidate. His conflicts centre round the question: what about the analyst giving the candidate his view of the validity of his application? This raises difficult issues related to forwarding the candidate's ability to assess his own capacities.

CANDIDATE'S ASSESSMENT OF HIMSELF

Let us start by considering an ideal state of affairs. The candidate has considered his application at length, thought over what is required of him by the Society, weighed up the amount of extra work that will be entailed, looked into his financial position and found it will be possible, consulted his family if he or she is married or close friends if not. All his deliberations have been brought piece by piece to his analyst who has analyzed the material in detail. The result will be a candidate who might surely put his own case before the committee. The odds are, in my view, that he would be accepted and I dare say that if asked his analyst would agree that this was a good candidate.

It is of interest that this method has never been employed directly in this Society. We started by combining formal criteria with the analyst's report. Later, two interviewers were added largely because analysts failed to organize their data well enough and tried to substitute categorical statements for an account of what they knew and on which their assessment was based. All the same, why is it that the committee has only asked the candidate to meet them in exceptional circumstances? It has never asked him to submit to them his own written self–assessment as far as I know, but has preferred to filter it through the interviewers. It is evidently supposed that the analyst and the interviewers will be in a better position than the candidate to do what we might hope he himself could do. There are good reasons for our procedure and I mentioned the alternative mainly to reveal the load of responsibility placed on the analyst and interviewers, which ideally would not be necessary.

Let us, however, remember that the object we set ourselves in analyzing our patients is to increase self–realization. If however, we, as a Society, represented by the professional committee who relies most on the training analyst for information, take responsibility for the candidate, we are supporting regression by treating the candidate as a child who cannot be relied upon to know what is good for him. I would conclude that the main reason why information is filtered through three people is this: whilst a candidate is in analysis his transference will extend to the Society and he will react falsely because of it. This sometimes happens in interviews, perhaps especially, when attempts are made to find out what kind of transference is active between analyst and candidate. This view is not always accepted for, I assume in order to treat the candidate as mature enough, training analysts have been known to tell the candidate why they have been turned down in spite of the injunction not to reveal what went on in the professional committee. On the whole, I think that the injunction is desirable because it facilitates the discussion in the committee, but there are difficulties in it for a training analyst and I have sometimes wished that I had not been present when a decision had been arrived at, especially when it is made on what I consider grounds which the candidate might benefit by knowing.

"THE SUPPORTING ANALYST"

Next let us consider why there are so few unaccepted applications for training. I have not looked up the files, but I should imagine a very considerable majority are accepted on their first application.

Now, if I am right that 80 per cent of this depends upon the analyst supporting his candidate, it may be because the training analysts are doing their job well. Whilst I think this is worth assuming till it is proved false, it has been said that training analysts are liable to support the candidate on principle. Let us therefore consider a number of pressures that predispose him to become, not a good judge, but a "supporting analyst". Though this attitude was observed by members of the professional committee, nobody has yet said what makes a training analyst take up a false supporting attitude. They are not very pleased and perhaps this is why they have not been listed. Here are the ones which seem to me worthy of consideration.

1 It is good to feel that the candidate is "your" candidate. Once you have felt this it is easy to take the next step and feel "because this is my candidate he is a good candidate".
2 It is good to feel "here is another future member of the Society who will understand what I am after through personal experience".

3 It is good to feel you are loyally supporting your candidate in what he wants or supposes he wants.
4 And if all these considerations are insufficient the analyst may shrug his shoulders and quiet his real judgement with: "Well, in any case it is only after training that the candidate will be in a position to judge freely whether he wants to be an analyst or no." This argument is very seductive because it is true enough, but has been used to evade the immediate issue.
5 The last consideration is much more serious: the analyst opposed to the Society's policy may seek to introduce candidates who will also be opposed to it. This is the only indefensible motive, if kept secret, and it should surely lead to the resignation of the training analyst. I do not think that in the long run any training analyst who has managed his psychotic trends would fall for long into the pitfalls of which this list is the exposition. However, they are all cogent factors in the training analyst becoming the "supporting analyst" and it is up to the committee and interviewers to spot them. Training analysts are liable to such defects which are in a sense a collective responsibility. Be it remembered here that all training analysts are elected by the Society – they do not apply for the distinction.

SOCIETY POLICY AND THE TRAINING ANALYST

In all this there is, I think, an implied need to get as clear a policy as is possible about what the Society as a whole is after and, if it is aiming at several ends, which of them carry priority. If the Society and so its committees cannot define aims, then each training analyst will have to make his own frame of reference. Here is one that could be considered.

a) The candidate is likely to become primarily devoted to analytic methods. He is a person who has or will develop a vocation. I suggest that in this case his analysis will have been of central importance for him and will result in a total effect reaching into every fact of his life.
b) The candidate wants to integrate analytic methods into another discipline: psychiatry, clinical psychology or religion, etc. If this aim is sustained it is not likely that the analysis will be so important to him as in the first group.

If these two groups are recognized and they correspond, as far as I can see, to the two kinds of members that we find in the Society, it would be worth making this explicit.

CONCLUSIONS TO HEADING

a) The more the Society's policy is made explicit, the more the candidate will be able to make up his own mind when application is appropriate.

b) The less policy is explicit (and available to all and sundry) the more acceptance will depend on the analyst's individual judgement and individual views as to what the Society ought to be.

To state my own view, I think the analyst's opinion is most valuable in relation to the ongoing development of the Society. As the 80 per cent is reduced the more can the analyst confine himself to the analysis of his candidate who would then increasingly become his patient.

All this has been thrown into relief by the candidate's application for training, now for the third heading.

ANALYSIS DURING TRAINING

Once the candidate has been accepted or rejected, the acute problem for the training analyst will have subsided. He can relax and continue his work. But it will not be long before he will notice a change and this will be connected with his candidate's view of the analyst's real or supposed role in the Society's decision. I have known acceptance contributed towards wrecking an analysis, rejection has never done so. There has always been some difference following acceptance. As a whole it represents a lessening of guilt and an increase in anxiety. It is highly desirable to analyze the situation but it is extra difficult because a change has happened in reality. The manifest anxiety is greatest between the application and the receipt of a letter from the chairman accepting or rejecting the candidate.

In the period of training one hears a great deal about seminars, the way they are led and the view expressed by colleagues: there are comparisons and rivalries with other trainees. Sometimes all this is interesting, sometimes irritating and it can act as a distraction from the analysis of the candidate rather more so than other kinds of information which any patient brings. It is somewhat harder work analyzing a trainee in that you have to make more effort not to get led down the tempting blind alleys that the candidate invites you to enter with him.

There remain the cases being taken on and the supervision. I can only say of this situation that whilst the candidate is acquiring the tools of his future profession some evident transference to the supervisor is inevitable; it cannot be avoided and it is more difficult to analyze than others of a like kind because the supervisor's conclusions about the candidate's work are going to be decisive in his acceptance or rejection. In fact, I do not think it can be analyzed adequately until the candidate has been accepted into the Society and supervision has ended. My reason for taking this view is that a family pattern has been set up and there is too much reality in the candidate's dependence on the parent figures. It is impossible to get round the fact that whether the candidate achieves his aim or not depends mainly on two people. He cannot afford to place enough trust in them since they do not usually, some never, reveal their opinion till it is expressed by acceptance or rejection.

APPLICATION FOR ASSOCIATE PROFESSIONAL MEMBERSHIP

I do not think that this need cause much heart searching to the analyst. By now the supervisor will know a good deal about the candidate's capacity to analyze patients and reports will be available from seminar leaders. The training analysts will already have defined the candidate's nuclear conflicts and all he really needs to state is how these have progressed. This view is not recognized but I hope it will be. However, application for acceptance or rejection as an associate member is a collective event in the sense that the training application is not. Thus it is a matter which the Society through its committees can much more truly decided.

ANALYSIS AFTER ACCEPTANCE OR REJECTION

It has been said that now the candidate can get some real analysis unhampered by anxiety about the training analyst's power over his future. This is only partly true; it happens more if training has mobilized too many defensives. It does not apply to those who have found out that they really want analysis for themselves. This is surely the only way that training will settle into its right perspective as furnishing them with the instruments they will use in their new profession.

With those for whom training has been used to strengthen defences, and this mostly applies to firmly rooted omnipotent fantasies, there will follow a struggle about continuing analysis which can now appear as a greater threat than before, but , whether they go on or no, the aim to get out of it will be greater and they will do so on the basis that since training is over they have got what they wanted, and are going to stop, if not now at least soon.

Assuming that these defences can be analyzed, there remains the field which we have already touched on – the supervisor and the candidate's patients. However astute the supervisor has proved to be, there will be a residual split in the transference which can only be analyzed and resolved after training has stopped and after the supervision has ceased.

Training does indeed help the candidate to forge good and useful instruments, but unless these are integrated into the analyst's personal experience they only too easily act negatively. The theories learnt and the methods used can easily result in the beginning analyst becoming isolated with what he has learnt. He can be functioning beyond himself and releasing affects from his patients which he cannot handle. The theories and methods still need further digesting. Even though this has been going on during training, the process cannot be completed without further analysis and with most this must involve a deeper regression than before. Inasmuch as training constellates oedipal patterns it has made pre-oedipal two-body analysis more difficult.

THE RELATION BETWEEN THE TRAINING ANALYST AND THE NEW MEMBER OF THE SOCIETY

If the new member has worked sufficiently through the delusional aspects of the transference, continuing analysis will not present insuperable difficulties. All the analyst can do is to make entry into the Society's life reasonably easy by behaving with ordinary discretion and especially refraining from exploiting the new member's identification with him, which is inevitable and desirable. As the analysis works itself out, and if the analyst does not seek to further the member's supposed interest inadvisably through an unresolved counter-transference, the new member may expect to settle into the Society, find and take his own place in it. I don't see any difficult problem for the training analyst, though on a number of occasions I have bumped into fantasies by members which seemed rather paranoid, based usually on undue influence of the analyst through the new member.

It is well enough known that analysts return to their training analyst for more analysis or they choose a new one. If they do the latter it strikes me to the advantage of the ex-candidate if he or she tells his training analyst and says why he or she is going to somebody else. I say it is to the advantage of the ex-candidate because I would expect the training analyst to know why, but his ex-patient may not know this.

THE TRAINING ANALYSIS ITSELF

So far, we have considered the special conditions under which a training analyst works and have not taken account of the training analysis itself. It is usually held that it is not to be differentiated from any other analysis. This is partly true and would be more so if the stresses on the training analyst were not different from and greater than in other analyses. It will be understood that there are numerous other differences besides those already listed, amongst which the length of analysis is the most prominent.

I have heard it stated in committee that an applicant should be told that he ought to go into analysis and that this would not differ from an ordinary analysis! Probably the statement refers to a procedure in which the self is placed in the foreground, i.e. a training analysis, like any other, must be a study of the self conducted in such a way as to benefit the candidate. This is why it is so important for the analyst to be clear about his own narcissistic aims and about his relation to the Society, and for the Society to realize just where the analyst is needed, so as to help them in choosing good candidates, and where he is not required.

It cannot be contested that the central feature of training is the candidate's analysis, yet more than once we have run up against situations in which training can be used by both candidate and training analyst to hinder if not prevent the development so much desired.

It is very unusual, however, for anybody who starts with the aim of being trained to continue avoiding personal issues for long, and it would be a very bad training analyst who did not succeed in analyzing the motives for training at all. I hope that most of you would agree that your analyses have done more than anything in driving home the dialectical nature of analysis, the two way nature of learning and the futility of operating techniques as instruments split off from the personality as a whole.

It is useful to look at origins from time to time because they give perspective to our deliberations. Training analysis began to be insisted upon from the discovery of the way counter-transference interfered with or even prevented the development of a psychoanalysis. Since then its importance has increased enormously. At one time it almost seemed to be considered that submitting to analysis was enough – technique became a bad word and the idea of the dialectic between two persons, analyzed analyst and unanalyzed patient, took over. I do not think such a position is or ever was tenable. But in rejecting it we must not throw the baby out with the bath water. We have seen the need for analysis to continue after training proper has stopped and that this initiates a further step in understanding the analytical dialectic. If the analysis has previously been good enough, the new member's patients, if any number are being analyzed, will ensure continuance of analysis since the beginning analyst will not have time to pick up the pieces into which he is liable to be torn and will ask for more analysis.

I think it is true to say that the emphasis on reductive analysis has increased as the years have gone on, though it is too early to say whether the trend is permanent or no. As one of those who is glad to see it happen, I have at the same time doubts as to whether in doing this we may not swing too far from Jung's later work. I myself cannot see that this is really so, however, and in any case if we are being one sided, it is worth it.

That reductive analysis is essential for the analysis of analysts seems to me more and more evident. It gets to the nuclear structures (archetypes) and does so by revealing the areas in which the ego is weak and unable to cope. It also provides a perspective and sense of proportion about training because other sorts of training have gone on before and the pattern of these can be regularly discerned repeating themselves in our training. Furthermore it can bring to the fore learning attitudes, even though they fail to operate if the candidate is working through a psychotic transference and the analyst cannot contain it. Lastly, reductive analysis brings under review collective standards and attitudes and leads to their reformulation in individual terms. After all, it is in line with our concept of individuation.

There seems, however, to be some confusion about what is meant by reductive analysis. It may be that this whole area requires more rethinking than I can give it here. It will, however, be worthwhile saying something about what it does and does not consist in. Reduction is a scientific procedure whereby complex structures are broken down into their simple component parts. Applied to our work it does not "reduce" the personality in the sense of belittling it; on the contrary its effect is just the reverse. It reveals parts of the personality which were repressed and so makes them available for development. "Reduction" and "analysis" are almost synonymous – each means reducing or dissolving a number of complex entities into their component parts. Thus in reductive analysis we aim to dissolve complex structures which stand in the way by repressing the more elementary forms which have not developed and obstruct development. In reductive analysis memories from childhood and infancy feature prominently and the patterns they reveal are used to understand disproportional reactions which are referred to the situation and time when they were relevant. Inasmuch as this discipline loads through repression to the non-repressed unconscious and may lead to concealed psychotic elements in the personality, it puts the analyst in a position to contain them and work them through. There is, of course, a risk here of a defensive psychosis developing, but in the case of a training analysis this risk is especially worth taking.

Why do I think that this procedure is essential? Quite apart from the need of any analyst to know in himself about the nature of infantile experience and its effect and place in adult living, training itself induces a regression and leads to the formation of new identifications with the analyst, the supervisor and the Society as a whole. If they are to be sound they need to be related to earlier ones which may need to be dissolved (analyzed) so that the development we hope to achieve is an evolution of the candidate's personality.

To conclude: my object in this paper has been to continue an effort which has been made by a number of our members over the years. It is to spell out a grammar of training so that we may in the end succeed in expressing what we do and make it widely known in clear and simple terms. When that is done we shall have done away with vague generalizations even though they may have stood us in good stead. The training analyst will not need, for instance, to recommend his candidate by reassuring the committee that the candidate is a person of the highest integrity. Such phrases can hope to be replaced by definable abilities for which we shall be to look.

Grammar, or should I rather say method, will not solve our difficulties but it can help to define where they lie and do much to make them manageable. We as a whole and the training analysts in particular are still learning, and I hope will continue to learn, from experiences. If anything remains vague we should aim to find out where it is happening; that is why I think developing a method is most important at the present time.

If this is going to be furthered and the interest of our members is going to be enlisted, it seems desirable to keep as open as possible a discussion which is liable to become exclusive and private. Arriving at decisions about specific candidates will probably always require closed meetings of committees, but the method of the proceeding and the principles on which the decisions are reached are best made as public as possible, so that they can be discussed and understood.

NOTE

1 The Society of Analytical Psychology was unable to provide details when this paper was delivered. Fordham estimates it as some time in the mid-1960s (ed.).

Chapter 7

Reflections on training analysis (1968)

INTRODUCTION

A 'Symposium on training' was published in 1961–62 in the *Journal of Analytical Psychology*. It was a first attempt to define the complex training situation and to start a discussion about its significance. Plaut, Newton and myself contributed from London and Hillman wrote on 'Training and the C.G. Jung Institute, Zürich'. In the subsequent interchange of ideas, Edinger from New York and Bash from Bern made valuable comments. Subsequently (in 1964) Stone wrote 'Reflections of an ex-trainee on his training'. This article was discussed by Marshak (1964) from London, who compared his experiences with her own.

These papers revealed such wide variations in the 'training situation' at each centre that different behaviour by training analysts would seem inevitable. For instance, though all symposiasts agreed that analysis of the candidate is the central feature of training, there was conflict over its meaning and practice. In my view, analysis could not cover the idea that 'Training is analysis' (Hillman, 1962, p. 8), for in this statement 'analysis' includes 'teaching and study'. In London the two are separated as far as possible because each is conceived to be essentially different (cf. this volume Chapter 3). There seems no possibility of reconciling this and other differences, which need first clearer definition than they have yet attained. My paper, therefore, is meant as a step in clarification.

It is, I think, startling that none of the authors in the 'Symposium' paid much attention to the training analysis. If it is agreed that, however it be conducted and whatever the term covers, its aim is to provide conditions under which the trainee can attain experience which will prove to be the basis of all his future work, it surely ought to be in the centre of the discussion. Hillman's attempt to place it there failed, as I see it, because he widened the definition so that the meaning of the term analysis became obscured. In London, analysis during formal training is conceived to be an essential part of the trainee's efforts to integrate what he learns intellectually with his own personal experience. If he does not succeed, the techniques of relating to his patients, taught in seminars and during supervision, will not be of much use to anybody (cf. this volume, Chapter 8).

The sketchy treatment given to the problems of training analysts is startling and has motivated my present essay. Because the subject is so complex I have needed to restrict my aims and so the discussion may seem to deal only with the surface of training. There will be no attempt to describe training analysis as a whole, and those who look for a complete presentation of this and other topics will be disappointed. Because training analysis is essentially like any other thorough one, a number of its characteristics can be assumed. I will now consider the more important ones so as to make clear that they are not in reality overlooked.

Training analysis is necessarily long. The 'candidate' will therefore have time to experience the unconscious and penetrate to its archetypal contents in personal infancy and transpersonal history (cf. this volume, Chapter 8). There will be time to investigate and consolidate the ego's relation to the inner world, to experience symbolic representations of the animus, the anima, the self, and the individuation process at work. So I shall not emphasize the activity of archetypal imagery nor consider whether, during training, particular images take on a different form from the ones that present themselves in other analyses. Training analysis is understood as an initiation and Henderson (1967) has shown that, in its various forms, initiation is a characteristic of analysis as a whole. I need not enlarge on his work.

My restricted aim, then, is to describe the conditions, that have proved their value in London, for training analysis to approximate an ordinary therapeutic analysis, and to consider how they, none the less, affect the training analyst and his patient. My interest in childhood, and the child in the adult, will become apparent: this is my special field of research, and it is patently applicable to training. One essential aim of initiation processes is to separate the adolescent from his parents and, while I think this formulation is crude in the light of present knowledge, it underlines the special place that the analysis of childhood must take in training.

A basic assumption in my thesis is that training analysis must be conducted by one analyst only if the earliest pre-oedipal conflict-patterns are to be adequately worked through: this proposition has been accepted in London. Elsewhere, on the contrary, it is held that two analysts of opposite sex are positively desirable so that the shadow, the animus or the anima may be adequately transferred to the analyst and made as conscious as possible. In my view this conception does not and cannot meet pre-oedipal needs because sexual identity has not been established nor has an organized shadow been formed. Also the infant part of the adult needs *only* one body; any other body is a fertile ground for stabilizing unrecognized illusions. In addition, whether the body be male or female has no meaning.

This formulation is sometimes met by saying that infant states can be identified and fantasied about with many people present, for instance in a group. Against this I would contend that they cannot either be reached or worked through in detail. The ego of a small infant cannot be used to identify himself nor have an adult-like fantasy about his infant state. He is himself that state, related first to parts of and then the whole of one person, his mother. In the adult likewise working through a regression to infancy is only possible with one person besides the patient present.

I fully recognize that regression to early infancy may not be necessary or possible in any particular case, but all the same infancy is there as an integral part of any analysis, albeit unconsciously. It is not going too far to say that the addition of a second analyst violates the infant–mother unity upon which a thorough working through of infancy and childhood depends.

The question of whether analysis of childhood gives sufficient attention to the shadow, the animus and the anima must at present remain an open issue. Only the shadow has so far been considered in any detail (Fordham, 1965), but there is every reason to suppose that the animus and the anima can also be dealt with satisfactorily. In childhood both figures are present in dreams, fantasies and early sexual life, and in addition it is clear that individuation processes take place very early on and can be observed in childhood as in any other stage of life (cf. Fordham, F., 1969, Fordham, M., this volume, Chapter 8 and 1969 and Jacobi, 1967). If this be true then a conclusion can be drawn. It seems inevitable that there are not two definable stages of analysis: a first occupied with childhood, superseded by a second in which individuation as a spiritual growth begins (cf. Hillman, *et al.*, 1962). For these reasons it seems likely that the assimilation of animus and anima occurs in the kind of analysis I am conceiving as fundamental.

One further introductory remark: I shall lay considerable emphasis on the need of the pair (training analyst and trainee) to trust the other persons involved in training and for them to have realistic grounds for feeling that the Society's business is well enough conducted for both to receive good enough treatment by the Society. I furthermore believe it is important for each of them to have opportunities for contributing towards the training process. Three papers published in the *Journal* (Newton, 1961, Stone, 1964 and Marshak, 1964) have looked at aspects of training from the candidate's position, and arrangements are made in the London Society for the candidate's views to gain expression.

THE TRAINING SITUATION

The papers from London did something towards building up the overall picture of the training situation there, but for present purposes further data need to be added. The Society requires that before applying for training a candidate should have completed 400 sessions of analysis, usually four to five times a week and not fewer than three. It is expected that most candidates will require three years' preliminary analysis, but the arrangements ensure that an exceptional candidate can comply with the regulations in two years. When he applies for formal training a candidate will be interviewed by training analysts. The two interviewers and the training analyst of the candidate will then report to the training committee (called the professional committee).

This body, which decided on the suitability or otherwise of the candidate, is usually composed of two training analysts, two professional members, and one other from any class of membership; the chairman of the Society and the director of training are *ex officio* members. The five members, not holding office in the Society, are elected each year and the *ex officio* members likewise but by different procedure which it is not necessary to describe.

I want to emphasize that the committee changes: new members are regularly elected to it and old ones retire. The system is therefore democratic and the tendency for an oligarchy to form is prevented. Besides ensuring the regular infusion of new blood from senior members of the Society, it has been found useful for one member – an associate member – to be included who has recently completed training. In this way a link is kept with the point of view of trainees to be considered by the committee. This arrangement is, however, still in an experimental stage, and the associate member is not necessarily elected every year.

When a candidate applies for training his training analyst is not allowed to vote for or against his acceptance. After the committee has heard what the two interviewers and the training analyst have to say and has asked questions and discussed their findings, a vote is taken when all its members feel ready to arrive at a decision about the candidate.

It is important to note that the committee's conclusion is not final; it is a recommendation to the council, the governing body of the Society, usually represented by its executive committee.

If a candidate is accepted for formal training this can begin. It lasts for two years and starts with a preliminary term of seminars twice a week on theory and technique. Then the candidate embarks on his practical work: first one analytic case then a second are studied under the supervision of two training analysts. Neither of them is the analyst of the trainee, and this is one way that analysis is kept from formal training.

After the two years have been finished, the candidate can apply for associate professional membership when he has submitted a thesis. Once again the members of the professional committee are asked to go into the trainee's suitability and the training analyst attends the committee meeting together with the two supervisors. On this occasion neither the analyst nor the supervisors have the right to vote.

The important elements in the design of these regulations are as follows:

1 That the analyst can, with the candidate's agreement, provide information without needing to identify himself with the decision to accept or reject his candidate for training or with his acceptance or rejection as an associate member of the Society.
2 If a training analyst or anybody else has definite or strong views about a decision, he is open to put them forward by addressing the council and its executive committee. It might be thought that this avenue for appeal to a higher authority is just an empty formality, but it has not proved to be so. On several occasions recommendations by the professional committee have been

> reversed or referred back for further consideration and special arrangements have been made to meet situations where opinion has been divided. Interviews with the candidate have been designed to answer specific questions or an interview between the candidate and the committee itself has been added to the usual procedure.

In addition to these avenues for discussion in committees, opportunities are provided for training analysts to meet together to present and work out their ideas in meetings of training analysts and seminar leaders or through consultations between them and the supervisors. These activities are desirable and sometimes essential.

The conditions outlined above have been developed over the years. Their aim is to minimize stress on the training analyst so that he can and does keep his analysis free from the influence of conflicts within the Society.

I shall from now on refer to the candidate or trainees as a patient, a term with disadvantages but which expresses very well the candidate's need for personal analysis and to feel that his meetings with his training analyst are for his own and not just his professional benefit. If the analysis is well conducted, it will not be long before a trainee discovers – even if he came overtly to further his professional ambitions alone – that he needs help with his own personal conflicts, i.e. his psychopathology. Then the term 'patient' comes to represent the true state of the candidate.

PSYCHOPATHOLOGY AND THE ANALYSIS OF CHILDHOOD

In the 'Symposium on training' Hillman lays special emphasis upon the teaching of psychopathology. His view is reinforced by Bash (1962) and contested by Plaut (1962). This important issue bears on what is required of the analyst. Two positions were taken up which I shall exaggerate for purposes of exposition: (1) psychopathology has to be taught and cannot be learnt about in analysis; and (2) it cannot be taught, but rather it needs to be discovered in the candidate's own analytic experience.

I lean towards the second position because it is dynamic and avoids a static, even formal, idea of psychopathology. If followed to its logical conclusion it would mean that at the end of his analysis a trainee would have experienced anxiety states, hysterical disorders, obsessional states, affect psychoses, psychosomatic disorders, and schizophrenic states, and he would have worked through to the psychodynamic roots of these states in the transference relation with his analyst. It would therefore become one of the training analyst's aims to provide conditions in which these states could be experienced.

Without subscribing to it I would point out that this large order is not as impossible as it seems. If regression occurs, the candidate will become a patient and will be in a position to discover the surface nature of the psychopathological categories defined by psychiatrists in so far as they relate to him. He will reach the affective sources from which some of them at least derive, and since the nuclear situations underlying systematic psychopathology are virtually universal, it follows that if the analysis goes forward well, the candidate's own psychopathology, which is analogous to, if not identical with, clinical entities to be found in psychiatric textbooks, will be discovered and elucidated.

This thesis depends upon the conception that psychopathology is the result of quantitative and not qualitative variations resulting from disturbed energy gradients; it is only true for some mental disorders so the extreme proposition cannot be generalized. A modification of it can be reached, however, and any training analyst can achieve it with his trainee. What is envisaged? (1) The candidate can hope to know about, become able to manage and transform the major part of his own psychopathology. With his experience in mind he can help patients having a psychopathology like his own. (2) Other damaged parts of himself may be so incompletely healed that under stress they present difficulty and require reworking through during the analysis of a patient. Others beyond transformation go to form a pathological nexus with the patient. (3) Finally the candidate will know where he is healthy and so recognize when he can only learn to understand his patients. In this he is essentially different from them and has more difficulty in empathizing with them.

I consider it essential to gain insight into these conditions because when – during any analysis – it comes to the crunch, what is learnt out of books, lectures, clinical observations, mental hospital experience and out-patient departments will be of little help unless the candidate has experienced and worked through his own pathology. Unless he has done so intellectual knowledge, which tends to be static, will become a positive obstruction in that all he has learnt will be used to bolster up defences, making them rigid when they might have been flexible.

Why then, it may be asked, is it necessary to acquire intellectual knowledge? The answer is complex and interesting, but it is not relevant here, except in so far as learning processes in training slant the analysis and in some ways intensify defences until the equivalent of what is taught be discovered in the trainee himself.

I have heard it humorously said that before a trainee can get any analysis of use to him he has to go through and complete five years of formal training analysis before he can get to the real analysis he wants. I think that, in these days, it would be an extraordinary state of affairs if this became true. Nevertheless, it does happen that the majority of good candidates will want, sometimes urgently, to continue their analyses after they have been accepted by the Society.

The continuation of analysis after training has finished is usual but it is sometimes made necessary in one particular respect: the candidate may not have dared, before acceptance, to make an all-out attack on his analyst without feeling somewhere that the analyst will retaliate by blocking his path to membership of the Society, even though the possibilities of his doing so are in reality very remote.

Before I became aware of the far-reaching importance of transference analysis, a patient who became a trainee presented quite serious problems because of his anxiety about attacking his analyst directly and in person. This major difficulty is one among others. While the essential features of the transference are the same as in ordinary analysis they present special characteristics. It is not my intention to go far into this problem, because both Plaut and I discussed it earlier (this volume, Chapter 3). I only want to emphasize that the candidate's position supports splitting of the transference: part of it being projected onto the Society, part onto the supervisors, and part going into group activities. This is not necessarily a disadvantage, but it does delay the working through of regressions to infancy.

In the 'Symposium' little stress was laid on the analyst's counter-transference, which also takes on special characteristics. The relation of the analyst to his colleagues and the Society is such that pressures are exerted on him to split his counter-transference and to regress just as his patient does also. Unless this is clearly recognized the infantile components in the training analyst's counter-transference relation to his patient may be overlooked. They are displaced onto the Society and his colleagues, leading to omnipotent defensiveness and to alliance with the infantile parts of his patient against the dangerous and often persecuting parent imagos represented by his colleagues: the supervisor, the director of training, seminar leaders or the professional committee. The liability for splitting to occur is one reason why it is useful for the analyst to attend the meetings of the professional committee when his candidate is being considered. Then he has an opportunity to sort out his own conflict patterns in ways that I shall suggest later.

An alternative way to manage the training analyst's counter-transference is for him to take no part in the acceptance or rejection of his candidate either for training or as a member of the Society. Thus the way is cleared, as it were, for more objective assessment of the candidate's merits. The advantage of this arrangement is its simplicity, but all the same, besides being of use to the analyst himself, analyst participation is, I believe, to the advantage of the Society in many respects. He can, for instance, provide information when his candidate's transference is such that nothing of it can be observed by the supervisors or other members of the Society.

This raises the vexed question of communicating confidential information. Its relevance depends first upon how the communication is done and next on how trustworthy the committee members are felt to be.

Plaut (1966) elaborated on the importance of the feeling of trust so I will not develop the matter here except to underline its importance in building professional relationships as a whole and of those within the Society in particular.

It may well be thought that the members of any well-functioning committee will trust each other enough, but in the confidential setting of the professional committee special claims are made on each member. As the training group's members are at the centre of the Society, how they are seen to perform their work is of great importance. It may be relatively easy for a candidate to have sufficient trust in his analyst but it not so easy for both analyst and candidate to feel confidence in the committee. By recurrently proving itself trustworthy it creates the necessary setting for information to be exchanged without reservation.

The training analyst's attending the committee is both a test of his trustworthiness and a symbolic act at critical stages in a candidate's career. This seems to me a powerful reason, in addition to the valuable information that he can communicate, for the training analyst's taking part in the proceedings of the professional committee.

There are many features of analyst participation in the committee's procedure of which I will instance a few. Any member of the training committee, and indeed the committee as a whole, is in a position to observe not only how good and useful the analyst's judgement may be but also whether it is at fault. If so, the committee members may help the training analyst in a number of ways. Idealization of his patient may become apparent in excessive praise or in attempts to explain away faults in his candidate which are quite transparent to anybody else, or in pleading for the candidate's acceptance or trying to swing the committee in his favour in unconvincing ways.

Again he may show that he feels it a personal offence if a candidate of his is turned down, and the reverse can also hold: angry with his candidate, an unfavourable account will be given, as if the training analyst wanted his candidate to be rejected and so, when he is accepted the analyst may find himself being disconcerted. If the committee functions well, besides making use of the training analyst's sound advocacy or critical assessment of his candidate, it can help the analyst to become aware of what has happened, to the benefit of his patient's analysis. In brief, the committee situation tends to show up the training analyst's counter-transference.

I do not want to over-stress the difficulties inherent in the set-up and its effect on training analysts, which is much more favourable than unfavourable. The training analyst's failings became apparent in the early years, and since clearer understanding of the nature and continuing importance of counter-transference in its positive and negative senses has received increased attention, the procedure has worked more and more smoothly.

To return to the subject of confidential information, I believe the dangers are overestimated. Because a training analyst will need to extract and compress essential information sufficiently to give briefly the information that is relevant, 'personal confidences' are beside the point. It needs skill to present only what is required by the committee and no more so to assist the training analyst in organizing what he knows, a printed guide has been compiled with headings together with an outline of what information may be assembled under each. When the necessary discipline has been acquired and the reason for it understood the question of confidence, in its ethical sense, does not usually arise. If it does and the analyst has to suppress relevant facts – he may be expected to inform the committee where it is necessary – it may well be asked whether the candidate is suitable anyway.

There remains the more complex question of whether it is desirable to divulge data from the analysis at all. I believe that there are valid rules about this which also apply to publication. Their existence only needs mention here, their discussion being outside the scope of this paper.

ENDING OF THE TRAINING ANALYSIS

The next topic I wish to raise is the more controversial ending of a training analysis. It is widely held in one form or another that the analysis of an analyst never ends. It is conceived that he needs to continue self-analysis for ever and this may be reinforced by repeated return to the original training analyst, to another analyst or analysts.

So why is it important to lay emphasis on ending, why not leave the whole process open-ended, so that the continuing self-analysis with recurrent doses of further personal analysis may occur, indeed it may be expected and approved of under the caption that because, in the sense indicated, an end to analysis does not and should not occur?

It is a matter of interest that very little has been written on the subject of ending by analytical psychologists. It seems, as far as I can discover, often to depend on intuition or such data as (1) the patient's history, embodying past separations, capacity to feel grief and gratitude, (2) the overt transference situation, (3) clues obtained from one or a series of dreams, (4) the reality situation of the new Society member, (5) an assessment of the ongoing individuating processes at work in the unconscious, and last, but not least, (6) the training analyst's counter-transference.

None of these are adequate by themselves and there are other important details, which cannot be gone into here, and which I am in the process of making the subject of a more detailed study. In any case, however, all of them need to be taken into account so that the end may be one which represents both a sad and a rewarding event. To achieve this is not easy. It needs, I am certain, work on the subject of ending as a phase of analysis in its own right.

I am convinced of the necessity for ongoing self-analysis and for accepting the analyst's need for further treatment. I want, however, to contend that the idea of continuing analysis should not be used to let training analysts become less rigorous in pursuing the work of ending than they might be with patients undergoing an overtly therapeutic analysis. So important do I think this to be that I believe basic training should take place in the area where the analyst is going to practise. I recognize that in the pioneering phase of analysis it has been necessary for analysts to be trained in centres away from the location of their future practices and especially in Zürich, but if this continues, unnecessary stress is inevitably laid on reality considerations such as money, family obligations and ultimate professional commitments. All these interfere with ending and so the analysis stops. For ending to take place there needs to be unlimited time available.

I do not want to expand further on the variety of factors that enter into ending. They are numerous and the analyst needs to make an assessment of them in individual terms. I rather want to draw to your attention the idea that ending is a problem for the training analyst himself, as well as the new analyst, by developing the idea that a pathological nexus develops between any patient and his analyst.

In the course of any long collaboration there grows up an amalgam of the analyst's and the patient's unresolved, and often unresolvable, infantile conflict patterns. We may expect the training analyst to know about them without necessarily being able to resolve them. If he cannot he can still interpret them – if the patient does not start to do so himself. His interpretation contains recognition that they cannot be resolved by himself alone and that in this area he is as much the patient as his analysand.

Let me illustrate briefly what I mean. Many years ago now one of my patients had been in a very long analysis and could not end because she had strongly entrenched beliefs about me into which she had no insight (delusional transference). It had taken me a very long time to recognize that I could do nothing about them and that I had not the inner flexibility, the passive resources, to let them be – so I simply regarded them as valid. The ending of the analysis depended in a large degree upon my recognition of this situation, upon my management of it, and the eventual interpretation of it to the patient followed by working through in detail all the events during the analysis where this situation had been mutually destructive. Only in this way could the analysis properly end with mutual sadness at parting and the feeling that this sadness was worthwhile because of the mutual rewards which would accrue.

We have been made familiar by Jung with the idea that the ill patient needs to be met with the analyst's health if the analysis is going to be therapeutic. This formulation is incomplete because there is a shadow to the ideal of health. In analysis we hope that disease and health may turn out to be the expression of a pair of opposites within the personality and that after analysis each will transcend the other. Unfortunately, this situation easily becomes idealized and so an illusion. In the life-span of any person there will have been situations which have resulted in irresolvable conflicts upon which pathological ego structures have been erected. However well analysis has been conducted and however complete, basically traumatic situations cannot themselves be changed. During analysis of any patient some of them will – through regression on the part of the analyst – enter into the analysis as part of the counter-transference and will interlock with the patient's corresponding primary conflict patterns forming a nexus which becomes part of the analytic situation. In many cases, perhaps all, unless the nexus is fully elucidated and its component parts sufficiently assimilated by the training analyst with the patient's full understanding, the analysis cannot end, it will be interrupted.

I think we can reasonably expect a training analyst and, indeed any analyst, to recognize the existence of this interlocking unresolved and unresolvable conflict situation. In the case of a candidate he cannot fail to have discovered through his own analysis and his supervision, that his patients represent over and over again aspects of himself for which he needs help because the patient is stuck at the same place as he is. Part of this state of affairs can be resolved, if not now, at least eventually: it contains counter-transference illusions. But as insight deepens the candidate discovers that he has a basic psychopathology whose content can only be thoroughly elucidated – nothing more can be done about it. Its contents are the actual traumatic situations of the candidate's childhood, supported by collective patterns organized to support them. He cannot truly accept these basically damaged parts unless his training analyst does so too. Recognition means that the training analyst is willing to let his damaged parts (his pathology) – of which his colleagues may be well aware and about which they tease him with varying degrees of humour or malice – have their place in his analyses of patients. Indeed it is, I suggest, the true basis of his motivation for practising psychotherapy.

I want to make it clear that this understanding is complex. It seldom if ever has anything to do with patients' omnipotent claims to know about their analyst's feelings, about his being 'the patient', 'the child' and so forth; these have no part in the core of the situation. Indeed it usually remains unconscious till the analyst, when it is indicated, leads the patient towards it explicitly or implicitly and, when he does do, confession is contra-indicated. All that is required is interpretation and working through of the specific incidents during analysis when the analyst could not respond to the patient and the patient, though perceiving it, was unable to grasp what had happened.

The experiencing of the interpersonal, pathological nexus suggests the theme of the 'wounded healer' referred to by Jung in the *Mysterium Coniunctionis* (1955–6, p. 121) and developed by Meier (1968). It is a complex topic on which Kerenyi (1960) has accumulated information. A healer who died of his wounds was Machaon, a warrior surgeon who had his own little army. He was said to have been killed by Eurypylos ('he with the wide gate', referring to the realm of the dead), the son of Telephoros, a child god: 'the finisher', who was also called Akeisis, 'the healer'. Achilles, also a healer, wounded Telephoros of Pergamon, who was told by the oracle: 'the wounder heals'. The archaic divine physician Chiron the centaur, who taught Asklepois and Achilles, was also wounded and the wound was incurable. Asklepois was not so much wounded as killed by Zeus because he resurrected the dead.

From this it would seem that the theme of the wounded healer refers to the hazards of the healer's work. So it would be necessary to look closer into the origins of the mythic patterns to find a true analogy to the pathological nexus. The connections with conflict and death surrounding the miraculous birth of Asklepios are probably more relevant. They relate to the theme of death and rebirth. I want to make it clear that the pathological nexus does not lead to rebirth; it is like the scar of a wound and this cannot be cured because it is the result of the disease. I believe that recognition of the irreducible psychopathology of the analyst, as an aspect of his shadow, is important for the maintenance of good enough relations between colleagues, besides providing the main motivation for conducting psychotherapy.

Perhaps it is going too far to say that its recognition is fully possible only when ending analysis becomes an aim, a situation in its own right. I am not saying that it is always a prominent feature of every analysis, but I do maintain that its full elucidation is frequently overlooked through insufficient concentration on reconstructing infancy and childhood, and because of this it is then displaced into the Society. This makes what is basically a rewarding job essentially disillusioning as well.

Chapter 8

Technique and counter-transference (1969)

PART I

Introduction

Analytical psychologists as a whole have paid little attention to the subject of technique. Yet without developing a clear picture of what analysts do – and that is what technique implies – data obtained in the analytic situation cannot be fruitfully compared, no scientific studies can be made and communication between colleagues becomes difficult, if not meaningless.

Besides Jung's publications, a number of books dealing with the practice of analytical psychology have appeared (cf. Adler, 1961, Baynes, 1955, Harding, 1965, Wickes, 1959). They are mainly expositions of Jung's classical methods of dream analysis, active imagination and amplification; they do not attempt to cover in detail the content of day-to-day interviews. This omission is sometimes deliberate, at least while analysis is in progress (cf. Kirsch, 1961, p. 171), and sometimes expresses anxiety lest study of the analytic situation, with a view to bringing analysts' activities to light, might interfere with valuable spontaneity in their relation to patients.

As an amplification of these doubts, reference has more than once been made to the alchemical analogy of the *vas bene clausum* (the well-sealed vessel) suggesting that such living matters cannot with safety be discussed outside therapeutic interviews (cf. Kirsch, 1961). These objections have not commended themselves to me. They belong to the 'secret tradition' composed of sayings passed on from one analyst to the other that are not discussed in detail nor submitted to precise formulation for critical evaluation. The influence of these private sayings depends very largely on exploitation of residual transferences and so are not intended for serious consideration.

In London, interest had been directed to elucidating what analysts do (cf. Moody, 1955, Plaut, 1956), and I myself contributed by making a study of the transference giving particular attention to the counter-transference (Fordham, this volume, Chapters 1 and 2, and 1964). That psychoanalysts have contributed in ways which have brought them very much nearer Jung's view of interaction between analyst and patient (cf. Racker, 1968, especially) has been valuable, and I shall make use of their work in this essay.

Jung's contributions

Since the studies conducted in London stem mainly from Jung, I shall begin by reviewing his observations on technique and how they developed over the years.

In his early publications he showed his grasp of experimental method and later of that of psychoanalysis, but it is in his correspondence with Löy (Jung and Löy, 1914) that this early position is most clearly stated; there he discusses psychoanalytic technique and writes that though 'there are general principles and working rules for individual analyses . . . the . . . analytic procedure develops quite differently in every case' (p. 272); thus early on he was aware, like Freud, of the need for flexibility in applying rules and of the individual character of the procedure.

In this correspondence he also lays stress on the therapeutic influence of the analyst personally – a theme which has been widely discussed – but it was in 'The therapeutic value of abreaction' (1921) that he made a most significant statement which applies to analysis, though he first considers abreactive treatment. He says that it is not so much suggestion that is therapeutic as the influence of the therapist himself: 'I would rather call it . . . his human interest and personal devotion. These are the property of no method nor can they ever become one; they are moral qualities which are of the greatest importance in all methods of psychotherapy' (p.132). He then goes on to apply this idea to the psychology of the transference conceived as 'the patient's attempt to get into psychological rapport with the doctor'. He not only analyses the situation but meets the patient's need for a realistic relationship. This requires honesty, for: 'How can the patient learn to abandon his neurotic subterfuges when he sees the doctor playing hide-and-seek with his own personality, as though unable, for fear of being thought inferior, *to drop the professional mask of authority, competence, superior knowledge*, etc?' (p. 137, italics mine).

This emphasis on personality and individuality is one root of the belief that technique is to be avoided. It was conceived as something that had little to do with personal qualities, did violence to the individual nature of the analytic process, and worst of all it could become disembodied. These techniques of the natural sciences aim to be and so, by implication, they are inappropriate.

It is of interest that Jung refers to the display of professional authority, competence and superior knowledge, qualities which a patient rightly expects his therapist to have acquired. That these introduce asymmetry into the analytic situation from the start is well–known and it will continue, though in diminishing proportion, as the analysis proceeds (cf. this volume, Chapter 1).

Jung here warned of dangers in the use of technical skills through a special case of the therapist using them defensively. He does not generalize, and he could not, for in his essay 'The relations between the ego and the unconscious' there are clear indications that he approves of the acquisition of techniques; he refers there to the 'synthetic hermeneutic method' and to 'the technique of differentiation between the ego and the figures of the unconscious' (1928). In 1931 he wrote of the 'principles of my technique' (p. 46), which has the 'aim to bring about a psychic state in which my patient begins to experiment with his own nature' and in another paper written at the same time: 'As is well known, one can get along quite well with an inadequate theory, but not with inadequate therapeutic methods' (1931a, p. 38).

Furthermore, he always gave reductive analysis relative importance though developing other definable procedures of his own: dream analysis and, though he tries to avoid applying the idea of a method to it, active imagination also; he further recommended the therapist to acquire a wide knowledge of mythology and comparative religion to use in the method of amplification – he surely did not mean these to be used to build up a therapist's defences!

Again and again he emphasizes the defensive uses to which technique can be put, and so I think we have to look into the roots of this theme: one of them stems from his relation to Freud. It was Freud, he believed, who emphasized technique and placed his authority behind it so that psychoanalysis became identical with its method: Freud, he said, insisted on 'identifying the method [of psychoanalysis] with his sexual theory, thus placing upon it the stamp of dogmatism' (1930, p. 324). To this he took vigorous objection – so here is an important source of Jung's critique of the uses to which technique can be put, and also, it may be noted, of Freud's theorizing. It may be noticed here that the two are conceived to be indivisible.

I would like to say in parenthesis that though Jung needed to take this stand, his concern about the future of psychoanalysis has not been borne out by its subsequent development, while ironically there has grown up a strong tendency to develop the very dogmatism amongst analytic psychologists against which he took such a strong stand (cf. Anon. 1963, p. 167; and Harding 1963).

I myself do not think of this tendency in such an unfavourable light as Jung did. To fight for a discovery or important element of theory or technique can, in my opinion, very easily lead to a seeming dogmatism that has a positive as well as a negative connotation, provided the theory or technique is worth fighting for.

To return to Freud, Jung divined in him a basic assumption which took over the rôle of a "*deus absconditus*" (1963, p. 148 f.), and gave a compulsive one-sided character to psychoanalysis. He struggled against it and thought he had resolved his own conflict by developing a theory of opposites which could lead him to say: 'the structure of the psyche is so contradictory or contrapuntal that one can scarcely make any psychological assertion or general statement without having immediately to state its opposite!' (1943, p. 77).

Jung seems to have conceived technique as a method based on theory. Whether this was in his mind when he expressed caution about theorizing (cf. for instance, 1938, p. 7) cannot be gone into here. In my view what he says is a plea for weighing the relevance of theoretical statements; if so he could not then reject methods. Whether a theory be true or false, whether it is useful or no, does not depend upon whether its opposite can be stated, but upon which of two mutually exclusive alternatives is the more true or useful in any particular context. Only when a theory becomes a conviction does a technique, based on it, become the exponent of a one-sided position and only then is the way open for it to be used as a rigid defence against irrational and unconscious dynamisms. Since Jung introduced many theoretical concepts of his own he could not in principle have been against Freud but only against identifying explanation with the scientific procedures of psychoanalysis as a whole. It may be noted here that some psychoanalysts conceived that Freud never did this (cf. Greenacre, 1968).

There can be little doubt that Jung was ambivalent about theorizing. Sometimes he seems to want a general theory that will explain psychic events, but he often emphasizes that there is none, with scarcely concealed satisfaction: there is, for instance, no general theory of consciousness, no general theory of dreams (1944, p. 43). Yet such statements were not true, even when he was writing, for Freud had constructed a theory of dreams, though it was not acceptable to Jung! It may be that his somewhat nostalgic wish for a general theory led him, as a compensation, to over-emphasize the irrational, unpredictable nature of psychic life: 'we have to reckon with a high percentage of arbitrariness and "chance" in the complex actions and reactions of the conscious mind. Similarly there is no empirical, still less a theoretical, reason to assume the same does not apply to the manifestations of the unconscious' (*ibid.*).

'The actual present'

When he was separating from psychoanalysis, another strand in his thinking is of particular relevance to my thesis: he criticized the tendency to investigate infantile memories at the expense of the 'actual present' (1913, p. 166f.). The issue he raised has proved of immeasurable importance and underscored the emphasis he develops on the interaction of analyst and patient, placing it in the centre of the analytic situation. This was well stated when, developing his earlier position, he wrote: 'By no device can the treatment be anything but the product of mutual influence, in which the whole being of the doctor as well as that of the patient plays its part' (1931a, p. 71), and then: 'For two personalities to meet is like mixing two chemical substances; if there is any combination at all both are transformed' (*ibid.*). Here is surely the root of his alchemical analogies and the concept of the dialectical procedure later brought into clear focus.

The individual and the collective

In 1935, he reapproached the individual nature of personal analysis. When discussing psychotherapy as a whole, he stated that there are two trends in the human psyche: one leads towards collectivism in social identifications, the other towards individualism. This individual–collective antinomy can be observed clinically: 'we can divide the psychoneuroses into two main groups: one comprising collective people with undeveloped individuality, the other individualists with atrophied collective adaption' (1935, p. 7).

In the second case of individualists, method and particularly reductive analysis, is the treatment of choice as a corrective to individualism. (Let it be noted that technique is here is linked with a therapeutic procedure). It is only when individuality is undeveloped that the non-technical dialectical procedure applies. 'Since individuality . . . is absolutely unique, unpredictable, and uninterpretable the therapist must abandon all his preconceptions and techniques and confine himself to purely dialectical procedure, adopting the attitude that shuns all methods' (1935, pp. 7–8).

The attitude expressed in his statement has exercised very considerable influence and has led analytical psychologists to claim 'unprejudiced objectivity' or 'enlightened subjectivity', to rely solely on intuition or to speak of using rules apologetically, thus qualifying procedures resulting from their application (cf. Fordham, 1968). In this confusion, which I consider unnecessary, they can gain some support from some of Jung's formulations, but not very much. In passages on method in *Psychology and Alchemy* (1944, p. 43 ff.) he seeks to establish his open-minded approach, but he goes on to expound his methods. They are the techniques of establishing the context of dream imagery either through associations obtained from the patient, the use of dream sequences (which can be taken as their equivalent) or amplification by using ethnological parallels. These techniques are clearly to be used: when writing of the patient's struggle for wholeness he says in the same volume (1944, p. 3) 'while the patient is unswervingly seeking the solution to some ultimately insoluble problem, *the art and the technique* of the doctor are doing their best to help him towards it' (author's italics).

There can be no doubt that Jung uses both theories and techniques not only to reduce excessive individualism to collective normality but in all sorts of ways, even if it be only 'make it a rule never to go beyond the meaning which is effective for the patient' (1931, p. 46). My reading of his position in 1935 is that he was overstating his case to highlight a worthwhile issue. In later essays, for instance his essay on the transference (1946) and in his last technical contribution to psychotherapy (1951), he is far less extreme – after all he developed a theory of transference and this cannot be done without modification of the position he took up in 1935. If the whole situation is conceived as individual and unpredictable there can neither be a description nor a generalized theory of the relation between analyst and patient.

In this perplexing situation, which stems from emphasis on the irrational, a formulation which Jung presented in 1942 in his paper 'Psychotherapy and a philosophy of life' (published in 1943) seems to me particularly enlightening. It shows where he thought technique could not, or rather ought not, to be applied. Starting from his earlier view he says that in those cases where a collective solution is not possible and so when individuation begins, the moral, ethical and philosophical assumptions of both patient and analyst come under review in the therapeutic situation. If the patient is to expose his convictions on these matters the analyst must do the same without reservation; it is in this situation that a personal confrontation takes place leading to further self-realization by analyst and patient alike. Technique then becomes undesirable, and 'explanation' becomes a defence whereby 'the possibilities of individual development are obscured by being reduced to some general principle' (1935, p. 11).

He goes further, to imply that, by force of circumstance, method is at an end, for the analyst's theoretical views, on which his technique is based, may well either prove broken reeds or need radical modification if the patient is not to be damaged by them. The moral conflict with the patient leads on to the important stage of transformation in which 'the doctor is as much "in the analysis" as the patient. He is equally a part of the psychic process of treatment and therefore equally exposed to the transforming influences' (1931, p. 72)

Summary

I have extracted passages from Jung's works that have proved significant to me. They sum up to show Jung's pioneering thought; therapy resulted from an alchemical-like interaction between patient and therapist. He held that sometimes clearly-defined techniques were indicated like reductive analysis, the synthetic hermeneutic technique and amplification, etc. Sometimes, however, when the individuation processes were constellated it was necessary to discard the use of defined methods and react more openly. Then a personal confrontation would result in which the therapist was conceived to be as much 'in the analysis' as the patient. In the course of putting forward this programme, he criticized a special authoritarian psychopathology evident among psychotherapists. It could be, often was, and still is, reinforced by medical training, which is thereby criticized. The attitude that it expresses depends upon an overcompensated persona which has become dislocated from the rest of the person so as to form a rigid defence – a false self, as Winnicott (1960) calls it. The rigidity was expressed in the unreal application of authoritative omnipotent attitudes. One further daring innovation was a criticism of scientific method when applied to personal interaction.

Personal note

My own formulations could not have been constructed without Jung's ideas and that is why I have worked over those that have been meaningful to me. From him I took the alchemical analogy, though in a way that initially made me give excessive importance to the analyst's internal life: to his particular qualities rather than his ability to manage them. Because I felt myself beyond techniques I did not need to use them. This led on to pursuing a subjective investigation and to understanding, contrary to my expectation, that the analyst's affects were responses to the patient and that then they were indeed a source for understanding the patient rather than himself; in this way I got out of a subjective bias. Thus arose the concept of a syntonic counter-transference (this volume, Chapter 1), developed as I started to grasp that what I thought of as part of myself was an introjected part of the patient.

My present position now depends upon another development: a concept of individuation outlined at the International Congress of Analytical Psychology held in 1965 (Fordham, 1968a), and will be further developed in a forthcoming volume *Children as Individuals* (1969). The concept which grew out of earlier work (Fordham, 1957a), is close to that worked further forward by Frieda Fordham (1969), who showed how individuation in infancy was consonant with Jung's basic definition. This position was also implied in 'The importance of analysing childhood for the assimilation of the shadow' (1965). Concisely, I hold that individuation processes can be shown to occur in all the stages of life that Jung differentiated (1931a) and that the non-rational open-minded attitude, which Jung adopted for individuation cases in later life, enters into and plays a significant part in an analyst's behaviour with all patients.

PART II

Technique

In the natural sciences technique has come to mean the skill of the scientist in using instruments of various kinds, whether mathematical or experimental. They are not subject to subjective or personal influence. Statistical techniques follow a logic of their own and an experiment, though designed by a person, operates without he himself having subsequent influence upon it. Can this concept be applied to interchanges between human beings at all and in particular between analyst and patient? That is to say, can there be a technique of analysis which has no relevance to the analyst as a person? This is surely the state of affairs which Jung, though he seems to be half hoping for it, discards when he says it is not available to the analytical psychologist (1944, p. 43). In spite of this it would be possible to interpret what he says to mean that when applying reductive techniques a scientific procedure is relevant but not when applying the dialectical procedure.

It will be apparent, however, that if the dialectical procedure be relevant to all analytic procedures (I was going to say 'techniques') then the analyst's personal reactions, far from being excluded, must be included in all of them. Therefore, if it is possible to refer to 'analytic technique', some modification of the 'scientific' concept, as I have formulated it, must be made rather than hankered after. Yet, while it is apparent that modification is required by the nature of the analytic situation, I mistrust excessive reliance on personal qualities. If there are dangers attached to the use of depersonalized or transpersonal 'scientific' techniques there are perhaps greater ones related to relying on the individual personal qualities of the analyst. He easily becomes idealized and so opens the door to such abuses as intrusive display of his personality or acting out his counter-transference.

Since technique enters into teaching, the subject may be developed by reflecting on a relevant and important feature of training. Technique, it will be conceded, involves reliable knowledge that can be communicated to candidates who under optimal conditions acquire it. As our knowledge of technique progresses and as we know more and more about the dynamics of the analytic situation, so our training improves and trainees start off from a better position as analysts. However, during supervision of candidates for membership of the Society of Analytical Psychology in London it often becomes clear that they cannot grasp and manage the problems their patients present because their personal conflicts and anxieties prevent them from doing so.

Many years ago, a candidate, a psychologist trained in reporting, revealed this particularly well. He could tell me in a sufficiently organized way how his patient behaved, what he said, and how he, the candidate, replied. Together we then worked out interpretations that he could use in detail and we predicted the results. After several successful applications of this procedure, it became apparent that he was not following up his achievements and ceased to be keen on proceeding as we had been; supervision then became more pedestrian, with his reporting, my commenting on case material, and his using what I suggested in various ways.

One feature in all this became clear to me: the candidate could not follow up the advantage he appeared to have gained. A number of possibilities for this state of affairs presented themselves, of which the following may be selected:

(a) his analyst had not been able to analyse the affective consequences of the exercise undertaken as part of supervision, because
(b) the affective implications of what occurred were far beyond the candidate's development. So the project we developed was only accomplished by splitting himself into an observing and thinking person. Thus he remained unconscious of his involvement in the process and this blocked further use of what he worked out in supervision.

From experiences in supervision besides this one, and also as the result of analysing candidates' counter-transferences to their patients, it became clear, once again, that an analyst must necessarily work within the range of his own affective possibilities. To push him ahead of what he can grasp affectively, even though he can comprehend the problem intellectually, of necessity raises his defences. It can lead on to exacerbating the false self, the very result which Jung rightly criticized. That the candidate refused to follow up the achievement was thus, in one sense, to his credit.

It is such experiences that seem to bring into doubt the relevance of the scientific method. However, it can be held that they merely indicate the interference of counter-transference affects, and so it would follow that had the candidate been further analysed he would have been able to pursue effectively the experiment that I initiated with him. He would be able to formulate interpretations and follow them up with others, or pursue other methods relevant to the material produced by his patient.

In training analytical psychologists the concurrent analysis and supervision of candidates is designed to prevent the misuse of technique and to ensure that what is learned is related at all points to the personal capacities and gifts of the trainee; thus the aim is to ensure that all transactions between analyst and patient remain personal in the sense that Jung used the term.

Having these ideas in mind, is it possible to formulate a concept of technique? I follow Jung in holding that analytic (or synthetic) technique cannot be defined as independent of human beings, as is usual in the natural sciences. It must include the personality of the analyst and refer to a differentiated part of the self which basically, by deintegration (cf. this volume, Chapter 1) is made available for the treatment of patients. Technique then cannot be defined unless it is thought of as including the person of the analyst. I suggest that if it be conceived of as the distillate of habitual behaviours by an analyst with differing kinds of patient, the problem can be made more manageable.

Technique, which I shall identify mainly with interpretation, then comes to depend upon the analyst's having achieved a sufficient range of experience and maturity. In addition he needs to have learned, in the personal setting of the analysis of patients, in supervision, seminars (later in discussion with colleagues), in reading and private reflection, how to refine his experience. As a result he will have acquired the capacity to communicate with patients, and abstract his experience with them into theories so that colleagues can understand, profit from and add to them. This formulation obviously covers only a part, though an essential one, of the total interaction between analyst and patient, for it only states the range of the analyst's ego development. But it is upon this that technique as defined must depend.

The definition requires qualification as follows: since the analytic situation is in essential respects unique and unrepeatable – hence the need to establish the individual context of any content under review – even the interpretation of the most familiar situations will contain variations in wording or phrasing and their affective content will differ from case to case. Variations in tones of voice and differing emphases not to mention facial and other bodily movements are inevitable and desirable so long as their relation to the patient is noticed and understood. It is important to grasp that though technique is essentially a scientific procedure, many interventions may be fruitfully compared to the work of an artist who uses his technical mastery in the service of a creative and individual achievement.

Since communications about technique to a third person or to a group or in a published essay alter the analytic events, often in significant respects, it can be claimed that to teach, to communicate techniques, to discuss technical procedures or to arrive at conclusions about what procedures are correct and what incorrect are all useless. Against this position, which I regard as due to idealization of technique and a wrong understanding of its nature, it can be held that, without great loss and with much gain, a moderate degree of abstraction and generalization can be used from which great advantages accrue. It becomes possible to compare notes with colleagues and to formulate techniques having validity in the social context which enrich and develop analytic practice with individual patients. In addition, more detailed matters can be gone into: studies can be made about the relevance of interpreting part of the patient's conflict or the whole of it, of activity or passivity on the part of the analyst, of timing interpretations and the quantity of them, of the meaning that the analyst's interpretations as a whole may take on in the light of the patient's positive or negative transference.

The problem that Jung opened up by stating that some patients need to become better adapted while others need to work out individual solutions can now be reconsidered. The difference between what Jung said and the ideas I have begun to develop is as follows: if *all* valid techniques are personal interactions between analyst and patient, then the individual element becomes an essential part of all interpretative and other analytic procedures. But this does not mean that all cases are the same; indeed, Jung's distinction still stands, as it were, macroscopically. It is only when the detailed microscopic analysis of the analytic situation is gone into that his distinction comes to be seen as quantitative rather than qualitative.

All patients are basically individuals: some are more or even overadapted, others are less grossly unadapted. A technique of interpretation is intended to increase the capacity of the patient for reflection about himself in relation to his analyst first and, as a consequence, his wider environment and his inner world. It has no other aim: it does not aim to remove symptoms nor render the patient normal or adapted, though if these results are in the patient's interest they will take place. All this leaves the patient to make use of technical procedure in his own individual way.

It may be added that when an analyst uses a technique he is affirming by implication that he has been over this ground before, that he is familiar with it and can respond easily and comfortably to his patient. The likeness of the analyst's experience with that of his patient leads, because of his familiarity with what is going on, to a capacity to project himself, i.e. put himself into his patient's place, or to introject, i.e., experience the patient's feelings inside himself: these twin processes form the basis for flexible and complex identifications necessary if he is to relate intimately (empathize) with his patient. By letting projections and introjections happen freely and relying on their taking place sufficiently, the raw material for interventions is provided (cf. Money-Kyrle, 1956). It is, to use an alchemical analogy, the *prima materia* of analysis.

The unconscious processes of projection, introjection and identification happen during listening to the patient. It is then that the analyst keeps himself open-minded, he 'puts aside preconceptions', and empties his mind as far as possible. Freud defined this attitude first in a classical phrase, 'evenly hovering attention'. When practising this 'technique', information is being collected and the analyst is finding out, through the activity of his attention based on unconscious processes, what is near the surface in the patient at this time.

On the basis of conclusions drawn from what the patient is saying *today*, an analyst makes technical interventions designed to clarify, explore and interpret the patient's communications. In this next step he draws on the whole of the knowledge of his patient that he has accumulated over months or years of analysis. The analyst distills the to-and-fro processes of projection, introjection and identification till he arrives at a position from which he can make an interpretative intervention in which he is flexibly involved. Under these conditions his intervention can be appropriate, he will estimate the patient's anxiety and make interpretations at suitable enough times; if he makes 'mistakes' these are of the order that can be retrieved (cf. Heinmann, 1960 and Strauss, 1960). The activities just described are part and parcel of 'routine therapy'. They only work with patients mature enough to use insights and are the expression of technique whose range increases with knowledge, experience and the analyst's personal development. The alchemical analog to this seems to be the use of a '*theoria* for effecting chemical changes' (Jung, 1944, p. 285).

In routine analysis it looks as if a part of the analyst has been set aside to act as an instrument much like the experimental instruments in the natural sciences. But this is only apparent because the unconscious processes, upon which the part relies, do not obtrude themselves. It follows that routine analysis of patients is conducted as if the analyst were using a 'scientific' technique with which he is thoroughly familiar. Under these conditions it is just as if he is conducting a sequence of experiments whose results he can predict and in which he is not personally involved. This state of affairs covers but reinterprets psychoanalysis as it has been developed over the years by many psychoanalysts (cf. Greenson, 1967). It depends upon establishing a therapeutic alliance that will hold through the interpretation and working through of resistances in the positive and negative transference.

The account of this procedure, which is necessarily brief and has been developed and elaborated in considerable detail elsewhere, implies that the analyst deploys his technique without the intervention of any counter-transference at all – an ideal that is, however, never reached.

Before proceeding to consider counter-transference – a term not much used by Jung – and its relation to technique, there is one feature of the analytic situation which needs attention: it is the analyst's style which expresses the individuality of the analyst. In the course of time each analyst develops his own characteristic way of analysing patients which is distinct from that of any other. It can be and has been held that the individual style is the central core of all analytical procedures. On this basis formal training becomes undesirable because it is essential for a trainee to find out in his own way, in relation to his patients, how to conduct analyses. Supervision and lectures and seminars on technique then come to be thought of as undesirable.

It is difficult to contradict this idea because style is by definition individual and ultimately uncommunicable, but even if the analyst's style is an essential feature of his practice, and I agree that it is, there is no reason to suggest that analytic training in which a personal analysis is a central feature can fail to expand the range and provide useful contributions to the development of his style.

It may fairly be claimed that Jung's special contribution was to a field where individuality was primary, but he did not say that techniques and methods were to be eschewed. This idea, already discussed above, is not the whole of Jung's thesis and so the generalization based on a part of it and made to cover the whole analytic situation cannot be justified by referring to his work.

Counter-transference

During the conduct of routine analysis, technique holds the patient, who ultimately, in spite of what he may project into his analyst's use of it, will be grateful to him. Counter-transference is easily managed and can be the part of the analysis that makes for empathy with his patient's conflict situations.

Analytical psychologists have developed a special interest in the counter-transference. It stems from the idea of the dialectical procedure and from Jung's situation that the analyst needs to be just as much in analysis as the patient. For this reason it can sometimes be thought that the analyst's having emotions about a patient means there is a counter-transference present in need of analysis. I cannot agree to this idea because the analyst can experience uncomplicated affects of two kinds: there are personal 'human' interchanges that occur most at the beginning or end of the interview, though they may also happen at any time that seems desirable. There are the more intense ones: love and hate, which can be directly relevant and so adapted to the patient's needs (in contrast to wishes).

Suppose a patient is truly deprived and worth love, then loving is appropriate; the same applies to hate of a patient when he means to be destructively violent. The only difference here between analyst and patient is in their differing consciousness. Since an analyst knows about his affects, he need not act on them but understands them as indicators and useful parts of the analytic situation. He knows that love and hate by analyst or patient can indicate either their basic unity or the inimical nature of their two personalities. Each can also contain realistic estimates the one of the other. The situation is the equivalent, in day-to-day work, of the confrontation that Jung conceived, though too narrowly, in moral, ethical and religious terms. Having laid emphasis on affective communications based on health the counter-transference can now be gone into in more detail.

The classical view of counter-transference, still frequently held as I have already mentioned, is this: it is undesirable and ideally takes no part in the analyst's technique. Its effects are held to be negative because an unconscious process is defended against and distorts the analyst's interventions. For instance, if the analyst is *not* analysing a patient in reasonable comfort and if the patient's behaviour, his illusions or delusions, disturb him in ways that are not to be defined and understood, then a negative counter-transference may be present. If he then finds himself making mistakes they are probably due to his counter-transference.

The following are examples of the undesirable-effects of counter-transference. (i) An analyst may reject the patient's transference by saying, 'I am not like that,' *when* the patient's projection requires interpretation. (2) He may defensively play a rôle which means he imagines that what he does or how he feels *necessarily* has a bearing on the patient's transference. He may then start to believe erroneously that expression of his good behaviour and good feeling will of *necessity* benefit the patient when well-meaning interventions are felt by the patient as impingements that interfere with the development of the patient's transference affects. These illusions and others like them can be grouped as counter-transference in its negative sense. A list of them would comprise the sum total of all the analyst's psychopathology; indeed, anything that an analyst says based on his unconscious which is defended against and so gives rise to illusions or delusions cannot be brought into relation with technique.

But is counter-transference always so negative? In 1957 I first suggested that it need not be so; I extended the use of the term and divided it up into illusory and syntonic parts. The illusory elements cover the negative undesirable elements in the counter-transference. Syntonic elements are basically different because, through introjection, an analyst perceives a patient's unconscious processes in himself and so experiences them long before the patient is near becoming conscious of them.

The significance of his experience may or may not be recognized by the analyst. But in either case it is of no use in the analytic process till the patient produces enough relevant material for the analyst to communicate what he has long 'known' to the patient. Only when the patient is on the edge of reaching an affect which the analyst has reflected inside him can the syntonic counter-transference be used. Before this the introject acts as a foreign body that often defines understanding.

It was these states that led me to use the term syntonic counter-transference and to think of the processes it represents as related to technique (cf. this volume, Chapters 1 and 2 and Fordham, 1964). Since then I have come to think that the clinical experiences subsumed under this heading seem better considered in terms of an introject that has failed to become reprojected. The two unconscious processes, projection and introjection, are thus considered valuable processes and, together with information gained by listening and observing, form the basis upon which technique rests. A syntonic counter-transference is thus part of a more complex situation. So conceived it helps to avoid two pitfalls:

1 Because the introject is of little use at the time, it becomes negative; since it deflects the analyst from his aim of working at the level which the patient has reached. It is relevant only to what is right under the surface and well defended against by the patient. Conceiving analysis as including not only the unconscious content being resisted but also the resistances themselves, it can be asked why does the analyst have the experience? If an analyst gets indirect experience through introjection which he often cannot understand, could it not be that he defends himself against the patient's own defences by knowing beforehand? Since he has no evidence of the source of his experiences, the conclusion I would draw is that he has ceased to listen to what his patient has

been saying because of his unconscious hostility to the defences which the patient seeks to communicate to him. In other words he treats the patient as if his defences do not exist. This illusion can lead to brilliant 'intuition' flair and the like that sometimes produces exciting results. It does not belong to analysis of the patient because the defences are ignored.

2. The introject may result in internal identification of the analyst's ego with it; then we may arrive at incarnating an archetype, a phrase used by Plaut in 1956. He postulated alternatives: either the analyst educates the patient or incarnates the archetypal image. His formulation, at the time very useful, like the syntonic counter-transference has unfavourable aspects – in particular it leads to the impossibility of the patient integrating the content of a projection. Here again there is often a concealed counter-transference illusion.

Each concept therefore highlights, or rather names, a state of affairs that all analysts can locate in the total analytical situation, but looked at in terms of the projection–introjection sequence the syntonic counter-transference can, like incarnating the archetypal image, be recognized as part of the unconscious communication process upon which technique rests. If either be considered in isolation it implies at best a temporary breakdown in communication to be located in the projective part of the analyst's work.

It is of interest that both these concepts, which rely on the study of events within the analyst, should be invented by analytical psychologists; they seem to have arisen from anxiety about the analyst's making projections and consequently overlooking the need for them. It is, I think, relevant to state that though there is little in Jung's publications against it and indications that he knew about the need for projection, nothing has been said overtly about its positive value. Jung's assertion that projections are part of the process of becoming conscious seems to have been overlooked and not applied to the analyst's work of interpretation. So the current attitude among analysts has been that projections ought to be taken back into the self and so integrated. Consequently there arose a tendency to exclusive subjectivism, i.e., if an analyst detected a projection from himself it was treated negatively and the tendency became established to aim at preventing projections. This view, however, can only refer to projections which created fixed illusions or delusions – it does not include those that are part of affective communication.

Gradually I came to realize that the practice was wrong, and, as a step in reversing this false position, I formulated the idea of the syntonic counter-transference. But because of the prohibition on projection I did not dare to think that the introject needed projection and so remained in a guilt-ridden subjectivism.

My inability to see the importance of projection, and I do not think I am alone in this, arose also from insufficient recognition of the essential infantile component in counter-transference. It is indeed only quite recently that I have understood that patients represent parental figures to the analyst in his unconscious. The angry attacks of patients are therefore treated as admonitions and condemnations that the infant part of the analyst needs, while their love and admiration are fed on by him and sustain him. Accordingly his infant part seeks to evoke these responses from his patient. These counter-transference responses have tended to be rigorously defended against because of the ideal analytic schema which ordains that an analyst ought to be in the position either of a parent or at least the equal of his patient all the time. If he is not, then the analyst easily rationalizes the situation and condemns himself to masochistic silence in the service of an idea which abjures a projection which it cannot prevent. An alternative seems to have been to rely on inappropriate 'spontaneity' which is then given infantile omnipotent characteristics as intuition which is really concealed projection.

The useful introject occurs while listening to the patient and provides material through which an interpretation can be formulated if kept at a distance from the analyst's ego. Then an internal dialectic can occur and if the analyst can also project himself, and particularly the infantile parts, into the patient and combine these with knowledge gained from the patient, a valid interpretation can result. The internal part of the dialectic may be almost instantaneous or prolonged, but it requires projection before an effective interpretation can be made. This situation was, I believe, indicated by Jung in the diagrams of crossed projections in 'The psychology of the transference' (1946, pp. 221) but he seems to have taken a more negative view of it than is being developed here. His presentation further lays emphasis upon culture and history so that the infantile roots of it become obscured from view.

An analytic episode

The following example illustrates the concepts being elaborated by considering the failure in interchange between a patient and myself. It was incompletely corrected with moderate ease and so helps to throw the process under discussion into relief. The example will introduce aspects of counter-transference evoked by and evoking psychotic-like patterns.

A woman, who had been virtually deprived of sex information till adolescence, had been puzzled about its effect on her in later life. One day she told me that her eldest son, aged about five years, had been playing a game in a bath. There was a big toy fish whose belly was split open. The boy put small fishes inside. The mother thought this an opportunity not to be missed and she started a rather long to-and-fro interchange about babies and how they got out – not, it will be observed, about the alternative understanding that the fishes might represent penises that are put inside the mother. The discussion continued till the boy jumped up excited and asked her to let him see her little door down below. She said 'yes' and after a pause added 'sometime' and changed the subject.

For a long time her own infantile sexuality had seemed problematic and I could not fully grasp its significance to her. I could feel into her situation and her unconscious anxieties and I knew very well what it was about intellectually, but neither she nor I could make headway in the transference because my ideas about it seemed to her plain nonsense or even delusions. On this occasion I pointed out that it seemed she had unintentionally seduced her son and then had to frustrate him, using a deception in the process. I offered this interpretation with rather careful choice of words because of previous unproductive clashes

After a pause and some further remarks by me relating this situation to her own childhood and comparing her behaviour with that of her own parents who were very rigid in their views about sex, I stated, with some irritation, that whatever their demerits they had not needed to resort to such manoeuvres. This was expressed mildly so as to give as few grounds as possible for what I feared would be felt as a damning criticism. It led to a very unexpected retort: 'It is you that want to look.' I felt bewildered, but recognized that some reply was required. As I could not produce one, I tried to locate the source of my state in myself first but without success, so there was a short pause before I replied, 'Maybe, but you remember that once you told me your husband only had to look at you to get an erection.' This made her silent and reflective.

The patient often has to be analysed through projective identifications of which her remark was one, and when working well with ordinary skill it would have been possible for me to let her develop this 'thought' into reflections about my emotions, perhaps speculation about my childhood, and sometimes she could work back to herself and, albeit rarely, find the situation in her childhood to which the transference referred. In this sequence interpretation could then have been used to relive anxieties and resistances that otherwise appeared insuperable without the warding-off activity that became necessary for me. My reply was defensive and so obstructed the ongoing personal interaction systems expressed in delusional forms.

All this was clear to me at the time, or shall I say within five minutes. But reflecting on this episode afterwards it became evident that my interest in the subject had made me stop listening in a way that included unconscious processes. Consequently my interest in the problem she presented led me to remain unconscious of the transference implication in her story. Had I been able to project myself into what she was saying I believe I would have succeeded in making in essence the following interpretation: 'Are you not telling me this because of a wish that I had behaved like you did to your son when earlier on in the analysis you gave me openings for doing so, and are you not reproaching me for my failure to take them up as your parents also did and so avoided your sexual interests and impulses when you were a child?'

This speculative interpretation is based upon analysis of my own counter-transference. I was predisposed to reproach myself and did so. This had blinded me to her reproach of me which was the one she levelled at her own parents whose positive virtues had made the faintest criticism of them almost impossible: their failings were put down, and with justice too, to the culture pattern in which they were brought up; but by this mature understanding she preserved them from the infantile attack that she needed to launch. 'Looking' featured in what she had been told about her father who used to sit beside her cot and gaze at her.

This example illustrated nicely the way in which my patient had represented her infantile sexuality in symbolic forms which as a child had kept her unaware of the instinctual sources from which the symbols sprang. The interpretation might have opened up avenues of investigation along these lines but it was not made because I had introjected her reproach and probably also the feeling of her parents that such matters should not be mentioned.

There is one element in my interpretation which related to the projective–introjective components in communication. If an analyst says 'you' to a patient it is worth remembering that the pronoun refers to a projection: 'I' likewise refers to the patient's projection introjected by the analyst. If this dual process is not borne in mind the situation easily leads to confusion and is a source of conflict centring on the meanings of the words 'I' and 'you'. It is the basis of many quarrels of children when they get into confusion about what each has said to the other.

What I have described illustrates the difference between being conscious or unconscious of a counter-transference. My patient's unpredicted behaviour had made me retreat into myself – syntonic counter-transference – and wait till I could find a way of managing what I had found out on previous occasions was a delusional transference. This had, in the past, frequently led to delusions of my own about myself as well as my patient. Then, her unpredictability had been far less manageable.

My recovery from it was, on this occasion, only so rapid because I had reached the point where, after many past failures, I could recover. The obstructing counter-transference was partly due to my establishing a masochistic 'policy' of not responding because I knew I could not spot the differences between her projection and my own position. When I could not I thought as follows: 'Well, perhaps . . .' then the way had become open to masochism. The next step would be to identify with the introject which happened when I believed that what she said was true. Then I had arrived at incarnating the projection. By following this up I discovered a delusion inside me and began to arrive at the technique of managing this patient's delusional transference, an essentially impenetrable psychotic-like state which needed to be reprojected.

Technique in psychotic states

In Chapter 7 of *The Psychology of the Transference* Jung says: 'The decomposition of the elements indicates dissociation and collapse of existing ego consciousness. It is closely analogous to the schizophrenic state, and it should be taken very seriously because this is the moment when a latent psychosis may become acute, i.e., when the patient becomes aware of the collective unconscious and the psychic non-ego' (1946, p. 265).

In this passage there is no indication how often the psychotic transference occurs. He makes it clear that the patient in this state need not be clinically psychotic but that the pressure of affect disturbs the analyst far more than during 'ordinary analysis', and induces regression to levels comparable to that of the patient. At this point it may seem justifiable to abandon technique and start relying on intuition. Jung, however, is quite clear that this is not enough. The therapist 'must hold fast to his own orientation; that is he must know what the patient means' and 'must approach his task with views and ideas capable of grasping unconscious symbolism' (*ibid.*, p. 268); then he adds: 'The kind of approach . . . must therefore be plastic and symbolical, and itself the outcome of personal experience with unconscious contents'. This is why 'we are best advised to remain within the framework of tradition mythology' (*ibid.*). All this can be taken as part of what I have included in the definition of technique which should therefore apply to the transference psychosis as much as to the transference neurosis.

So that there can be no ambiguity I must state that I do not use mythological knowledge in analytic sessions. How Jung used it in therapy is not at all clear from reading his publications, in marked contrast to his convincing demon- stration of its value in deepening understanding of dreams and fantasies outside analysis. My own personal experience of it in analysis was far from satisfying in that it too easily introduced intellectual defensive systems into the therapeutic situation.

When Jung writes in the same context, which implies the use of mythology: 'Whenever possible I try to rouse the patient to mental activity and get him to subdue the *massa confusa* of his mind with his own understanding.' This is in line with what analysts, I conceive, try to do all along – but how? If this be translated to justify setting the patient to learning about myths by reading books, this can easily result in the very warding off of the transference of which he accuses Freud (Jung, 1946, p. 171).

This interesting issue is not essential to my thesis, whose discussion can better be furthered by asking: is it possible to refer to a technique of managing a transference psychosis in the same way as a transference neurosis? If we follow Jung the answer seems to be yes, but because of my reservations I think that the problem needs more sorting out and here I have found the work of psychoanalysts impressive.

Some claim that they can approach this area by using interpretative techniques alone and that affective involvement with the patient is not a special feature (Rosenfeld, 1965). Others like Margaret Little (1957 and 1960), Searles (1965), and Winnicott (1947 and 1960a), consider the analyst's affects are so important that psychoanalysis in its classical sense cannot be conducted. Little holds that the analyst's 'total' response to the patient is essential. She conceives that it is important to rely on and use the counter-transference and that to rely on technique as defined by the majority of psychoanalysts is insufficient (cf. supra, p. 106, Little, 1957, also Bion, 1955). She notes the elements of surprise and arbitrariness and these clearly prevent the deployment of controlled technique which relies on the analyst's predicting the outcome of his interventions.

However, what seems at first surprising, chaotic and uncontrollable can perhaps be subjected to analytic observation and brought within a describable framework. Jung had already done this, but Searles' researches into the psychotherapy of schizophrenia, in which the 'therapeutic alliance' – as previously understood – is out of the question, is of special interest.

His work complements and expands Jung's description by showing how it feels personally. He states openly that the therapist's comfort, his hate and love of the patient, are good and reliable indicators for therapeutic action. For instance he defines a first stage in psychotherapy of psychotic patients in which the therapist feels unrelated to his patient. From this he infers the cause: the patient is reacting to him as inanimate, an animal, a corpse, an idea or something essentially *not human*. During this period the therapist experiences definable affects, but first and foremost he needs to see that he himself is at ease. Having achieved this over a prolonged time he begins to hate the patient and this ushers in a totally destructive transference of a delusional kind.

In both situations, he conceives that the counter-transference becomes an indicator of the transference. Next there is a phase in which love begins and the analyst becomes deeply involved in it. Are these experiences to be classed as counter-transference or are they 'healthy' responses by the analyst? They are experienced in a modified form in many thorough analyses, indeed if Jung's essay to be taken as a paradigm of a complete analysis they may be expected to occur always.

In my view Jung's thesis justifies an extended use of the term 'counter-transference' to cover these experiences (cf. this volume, Chapter 2), yet he does not use the term except with reference to Freud. This was probably because he interested himself in meeting the psychotic-like needs of his patients and his reactiveness did not correspond with counter-transference illusions. At first-sight there seems to be an essential difference between the therapist's response to the psychotic transference and his responses to a transference neurosis in routine analysis. There is less mental control exerted by him than when he is being an analyst using technique in its classical sense and he needs to rely on his affects much more than in his mind. But his affects are not disruptive to the progress of analysis and are needed urgently by the patient. Searles means, if I understand him, that without the analyst's remaining comfortable, without his hate or without his love, the patient cannot begin to make any sort of transference relationship; this is apparently not so when there is transference neurosis.

On these grounds it becomes questionable whether the therapist's work with a psychotic transference can be thought of as technique. Nevertheless Searles succeeded in mapping out the course that affects regularly take and thus, he has gone far towards defining a technique of therapy for psychotic patients. It is of interest to look in passing at other situations that Searles states can occur and need to be recognized; the patient needs the therapist to do his thinking for him, he nullifies all the efforts of the therapist to be helpful, the patient treats the therapist as ill or seeks to help him in his diseased state. If anything is to be done the analyst needs to work inside these delusional reversals of the part of an analyst in analytic therapy.

Researches into the psychopathology of clinical psychoses and borderline states have given most impetus to the study of counter-transference. Because of the unremitting pressures that these cases exert on the analyst, there have been tendencies to introduce proceedings based on the acting out of affects, or through unconsciousness to introjection of the psychosis (cf. Jung, 1946, p. 171f, and Meier, 1959, p. 32). Each can now be seen as those manifestations of counter-transference which have here been defined as incarnating it or behaving syntonically. On the other side under these pressures the aim of furthering and deepening analytic work has been abandoned and it has been changed to mobilize ego defences (cf. Federn, 1953)

It is not my intention to discuss the analytic psychotherapy of psychotic disorders, though there are indications that they can be better understood by more penetrating understanding of counter-transference. I have wanted rather to show how the study of counter-transference in these cases has led on to extending the idea of counter-transference into the framework of classical analysis itself. Searles showed how a psychotic transference seems to attack the classical technique and so, if I am correct, the first step must be to analyse the structure of technique in the neuroses. The difference between the transference/counter-transference set up in the minor disorders and the psychoses then seems to be quantitative rather than qualitative.

If a careful study of the analytic situation be made this is often quite easy to demonstrate. There is a modicum of truth in the delusion of a patient that the analyst is ill and urgently needs the help of the patient which the analyst could fall for by incarnating the delusion and conclude that he was getting treatment for himself; this means he has regressed to an infantile position. But in any analytic situation there lies the potential for this to occur. The technique of asking the patient to produce his ideas, feelings and affects with as little restraining as possible, initiates a transference situation, but it also provides the ground for the analyst's feeling like an infant being fed in various ways: being given good food that he can digest and enjoy or being stuffed with food he does not want or cannot make use of, and this can lead on to regression to persecutory levels. He may be expected to be conscious of these affects and in the counter-transference neurosis they are manageable; but when the transference becomes delusional his own persecutory and depressive feelings become much stronger and less easy to manage. In this situation he will hope to react, if not with technique, at least with affective flexibility. It is true that often he ceases to be an analyst in the usual sense, but this is due to the strength of the affects rather than their nature.

Having recognized this state of affairs it becomes clearer that the counter-transference can become an indicator of the patient's transference. So the analyst has acquired an instrument that he can use. Counter-transference becomes one – but not the only – source of information about the patient's transference. So long as the analyst is conscious of the part his unconscious processes (and defences are among them) play in his interaction with his patient, his ego can analyse and use this information as part of techniques whether it be in neurotic or psychotic states. This conclusion provides a basis for working out in day-to-day analysis what Jung formulated as the dialectical procedure.

Summary

The subject of technique has not received the attention it deserves. Study of Jung's position shows that he laid varying emphasis on it. Sometimes he estimated it highly, sometimes thought it ought to be eschewed. Analysis of his statements show that his ideas settled round the differing needs of patients. Some needed to become adapted, and for them a rational technique was required; others, needed to individuate, and required a confrontation with the analyst from which the dialectical process derived.

In this paper the differences between patients are conceived to be quantitative and individuation is understood as a continuing process from birth to death.

The concept of technique applies very well to analysis of the transference neurosis when it can seem as if the analyst is applying interpretation in much the same way as a scientist applies his experimental procedure. But this is not a true picture for there is a dialectic to be found on the one hand in the interaction between the ego of analyst and patient and on the other in unconscious projection–introjection process.

Taking a wide view of counter-transference enables a deeper understanding. It lies at the root of technique, and is indeed the *prima materia* out of which technique is distilled.

In the last decade analysis of the psychoses has introduced a new dimension to analytic skills. Psychotic and borderline cases require a more reactive kind of behaviour by the therapist. Handling unexpected and more openly irrational data produced by patients leads to a transference psychosis and to a correspondingly complex counter-transference. The work in this area of therapy is reviewed, evaluated and brought into line with Jung's position. It has converted counter-transference from an unwanted and undesirable intrusion into a useful instrument in the hand of the analyst: transference evokes counter-transference, and vice versa.

Chapter 9

Reply to Plaut's 'Comment' (1970)[1]

Just as my paper 'Technique and counter-transference' stimulated Plaut (1970), so has his 'Comment', in the last issue of the *Journal of Analytical Psychology*, stimulated me in a number of ways, some of which I believe it will be profitable to develop.

To start with a disclaimer. The almost complete absence of the term archetype in my article is not due to its being 'omitted' but is the result of considering technique as a manifestation of ego functioning.

Let me next answer a reproach: am I wrongly attributing to him the term 'incarnating the archetype'? In his original paper Plaut (1956) refers more than once to 'incarnating it', referring to the archetypal image. While he may be right in reproaching me for inexact attribution and for not including the term 'image', it remains that the phrase 'incarnating the archetype' has been widely used as a shorthand and I must record in my defence two observations: 1) I did not put the phrase in quotation marks, and 2) in the phrase 'incarnating the archetypal image', the word 'image' is redundant because an archetype could not be embodied without there being an image.

I believe that I was also in order to interpret (i.e. to 'misrepresent') a formulation that was obscure in a number of respects. Clear definition is not always necessary or desirable and it is not my intention to criticize so long as the formulation be recognized as imprecise and that it will provoke differing understandings and interpretations by others. That interpretations of such formulations often appear to the originator as 'misunderstandings', 'misquotations' and the like, is more or less the rule, so I need only say that to me the religious association to incarnating was not important; I recognize, however, that in saying so I must state my difficulties more clearly than I have done in my paper. There I compressed my thoughts unduly and so I welcome this opportunity to expand them.

In the first place Jung's case that Plaut cited showed that the patient could distinguish Jung from the daemonic image as in an ordinary transference. When Plaut cites Jung as saying 'There is no way of getting out of the toils of the unconscious except for the doctor . . . to acknowledge himself as the image' (1943, p.90) Jung means, as I understand it, that there is no point in denying that he was representing the projected image to the patient and that it would be merely interfering to use either interpretations of a reductive kind or defensive common sense. Plaut refers to the latter when he says that he could think: 'Oh there is quite a lot in what she says' or 'I am nothing of the kind' (p.18).

I would understand that Jung would think somewhat as follows: 'This is an archetypal experience that transcends both the patient and myself, it is religious in nature and represents a religious need of the patient.' He would communicate the substance of this idea to the patient as he says in another context (cf. 1935, p. 131). Thus Jung does not do anything like incarnating the daemon but continues with interpretation. Yet this passage, as if to introduce the subject of incarnating, precedes Plaut's three main points: 1) That the archetypal image must be recognized and distinguished from the patient's conscious demands. This is clear to me though the distinction is not so easy and sometimes not possible or desirable. 2) That the unconscious affects the analyst is also in line with my experience.

It is the substance of his third point, where he refers to incarnating and the need for distinguishing the ego from the archetypes, that I would find obscure for the following reasons: Plaut chooses as an example the animus figure (a part of the woman) to be incarnated. As a man he cannot 'become what the patient's unconscious asserts' (1956, p. 18) because the animus in her own unconscious cannot by definition be a part of him; only if he introjects this image can sense be made of his thesis. Once introjected then consideration of its relation to the ego becomes relevant (I assume he means the conscious parts of the ego). This is the basis on which I assumed that Plaut's thesis involves introjection. I would also say so if the image was any archetypal image at all, but for a somewhat different sense: the image though collective basically has individual characteristics and its associative connexions are significantly and usually drastically different in any two people. I added identification because of the word 'become' in Plaut's phrase, 'Then I would *become*'. I recognize that Plaut states that incarnating occurs 'without identification' (p.19) but this does not convince me, though it is just possible that we are using terms in different ways. Only if he had said 'become *for the patient*' in the sense of it being the patient's experience, can I conceive that there would be no identification, but then there need be no introjection either.

In spite of these formal objections, I think I know very well what Plaut was aiming at as I hope I showed when I used his idea in an earlier paper (this volume, Chapter 1, p. 36). In analytical psychology there was, at the time, a view that the transference of infantile characteristics though inevitable was undesirable; they needed to be dissolved by the application of explanatory principles or reductive criticism. On the other hand, when it come to archetypal forms, education was often applied. At that time I was coming to understand that the centre piece of analysis was the interpretation, living through and integration in the transference relationship; of affects having infantile and archetypal characteristics. Their interpretation, I observed, need not have the supposed critical reductive aim but was rather a means of elucidating and clarifying affective processes and all their associated connexions. These affects may form the basis of a 'wonder world' which Plaut wishes to preserve; I don't think there would be much disagreement between us on this score, so I can go on to say that incarnating, whatever it meant in detail, laid emphasis on the affective interpersonal transference relationship. More recently Davidson (1966) compared it to action imagination and this develops interestingly my earlier remarks on the relation between the two (this volume, Chapter 1).

That I now think the experience can be expressed in relation to the functioning of projective, introjective and identification processes is because they go a long way to explaining inaccessible transference processes, especially where a transference of delusional intensity predominates. With these ideas I have found it possible to extend the applications or interpretations , I believe beneficially.

Next: I am not at all easy when Plaut says that an analyst would 'be wiser to reproject' (p. 93) nor that 'there is a place for the analyst to incarnate an archetypal image'. Projection and introjection are unconscious processes, and are not usually under *control* of the conscious parts of the ego; much less so during analytic interviews where the analyst's attention is focused on his patient. Afterwards and sometimes, as in the example I gave where the part of the interview I recorded became a subjective experience, it is possible to work on the disorder. If therefore he thinks that an analyst can, as a matter of technique, project or introject then I would like to know how it is done. According to my view what he proposes is magic in its formal sense; by which I mean that a manageable model is made of the real unmanageable situation, then by manipulating the model in the desired way, a result follows which may or may not happen: sticking pins into a wax model of a person may (or may not) take place where the person has pains. Whether it does so or not is not a matter of technique because it is unpredictable.

Then on to the subject of 'distillations'. Interpretations rely on the analyst's capacity to distil (mostly unconsciously) the data they provide. Distilling, I suggest, could mean sorting out false perceptions from the true ones which accord with observations – the others, the false ones, do not.

To approach the subject of antecedents. The term style is not new – it can be found in the literature and papers that have been written on it. I meant to use it in an ordinary sense, and it was evidently precise enough for Plaut to understand what I meant, though he used it in ways that I did not intend. No doubt it will get used and given meanings not thought of by me and I may object. His linking it up with the personal equation and personality seems to me unwarranted, because I think the personal equation is the stuff of one analytic relationship; but all the same, if he finds it useful it will be interesting to see the result of his thoughts.

Next, Plaut claims that the 'positive aspects of the differentiation (between transference and counter-transference) had not yet been described' when he wrote his paper published in 1956. This statement is perhaps not altogether surprising in view of the rather inadequate level of communication between analysts at that time. But it may be worthwhile showing that the idea of positive counter-transference has a history.

The discovery had an indirectly positive result in that the distinction led to instituting training analysis in the early days of psychoanalysis. It was implied in Jung's 'The therapeutic value of abreaction' (1921) and developed into the idea of the dialectical process. It was rather specifically expressed in 'The psychology of the transference' (1946) though the term counter-transference was only used in a footnote. By 1956 the sense of it was being discussed and Moody had published an interesting example of the value of acting out the positive counter-transference in 1955. In 1957 my concept on the syntonic counter-transference had been published and had been discussed in the S.A.P. over a year before. Among psychoanalysts the subject was being gone into intensively and ironically before analytical psychologists! In 1950 Paula Heimann published a paper 'On counter-transference' in which she specifically wrote on its positive aspects. In 1951 Margaret Little had written 'Counter-transference and the patient's response to it'.

No doubt Plaut, like myself, was ignorant of the developments taking place in psychoanalysis. I thought my idea of the syntonic counter-transference was original and I was only later to discover that Paula Heimann was seven years ahead of me. Since then I have paid close attention to psychoanalytic writings and I owe much to them. In estimating the importance of projection–introjection systems in the normal counter-transference for instance I owe much to Money-Kyrle and I have lately learned a great deal from Racker, whose book was published after a late draft of my paper had been completed.

In his 'Comment' Plaut raises another question of interest to me. He thinks that a clue to a solution of his uncertainty may be found in the analyst being ready to let himself become the 'first not-me possession' and he links this with Winnicott's idea of 'transitional objects'. Now one of the essential features of the transitional object is that it is *not* a person. It is a bit of fluff, a rag or a doll, etc. It therefore seems to be wrong to put it in this way. Yet the process of discovering that the mother (as breast, arms, etc., etc.) is not me and yet belongs to me, though not clearly defined or known about, is different from the transitional object as I understand it from Winnicott's writings and my own observations. In my understanding the transitional object is a very early self-representation (Fordham, 1969) so it would be confusing to assume that when the analyst is felt to be a 'not–me possession' that he has become a transitional object. All the same Plaut's proposition is pertinent, especially as Jung laid emphasis on 'not-me' archetypes.

NOTE

1 In his 'Comment', Plaut states that the phrase 'incarnating the archetype' does not occur in his piece. He discusses the residue of metaphoricity in new concepts, critiquing Fordham's use of the word 'style' and 'distillation'. He claims that the religious connotations of incarnation are the reason for the misquotation. He suggests a culinary alternative to the term – 'the analyst may allow himself to be edible, provided he is reasonably sure of surviving' (Fordham *et al.* 1974, p. 295). Plaut comments on this interchange in 'Fred Plaut in conversation with Andrew Samuels' (Samuels, 1989) (ed.)

Chapter 10

The interrelation between patient and therapist (1972)[1]

A characteristic feature of analytical psychotherapy is its emphasis on individuation. As a baby each of us started from being a discrete unit. Each came into relation with his mother, experienced first as a diffuse ill-defined affect with a focus on the mouth since at first there was no mother 'out there'. Each was dominated by the pleasure principle: what was satisfying was pleasure, what was not was pain. Because a baby cannot separate out what is him from what is his mother, the early relation is conceived as a state of periodic identity or fusion with the maternal environment. Complex processes lead to his distinguishing himself from her; they involve pining, primitive guilt, a growing sense of external reality, rudimentary recognition of psychic reality and capacity for love and gratitude. These feelings, linked to the growing acuity of perception and motor skills, give rise to the basic pattern of individuation, i.e. separation from primitive identity by increasing self-awareness (cf. Fordham, 1969); the pattern repeats again and again throughout life till the development which Jung emphasized in later life is reached. This time it does not take place in the setting of mother and infant but in relation to social and collective forms it involves relating religious and philosophical attitudes to the individual, and the whole sequence is thought of as growing self-realization.

This very compressed statement is necessary because most therapists – involved as they must be with complex psychopathology – have a frame of reference against which they judge success or failure, the subject of this congress; that of individuation is used by analytical psychologists: if it be fostered there is a measure of success, if not, there is failure.

Before proceeding, a word on terminology: the word therapist will refer to all those who treat patients to their benefit, i.e. who further individuation, wittingly or unwittingly. An analytical therapist, sometimes called 'analyst' for short, is one who is trained in analytical psychology.

The particular subject of this meeting is the interrelation between patient and therapist, and the idea of individuation that led Jung to develop a special view of it. Besides saying that because of the individual character of any patient's solution to his conflicts, the therapist must not believe he knows because he cannot know what is right for the patient, Jung affirmed that it is usually necessary for the analytical therapist to consider himself in the therapy with the patient and that, in any successful outcome of the dialectic between the two persons, the analyst will need to change or even be transformed along with his patient (Jung, 1931a, pp. 70 ff.).

This radical view has sometimes been used to invalidate the use of definable techniques of treatment (cf. this volume, Chapter 8), which Jung sometimes conceived as the equivalent of medical prescriptions, i.e., something like a medicine that a therapist decided to apply so as to resolve a localized disease process.

During his professional life he oscillated, but it may be said that he increasingly emphasized the importance of the therapist's personal interaction with his patient over against the use of definable techniques which could be learned as in the natural sciences or in medicine. However, he left behind him a sufficiently open field of study for others to take up. I can best enlarge upon it by considering the controversies that have arisen over the training of analytical psychologists.

The issue centred on whether the practice of therapy could be taught. Theory and its less abstract correlate mythology did not present a problem, but the more intimate relation between patient and therapist did: what was to happen when the candidate took cases under supervision; how flexible was supervision to be and was it to be thought of as a special aspect of the candidate's analysis or no? Here the lines divided between those who thought that techniques, formally separated out from the candidate's analytic psychotherapy, could be taught with benefit by a supervisor: how to listen to the patient, how and when to intervene, how to detect transference and counter-transference manifestations and how to interpret them.

Those who opposed this procedure feared that if all this were done the spontaneous dialectic between two individuals would be disastrously impinged upon and even destroyed by excessive control or indoctrination (Hillman, 1962, p. 14); consequently, supervision was limited or confused with analysis, which for training purposes had to be modified in terms of the 'training goal' (ibid., p. 9); the formal teaching on topics of cultural interest, general theory, knowledge of mythology and psychopathology were added. This controversy inevitably provoked questions as to the nature of technique, which I will now consider.

Training analysis aims to make the future therapist sufficiently flexible so that he can influence and be influenced by his patient and can go on changing and developing as he conducts therapy. Assume that a future therapist's own analytic therapy has been rather effective and has sufficiently accomplished its aim. As there is no detailed training by a supervisor when the trainee starts to treat patients, he will find that they can be rather bewildering; he tries to use what he has learned in his own analysis and when it does not work he may begin to feel disillusioned. However, through his own analysis he will often have been disillusioned so he can mobilize interest. After a variable time he finds out what he can do and what he cannot do and gradually develops his own personal style of analysis which he settles into. The next step is to find that there are regular features in what he does.

This leads to understanding the nature of his technique. It is the formulation of ways he has reacted reliably with his patients; his behaviour has even become a routine which is – I would emphasize – related at every point to his own personal experience.

The same problem can be approached from a different angle by focusing on the nature of interpretations. These are, like generalized techniques, discoveries and in essential respects are each time individual and unique. Within the time allotted to any single interview a good analyst must, in my view, start from a deliberate and cultivated open-mindedness as to how the patient will construct his communications this time; the patient talks and as he does so rapid changes take place in the analyst called empathizing; he listens, put parts of himself in the patient's place or feels the effects of what is being communicated inside himself; in so doing he lets the unconscious processes of projection and introjection come into action.

While this is going on he still does not know what it is all about till something specific happens in the patient's communications; it may be that the patient will pause or seem confused and at this point the analyst suddenly knows what it is about: he is in a position to communicate the reason for the patient's anxiety to him; communication may or may not be necessary and may or may not be made. This account is optimally accurate, by which is meant that if the analyst is functioning well it takes place like this; however, the period of empathizing and uncertainty varies from a few seconds to a whole interview. This bit of description is intended to show not only something of how a good intervention takes place but also why it will be couched in ordinary language and does not require the use of technical terms: they would be intrusions into the essential personal and individual details which make the communication relevant.

By stating the part which an analytic therapist plays, how he develops a technique and applies it in a particular way, I am sketching one side of the transaction between patient and therapist because of a bias. It is the one which had led to careful scrutiny of the counter-transference by analytical psychologists, because of the importance, sometimes excessive, given to the analyst's personality. However, Jung contributed significantly to the patient's transference especially by applying alchemical parallels and relating these to other social and religious data (Jung's 1946). In doing so he aimed to underline the archetypal nature of the transference in individuation: it follows a definable path if the patient's need is met well enough by the therapist.

In theory the analyst's capacity to empathize is based on his affective knowledge of the archetypal experience in this patient's material. At this level both patient and analyst would be identical were it not for the individual form which each has given to their archetypal structures. Whereas the patient is relatively unconscious, the therapist is relatively conscious and so in many areas he can meet the patient's affects with ease; for his part the patient has insights of his own or can make use of what the analyst provides. This state of affairs may be called ordinary analytic psychotherapy (cf. this volume, Chapter 8).

Jung however was not so much interested in this field of experience, but rather in that area in which insight was less important; in the place of it he came to rely on experience and process. But where insight is not possible we reach the level of delusion and hallucination though not necessarily in their psychiatric sense. In this area it is not known how to rely upon the techniques which are useful in ordinary analysis because there is no centre or self-representation to which reference can be made. Consequently, instead of treating the patient's behaviour as merely pathology it needs to be understood as containing valuable elements.

A colleague (a psychoanalyst) once remarked to me that he tried to give his candidates a psychotic experience. I believe he meant to think of it as a valuable experience, not just in the sense of making it easier to meet psychotic parts of a patient but as needed and positive for the future psychoanalyst.

Those who have read Jung's *Memories, Dreams, Reflections* (1962) and have grasped it will recognize what is meant; Ellenberger (1970) has recently coined the term 'creative illness' for it. Thus the experiences which Jung underwent were crucial to his psychological formulations which grew out of it (cf. Hubback, 1966); without them there would be virtually nothing that is characteristic of him.

It is this attitude which runs through the work of analytical psychologists, whatever varying importance they give to defining techniques.

NOTE

1 This paper is a slightly modified version of the author's contribution to a conversazione held under the auspices of the British Psychological Society during the 5th International Congress of Analytical Psychology in London, September 1971.

Chapter 11

Jung's conception of transference (1974)

INTRODUCTION

It is sometimes said that you can find anything in Jung's writings – implying that he did not know his own mind. I am not of this opinion. There are variations and minor contradictions in his writings on transference, often where there is still controversy today, but, by studying his publications as a whole, a basic consistency running through it all can be clearly defined.

There are, however, important changes in his views that cannot be attributed to the delineation of opposites. More needs to be known of the context in which they were made, for this is either omitted by Jung altogether or not given in sufficient detail. I shall suggest tentative solutions, hoping that in the course of time more information, which may make a better and more reliable conclusion possible, will become available. But even if we knew all the sources of vacillations and even reversed conceptions which are, let me say, like those almost anybody who published so much would make, it would still be necessary to bear in mind Jung's own comment on his method of exposition: 'not everything I bring forth is written out of my head, but much of it comes from the heart also, a fact I would beg the gracious reader not to overlook if, following up the intellectual line of thought, he comes upon certain lacunae that have not been properly filled in' (Jung, 1917, p. 118).

In this paper I shall be bringing together much that is familiar. Is it worthwhile looking again at what we knew long ago? Clearly I think so and my reason is this: to look from time to time at the foundations and incomplete superstructure of a house still in the process of being built shows what is firmly built and what is still in the process of construction. To stand back and look at what has been done helps to orientate us when occupied with details or some particular part of the whole and, most important, makes it impossible to believe that one part is the complete structure.

PART I

'The theory of psychoanalysis'

In 'The theory of psychoanalysis' Jung began to formulate his ideas about transference. In that collection of lectures, delivered at Fordham University in 1912, he asserts: 'Thanks to this personal feeling Freud was able to discover wherein lay the therapeutic effect of psychoanalysis' (Jung, 1913, p. 190). It was, he says, in the transference. At first, analysis may proceed without evidence of its presence and therapeutic effects may be achieved as patients revive memories, abreact traumatic affects, penetrate into secret and previously repressed areas. But the result of the analysis is not always beneficial – indeed there are patients who pursue the search for historical material 'without making the slightest improvement' (Jung, 1913, p. 191). In these cases especially, the answer lies in interpreting the infantile attitude of the patient to the analyst for 'all those sexual fantasies which cluster around the imago of the parents now cluster round him' (Jung, 1913, p. 190), producing an erotic transference composed of 'memory images of the parents'.

At this stage transference is far more important than analysis of the patient's history, because the analyst is at once assimilated into the family *milieu* and, at the same time, is outside it and related to the real world. In this sense transference becomes 'of great biological value to the patient'; and is 'a bridge across which the patient can get away from his family into reality' (Jung, 1913, p. 190). So, he continues, the 'bond is one of the most valuable social factors imaginable' (Jung, 1913, p. 199). And he adds that besides sexuality there are moral, social and ethical components which become the analyst's allies once they have been 'purged' of their 'regressive components, their infantile sexualism' (Jung, 1913, p. 199).

It is the infantile contents especially that can make transference 'a powerful hindrance to the progress of the treatment because the patient assimilates the analyst to his father and mother' (Jung, 1913, p. 191), and the more he does this so much the more will transference do him harm. It is therefore essential for these parts to be, as it was called, severed – how can this be done? Besides interpretation, which makes the nature of the transference conscious, there arises, Jung says, a battle within the patient who fights against the neurotic forces and infantile demands, but at the same time the patient shows resistances to sustaining the conflict so as to reach a successful conclusion. He may bargain with the analyst like a child who wishes to get presents from his parents; alternatively he may seek out 'special adventures' (Jung, 1913, p. 198), which the analyst must not prevent since they may contain value for the patient. Jung is very specific on this score: 'we have to let the patient and his impulses take the lead, even if the path seems a wrong one. Error is just as important a condition of life's progress as the truth' (Jung, 1913, p. 200).

As to the analyst himself, the patient perceives characteristics of his personality and makes them part of himself, and these help in constructing the bridge to reality. The analyst's personality is therefore crucial, and he must be mature if he wants to help his patient in the correct direction; Jung defines characteristics that he must have overcome: isolationist tactics, auto-erotic mystification, infantile demands which if unacknowledged 'may identify themselves with the parallel demands of the patient' (Jung, 1913, p. 199). For these reasons a personal analysis of the analyst is essential and he will be astonished to find how apparently technical difficulties will simply vanish as the result of it.

Another facet of this essay is Jung's comparison of confession and transference with practices of the church: they are, he says, 'a brilliant method of social guidance and education' (Jung, 1913, p. 192). But, he continues, a modern person consciously or unconsciously has become disillusioned by the church and strives for something different: to 'govern himself and stand morally on his own feet' (Jung, 1913, p. 193). It is thus the aim of analysis to help in this direction and so the best result is when a patient becomes 'in harmony with himself, neither good nor bad, just as he is in his natural state' (Jung, 1913, p. 196). In striving towards wholeness, which involves severing the transference, Jung reminds us, 'only certain religions demand this of the individual, and it is this that makes the second stage of analysis so very difficult' (Jung, 1913, p. 197).

'Some crucial points in psychoanalysis'

In the same year (i.e. 1913) as he delivered his lectures,[1] he was corresponding with Dr Löy and his letters contain additions and amplification of themes already considered. He perhaps lays more emphasis on the social and moral content of transference and conceives the sexual fantasies more favourably as analogies which are related to empathy, adaptation and the 'urge towards individualization' (Jung, 1914, p. 284). And again the apparently sexual character of transference leads on as a bridge to higher empathy, to the value of the personality and so to the 'road to freedom'. There is some interesting detail about the positive and negative transference related to the father imago; he gives positive and negative valences to love, hostility and rebellion; for a patient who is an 'infantile rebel', a positive transference is an achievement while a negative one just repeats the old pattern and is a 'back sliding'; for a patient showing 'infantile obedience' the state of affairs is reversed. Consequently an apparently negative transference is positive and can further individualization. Finally, there is the more specific idea that 'the patient's libido fastens on the person of the analyst in the form [not only of sexuality but also] of expectation, hope, interest, trust, friendship and love' (Jung, 1914, p. 286).

'The therapeutic value of abreaction'

By 1921 in 'The therapeutic value of abreaction' Jung's ideas have developed further and he introduces new ones. (1) 'The therapeutic effect comes from the doctor's efforts to enter into the psyche of his patient, thus establishing a psychologically adapted relationship' (Jung, 1921, p. 134). (2) The degree of transference varies with the understanding between doctor and patient: with good understanding transference is moderate, with poor understanding it becomes intense and sexualized. The importance of the real relationship between analyst and patient is stressed when he says that after a thorough analysis 'the patient's claim to . . . human relationship still remains and should be conceded, for without a relationship of some kind he falls into a void' (Jung, 1921, p. 136).

In this context he makes a very sharp attack on the 'exclusive reduction' of a patient's material to its sexual roots. It is his most vigorous one and it is difficult to understand why he made it so strong. Exclusively sexual reduction, he says, 'is a shocking violation of the patient's material'. It ignores the creative elements in the patient and leads to blocking of outlets so that the patient clings in a 'conclusive erotic transference *unless he prefers to break off the relationship in hatred*' (italics mine) (Jung, 1921, p. 134). 'In either case the result is spiritual desolation' (Jung, 1921, p. 134). So exclusively sexual interpretation becomes 'a gross technical blunder' (Jung, 1921, p. 135), 'for it constantly destroys the patient's every attempt to build up a normal human relationship by resolving it back into its elements' (Jung, 1921, p. 135).

But if adaptation takes place 'in spite of all this . . . it will have been at the cost of many moral, intellectual and aesthetic values whose loss to man's character is a matter for regret. Quite apart from this major loss, there is the danger of perpetually brooding on the past, of looking back wistfully to things that cannot be remedied now' (Jung, 1921, p. 135).

All this reads like an attack on psychoanalysis. But to what purpose? In 1918 Freud had criticized the 'Swiss School' in an address, 'Lines of advance in psycho-analytic therapy' (Freud, 1918), delivered to the Fifth International Psychoanalytic Congress; then he grossly misrepresented Jung, so it is possible Jung was retaliating; but, if so, he seems to misfire for, in 1920, Freud had already published 'Beyond the pleasure principle' (Freud, 1920). There are two other alternatives: (1) that he had come across cases which had been badly handled; or (2) he had personal experience of difficulties with his own patients over their sexuality. I feel sure Jung had a reason for his attack which seems to be based on considerable affect – it 'comes from the heart'.

Having given his view of a problem, which can still exercise analysts, Jung continues in very definite terms. Properly handled reductive analysis is essential for 'The transference phenomenon is an inevitable feature of every thorough analysis' (Jung, 1921, p. 136) and relationship is impossible until all the projections have been consciously recognized and resolved.

'The touchstone of every [successful] analysis . . . is always this person to person relationship, a psychological situation where the patient confronts the doctor upon equal terms, and with the same ruthless criticism that he must inevitably learn from the doctor in the course of his treatment.' In this way instead of the 'slavish and humanly degrading bondage of the transference', the patient 'discovers that his own unique personality has value, that he has been accepted for what he is, and that he has it in him to adapt himself to the demands of life' (Jung, 1921, p. 137). 'Our task is . . . to cultivate and transform this growing thing until it can play its part in the totality of the psyche' (Jung, 1921, p. 138). This is a clear statement that transference is goal-seeking and that the doctor becomes a real person as well as an analyst, the recipient of the projections which he reduces.

Discussion

These three papers may be considered together. They cover the ideas and practices before 1926 when Jung wrote the first of his *Two Essays on Analytical Psychology* (1916/1928).[2]

The early period is revealing of Jung's consistency; it is indeed astonishing to find the core of all his later ideas and practices unambiguously set down in print, though, as will be seen, at one time he withdrew from the almost excessive importance he first gave to the transference as the effective element in the 'here and now' as it is called nowadays.

It is of interest that he attributes the discovery of the therapeutic importance of transference to Freud. This, I believe, is open to doubt. Though we may learn more about this from his correspondence with Freud, according to my reading of the literature the therapeutic effect of psychoanalysis is supposed by its exponents to stem *not* primarily from the transference, but from the making conscious of the unconscious enshrined in the famous epigram, 'where id was there ego shall be'. Even today the position of many psychoanalysts is far from the one Jung attributed to Freud. In a recent symposium on the subject at the British Psychoanalytic Society there was very little emphasis on transference as a situation from which therapy stems. Jung's position is reflected not so much in classical psychoanalysis as in the work of Little (1957), Heimann (1960), Strachey (1934), Racker (1968), Searles (1965), and Milner (1969); but space does not permit me to enter into this subject.

Jung went along with Freud in recognizing the incestuous, erotic and infantile characteristics of transference, as well as accepting its resistance phenomena. Where he went beyond psychoanalysis is in his emphasis on the goal-seeking and therapeutic function of transference in which the real personality of the analyst became highly significant. His emphasis on transference as a potentially therapeutic situation and on the real personality of the analyst seems to have been his own particular contribution. The idea that once the projections have been recognized and resolved, a bridge to reality can be made with the aim of attaining moral autonomy, defined, even in 1913, as the 'urge towards individualization', is characteristic and central in the development of his thesis. The social and religious, moral and ethical meanings of transference are also much more important to Jung than to Freud.

I have paid rather close attention to the negative transference and want to make a further comment upon it because it receives so much attention today and the management of it has been considerably advanced.

There is only one direct reference to it as such: where Jung says that for obedient patients a negative transference is valuable, etc. There is also reference to the patient with a compulsive transference who breaks off the relation in hatred; but this he attributes to the 'exclusive sexual interpretation' and so cannot be conceived as transference but an adapted response. One other possible indication of it is given where he says the analyst is confronted by his patient as an equal and critizes with the same ruthlessness that he has 'learned from his doctor'; but this again does not define negative transference, though the patient's criticism might very well contain it. So it does not seem that in this early period Jung had scrutinized the patient's hostile and critical attitudes much for transferred matter.

PART II

'Two essays on analytical psychology'

In the *Two Essays* (1928) Jung began to relate transference to individuation in much more detail. He also made his position about reductive analysis more evident, and there is clarification of what he means by the personal unconscious; it contains what is now commonly called 'whole object psychology': the *persons* in the patient's past whose imagos are transferred to the analyst comprise 'father, mother, uncle, guardian, teacher etc.'. They contrast with the archetypal transference which he introduces here for the first time and which he approaches through the idea of disposable energy – already broached in 1913 – as follows: 'Let us suppose that [a] patient is "analysed", i.e. she has, through the treatment, come to understand the nature of the unconscious thoughts lurking behind her symptoms and has thus regained possession of the unconscious energy which constituted the strength of those symptoms. The question then arises: what to do with the so-called disposable energy?' (Jung, 1917, p. 61). Since the patient's fantasies have now transferred themselves to the doctor 'they must be cauterized, i.e. resolved by reductive analysis and this used to be called "severing the transference". Thereby the energy is again released from an unserviceable form, and again we are faced by the problem of [the energy's] disposability' (Jung, 1917, p. 62).

At this period Jung was again rather definite that the patient can become free of this personal transference and can indeed cease to be infantile. The next stage in analysis is that in which the structural elements of the personality are projected. The case that he cites in illustrating his thesis is often quoted. It is of a woman patient with masculine traits of which she is unconscious. Jung identifies them and then asks himself where can the masculine parts of herself be located? Deciding that they must be projected, he asks his patient how he appears to her when she is not with him and she reveals: '"Sometimes you seem rather dangerous, sinister, like an evil magician or a demon. I don't know how I ever get such ideas – you are not a bit like that"' (Jung, 1917, p. 89).

From this Jung proceeds to the distinction between the human and non-human parts of the psyche and the need to make a sharp line of demarcation between the ego, or subject, and the non-ego. It was in this way that he gained access to the archetypal images and could interpret with references to them. They were 'raised to the subjective plane', which in effect means that the transference was interpreted as parts of the self and thus the way was opened to the use of active imagination and the dialectical process between the ego and archetypal forms.

I would like to remind you of an especially interesting example in these essays which bears on the resolution of the archetypal transference. Again it is of a woman whose transference imago becomes 'blown up'. In spite of insight into the personal meaning of the transference, the father imago became combined with saviour and lover and did not dissolve. Dreams, Jung found, referred to him and his person distorted in a remarkable way. Sometimes the figure was of supernatural size, sometimes he seemed extremely aged, then again he resembled her father, but was at the same time curiously woven into nature, as in the following dream: 'Her father (who in reality was of small stature) was standing with her on a hill that was covered with wheat-fields. She was quite tiny beside him, and he seemed to her like a giant. He lifted her up from the ground and held her in his arms like a child. The wind swept over the wheat-fields, and as the wheat swayed in the wind, he rocked her in his arms' (Jung, 1917, p. 129).

The analysis gradually ended and Jung concludes that these dreams reflected a shift of emphasis away from personal to transpersonal functions leading on to the self: 'a kind of subterranean undermining of the transference [took place]. Her relations with a certain friend deepened perceptibly, notwithstanding the fact that consciously she still clung to the transference. So that when the time came for leaving me, it was no catastrophe, but a perfectly reasonable parting.' 'I saw', he continues, 'how the transpersonal control-point developed – I cannot call it anything else – a *guiding function*, and step by step gathered to itself all the former personal overvaluations; how, with this afflux of energy, it gained influence over the resisting conscious mind without the patient's consciously noticing what was happening' (Jung, 1917, p. 131).

There are difficulties in this presentation, especially on the subject of idealization and destructive and hostile fantasies and impulses associated with it which may very well have undermined the transference; however, whether this reflection be true or false, the concept that there is an inherent evolution in the transference in the direction of individuation is an important addition to the clinical picture. It had been present in his early views but in terms of a more or less conscious striving towards a goal; here the idea had become deepened and enriched.

PART III

'Analytical psychology – its theory and practice'

The Tavistock Seminars, delivered in 1935 (Jung, 1968), contain, in the lecture about transference, more directly clinical matter than is found in any of his other publications and there are a number of illustrative vignettes which could profitably be made the subject of discussion: (1) The case who came from an intellectual analyst and who was a 'sanguine', feeling type. Jung's expression of affect, he says, made all the difference. It is in relation to this case that he gives the best statement I know about why he does not use the couch: 'So, in order to be able to show my patients that their reactions have arrived in my system, I have to sit opposite them so that they can read the reactions in my face and can see that I am listening' (Jung, 1968, p. 157). (2) The case in which Jung dreamed of a woman and told her his dream to her benefit. Incidentally, the case was posthumously published in more detail and there were further very severe difficulties. (3) The auto-erotic woman whom Jung worked with; he did not interpret the transference until one day she burst out with 'I love you'. He explains his behaviour, which included not interpreting the transference, saying, 'You have to accompany the process and lower your consciousness and feel along the situation . . . otherwise he [the patient] feels too awkward and will have the most terrible resentments afterwards' (Jung, 1968, p. 170). This may be the type of case he referred to in his earlier generalization.

Then there is a list of the causes of transference which is once again taken to be essentially erotic: (a) the projection process; (b) analysis itself; (c) provocation of the analyst, 'by insinuating the wrong things, by arousing expectations, by making promises in a veiled way' (Jung, 1968, p. 170). In this context he comments: 'An analyst is not allowed to be too friendly . . . . Leave people where they are' (Jung, 1968, p. 170).

In this lecture he first introduces the important idea that emotions are contagious and that for the analyst to resist them is undesirable: he cannot fail to be affected and had better accept this fact. Most contagion takes place 'when the contents which the patient projects into the analyst are identical with his own unconscious contents' (Jung, 1968, p. 157). The unfortunate effects of transference, he says, are not only on the patient but also the analyst who, under the influence of projection, can become infected – ill from an induced psychosis or even physical disease.

Jung comes back more than once to the idea that to be cured a patient must have a transference. He appears to be against it, but is mainly attacking the compulsion implied in the word 'must'. In doing so he arrives at the curious statement: 'A transference is always a hindrance; it is never an advantage. You cure in spite of the transference not because of it' (Jung, 1968, p. 169). This is a feeling statement, as I understand it, apparently reversing his earlier and later views on the matter, and what he says is even contradicted by the case of the auto-erotic woman he cites shortly before. But, he goes on: in spite of all this the transference is a fact that has to be dealt with and there are treatments for it: (a) reductive analysis; (b) discrimination between personal and impersonal contents; leading to (c) objectivation of the impersonal images, the procedure that was put forward in the *Two Essays*.

Jung's ambivalence about the transference comes out very clearly in this lecture and there is an echo of it when he tells in 'The psychology of transference' that he prefers a light transference or even cases in which there is none apparent.

Why has Jung become so critical and self-contradictory about transference analysis? It may have been partly because he was speaking to psychotherapists who were divided on this subject. At the Tavistock Clinic, Hadfield, one very influential member considered transference irrelevant though there were others, especially Bion, who contested his view. In addition, when he refers to transference the audience would have been thinking of the analysis as the making of unconscious contents conscious and this, according to Jung, would mean omitting altogether the ongoing archetypal transference elements leading to individuation.

Another contributing factor may have been that his discussion of transference was requested by the seminar members when Jung was in the middle of developing his amplification of an archetypal dream. He appeared to accept the request with equanimity, but I find it difficult to believe that he was not irritated and disappointed at the reception his cherished skill in handling archetypal material had received. One overstatement could well be accounted for as a dig at those who had so summarily rejected this vital part of his work: 'If there is no transference so much the better. You get the material just the same. It is not transference that enables the patient to bring out his material; you get all the material you could wish for from dreams. The dream brings out everything that is necessary' (Jung, 1968, p. 170). Whether it was in the heat of the moment or by design, Jung does not here make the case against transference quite as strong as it sounds, for it is not essentially the material that is important but its distribution: its relation to the analyst is the point at issue and only secondarily 'the material'.

While there are unsatisfactory features of Jung's critical assessment of transference in these lectures, nonetheless, if taken in conjunction with two other papers ('The principles of practical psychotherapy' and 'What is psychotherapy?') it is revealing. In the former he divides up therapy into methods of influence and those in which 'the therapist is no longer the agent of treatment but a fellow passenger in a process of individual development' (Jung, 1935, p. 8). This distinction is linked with very practical action, for he writes: 'all methods of influence, including the analytical, require that the patient be seen as often as possible. I content myself with a maximum of four consultations a week. With the beginning of synthetic treatment it is of advantage to spread out the consultations. I then generally reduce them to one or two hours a week, for the patient must learn to go his own way' (Jung, 1935, p. 20). And again: 'I manage in difficult cases with three or four sittings a week. As a rule I content myself with two and once the patient has got going, he is reduced to one' (Jung, 1935a, pp. 26–7). Here he defines one objective in reducing interviews: it is for the patient 'to free himself from my medical authority as speedily as possible' (Jung, 1935a, p. 27). This pattern of therapy, dependent upon developing an internal dialectic between the ego and the archetype, has dominated much of the psychotherapy conducted by analytical psychologists.

In this method the patient and analyst work together on the material meaning mostly dreams and active imagination. It is probably this idea that made Jung emphasize the importance of doing nothing to highlight, bring out or, at worst, provoke a transference. Following his line of thought, the therapeutic effect would come not from transference but from the patient's adapted appreciation of the therapist's personal qualities, from introjection of them and identification with them as a means of making a bridge to reality. To this evaluation must be added the archetypal evolution, represented in the transference, that leads the patient towards greater individuation.

PART IV

'The psychology of the transference'

'The psychology of the transference' is difficult to assess and Part Two makes considerable demands on the reader: some knowledge of alchemy is essential and also its relation to Gnostic and Christian doctrines. Its strong historical orientation, though fascinating in itself, does not meet day to day analytical work and leaves one often stranded in a symbolic world that has to be translated if it is to make much sense to more than a few patients. Furthermore, it also contains a complex of viewpoints, genetic, social, clinical (as well as historical) that interlace so as to create difficulties if the reader is looking for clinically orientated ideas with which to organize observation of patients in analysis. Jung defends himself from this reproach by saying that the volume is not for beginners, but for those who have already been 'instructed in such matters', meaning, I assume, how to manage and interpret transference – for interpretation is essential. However, where is such instruction to be obtained, for it must be extremely detailed, if not from this work?

In spite of these difficulties the overall thesis is clear: transference can reveal all the stages of the individuation process: the alchemists projected it into matter, the patient projects it into the analyst who, through his own experience of individuation, becomes involved in an emotional dialectic with the patient.

In general, Jung's practice remains the same: there must be analytic reduction of projections so that a real relation to the analyst may emerge as self-realization increases.

Again, there is the assumption of a preliminary stage of confession and analysis with insight before the unconscious content is constellated and the transference begins. Jung suggests that a great deal can be done in this way, and even that a sort of preliminary goal can be reached; we read that there are those who think it has been achieved 'once the unconscious contents have been made conscious and theoretically evaluated' (Jung, 1946, p. 278). Be that as it may, the onset of the archetypal transference starts in the unconscious. It may not be recognized at all at the start and only appears in dreams heralding its onset. Jung gives illustrative examples of significant contents: 'A fire has started in the cellar, or a burglar has broken in, or . . . the patient's father has died in it [a dream] may depict an erotic or some other ambiguous situation' (Jung, 1946, p. 183).

Jung then describes the case of an elderly woman whose dreams lead back to a picture she drew; it has analogies in it to the alchemical pictures in the series to be discussed. There is a serpent woman with a serpent rising from her genitals (to be equated with the fountain in the picture of the alchemical series), the five-pointed golden star, the bird flying down with a twig in its beak which has five flowers, four arranged as a *quaternio* and one, the topmost, is golden and, Jung says, is 'obviously a mandala structure' (Jung, 1946, p. 185).

It seems to have taken much work on resistances before the transference emerged. What was this like? Here reference to the description tells us: 'The doctor by voluntarily and consciously taking over the psychic sufferings of the patient, exposes himself to the overpowering contents of the unconscious and hence also to their inductive action . . . [thus] doctor and patient find themselves in a relationship founded on mutual unconsciousness' (Jung, 1946, pp. 175–6). An *abaissement* (a 'foggy' state) occurs till 'one finds oneself in an impenetrable chaos, which is indeed one of the synonyms for the mysterious *prima materia*' (Jung, 1946, p. 187). The doctor becomes confused and disorientated almost as much as the patient; fortunately not quite as much for 'all the time the doctor's knowledge, like a flickering lamp, is the one dim light in the darkness' (Jung, 1946, p. 198). Ethical qualities, patience, tolerance, courage, faith are essential and 'The doctor must go to the limits of his subjective possibilities, otherwise the patient will be unable to follow suit' (Jung, 1946, p. 199) for 'sometimes the patient has to cling to the doctor as the last remaining shred of reality' (Jung, 1946, p. 199), in face of his 'autoerotic affects and fantasies' (Jung, 1946, p. 268).

The alchemical pictures and text develop in a sequence which is rather orderly, but it is emphasized both by the alchemists with relation to the *opus* and by Jung with reference to the progression of transference, that the stages are not standard and vary within wide limits. For convenience I will follow the order which Jung has used.

After a sort of preliminary statement (Picture I) there is the human encounter; it follows a conventional form, presumably within the doctor–patient or other equivalent formula (Picture II). This leads on to the analysis of their personal unconscious and its incestuous contents. Once again there is a very positive assessment of transference: '[it] . . . gives the patient a priceless opportunity to withdraw his projections, to make good his losses and to integrate his personality' (Jung, 1946, p. 218).

Picture I

Picture II

Source: All pictures are from the *Rosarium philosophorum* (1550); reproduced in Jung's *Collected Works*, Vol. 12.

Picture III

Picture IV

Picture V

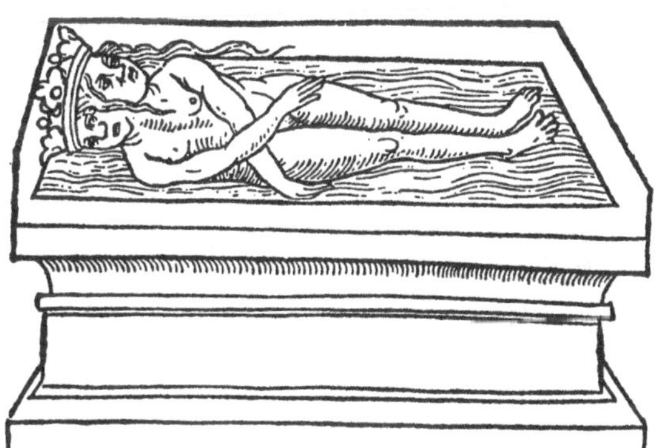

Picture VI

Picture VII

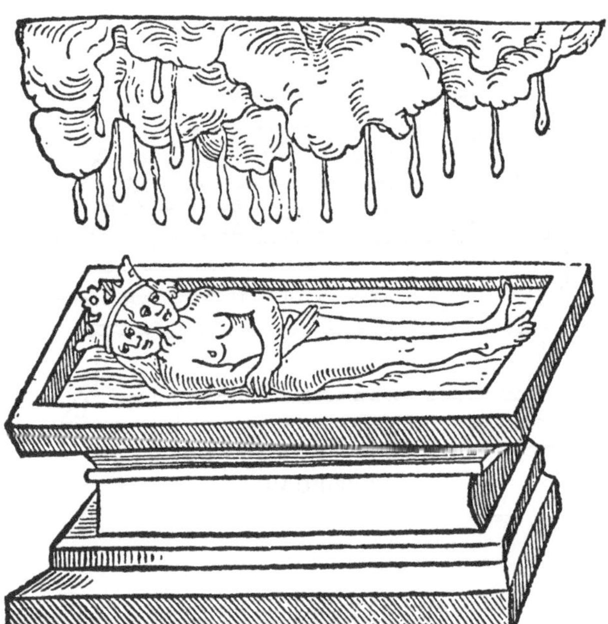

Picture VIII

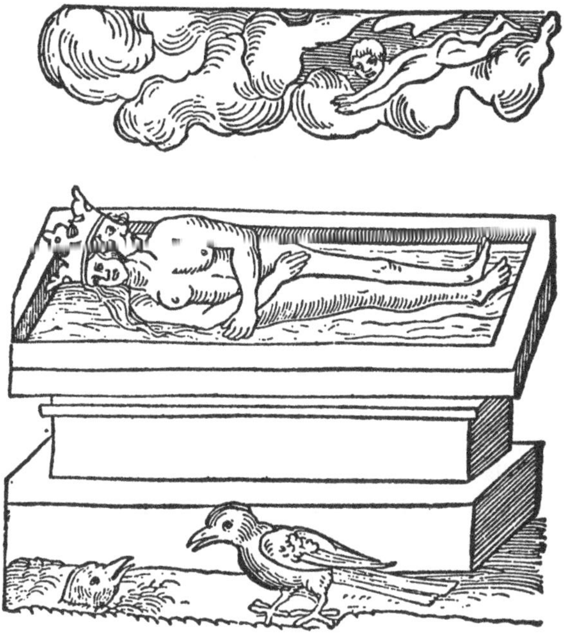

Picture IX

Picture X

There are at this stage many indications of incest which Jung conceives for the first time, following Layard, as a true instinct that blends like with like and so is the *prima materia* of individuation. To the extent that transference is projection, and nothing more, 'it divides quite as much as it connects. But experience teaches that there is one connexion in the transference which does not break off with the severance of the projection. That is because there is an extremely important instinctive factor behind it: the kinship libido . . . [which] wants the *human* connexion. *That is the core of the whole transference phenomenon . . . relationship to self is at once relationship to our fellow man, and no one can be related to the latter until he is related to himself*' (Jung, 1946, p. 233) (italics mine). And again the end is not in sight when the projections are broken, the connexion whether based on love or hate may collapse but the problem has only been postponed for 'behind it there stands the restless urge towards individuation' (Jung, 1946, p. 234).

There follows a diagram of the interrelation between analyst and patient when the animus and anima are becoming conscious. It is, as far as I know, the first statement in any detail from any source that gives value to the transference/counter-transference set up alongside the real relation of analyst to patient. Before this there are specific examples and also general statements about psychic infection given in the Tavistock Lectures – here is a quite clear account which could be spelt out in more detail if necessary.

In paragraph 423 (Jung, 1946, p. 221) he adumbrates the component parts as follows: these are,

(a) An uncomplicated personal relationship;
(b) A relationship of the man to his anima and the woman to her animus;
(c) A relationship of anima to animus and vice versa;
(d) A relationship of the feminine animus to the man (which happens when the woman is identical with her animus) and of the masculine anima to the woman (which happens when the man is identical with his anima).

This pattern, based on a *quaternio*, Jung compares at some length with two fairy tales (one Icelandic, the other Russian), with the Christian mystical union, with alchemy, with the incest motif in the pagan mythology, with cross-cousin marriage systems of primitive communities, and, finally, the disorganization of our exogamous marriage system at the present time resulting from the freeing of the endogenous incestuous tendency from containment in religious life. Because it binds like with like it lies at the roots of collectivism (mass-man psychology) which tends to throw up saviours and leaders to express and exploit group identity.

All this is part of a social theory of transference to which he adds a historical dimension by linking the gnostic anthropos doctrine through neoplatonism and alchemy with the transference situation and individuation. Therefore transference 'is vitally important not only for the individual but also for society, and indeed for the moral and spiritual progress of mankind' (Jung, 1946, p. 234).

In Picture III the royal pair are naked. This expresses a state of affairs which comes about when the persona has proved an inadequate container of affects and so a naked confrontation is needed. The shadow emerges, therefore the honesty and truthfulness of both partners in the enterprise are tested to the full.

Picture IV. The pair descend into the bath (the unconscious) and a 'night sea journey' begins leading to Picture V, the *coniunctio* proper resulting from assimilation of the unconscious. Jung makes renewed pleas for patience: 'although the patient is – from the rational point of view – equipped with the necessary understanding and neither he nor the doctor can be accused of any technical negligence or oversight' (Jung, 1946, p. 253); the transference cannot be severed. So 'Above all one needs forbearance and patience, for often time can do more than art' (Jung, 1946, p. 245). Furthermore the analyst must not assume he knows: reasonableness will not work any more because it tends towards severing the transference and this is not indicated. There is here a warning against taking the frank eroticism of the picture 'pornographically'. I am inclined to believe that Jung is thinking of the dangers of sexual interpretation but also of the eroticized transference here in which all insight is swept away by the patient's sexual excitement. With this in mind his seemingly excessive insistence on the mystery and symbolic nature of the material can be understood.

Picture VI, 'Death'. Here the assimilation of unconscious contents has led to death of the ego; since death of the ego (of the old personality ideal?) makes way for the self, the alchemists' death–rebirth sequence is gone into at some length. There is a fusion between king and queen (ego and anima) so that a hermaphrodite is formed. It can be inferred that there is now a tendency for unconscious fusion between analyst and patient through animus and anima conjunction, but there is little more to be gleaned about the nature of the transference itself; indeed, it seems that it is the real personality and experience of the analyst that counts more.

Picture VII, 'The ascent of the soul'. Further disintegration takes place, ego consciousness has collapsed. The soul is lost and ascends to heaven. Again patience, courage and faith are required and the approach should be 'plastic and symbolic, and itself the outcome of personal experience with unconscious contents' (Jung, 1946, p. 270). Jung continues: 'Therapy aims at strengthening the conscious mind, and whenever possible I try to rouse the patient to mental activity and get him to subdue the *massa confusa* of his mind with his own understanding, so that he can reach a vantage point *au-dessus de la mêlée*' (Jung, 1946, pp. 270–1). Again Jung evokes the optimism of the alchemists and adds that: 'At this point, unpalatable as it is to the scientific temperament, the idea of mystery forces itself upon the mind of the inquirer, not as a cloak for ignorance but as an admission of his inability to translate what he knows into the everyday speech of the intellect' (Jung, 1946, p. 272).

Picture VIII, 'Purification' – the whitening stage. The evocation 'whiten the lato and rend the books lest your hearts be rent asunder' leads Jung to apply type theory to the state of affairs: the intellect (thinking) is no longer effective and in fact a positive hindrance; it is here that primitive feelings linked to affect (because it is the inferior function?) become the focus of attention and involvement. There is even greater splitting so that a schizophrenic-like condition emerges which would mean the emergence of a delusional type of transference where insight is impossible; however, this can result in a more meaningful relation in which the real person of the analyst, which was there before, of course, becomes more important as the self gradually crystallizes. So it is in this area that the analyst's affective reactions become more and more significant.

Pictures IX and X, 'The return of the soul' and the 'new birth'. There is, I think, nothing in these last two sections which bears directly upon the theme of transference as projection. The return of the soul vivifies the body and from this conjunction the self is formed. Jung here expresses himself almost entirely in symbolic language since he has reached the stage at which the self is coming into being. It is in this light that I read John Pordage's letter to Jane Leade and the poem about the hermaphrodite. It is I think rather striking that Jung remarks near the end: 'I have never come across the hermaphrodite as a personification of the goal, but more a symbol of the initial state, expressing identity with anima or animus' (Jung, 1946, p. 319). It implies that there is something wrong with the alchemical sequence if looked at from the point of view of individuation. I am not convinced that the alchemist's ignorance of projection accounts for it.

PART V

A clinical application

This completes my review of Jung's researches. It is apparent that there is a consistent and coherent growth in it all and Jung is very clear that with suitable modification the symbolic material can be observed in clinical data. No doubt with this in mind he cites in his 'Introduction' a patient who had painted a picture having analogies with pictures in the *Rosarium* series. Presumably the patient's transference went through the further stages like those which Jung subsequently elaborates. So would it not be possible to make further clinical translations? I believe so, and the following example of how the symbolism can be read in clinical terms illustrates what could be done over and over again.

Taking Picture VI ('Death') and Picture VII ('The ascent of the soul') together, they can be considered in two ways. (1) 'Death' may be projected. In the case of a male analyst a female patient may be identified with the animus. This would mean that the patient is possessed of qualities of the spirit and would detach herself from the useless (dead) analyst. She, animus fashion, has the solution and either departs from her useless analyst by destructive splitting or seeks to bring him to life by embracing him with her supposedly vivifying opinions. (2) Alternatively, if the patient feels dead (i.e. is depressed), then the analyst is imbued with her animus, so that he is felt to pay no attention to her but simply offers interpretations which are felt as abstract, intellectual and remote;

nonetheless, the hope of life is, unconsciously, contained in him. Partly through introjection of the projection the analyst does not despair but feels the necessity for the patient to use him in this way.

PART VI: DISCUSSION

The most impressive feature of Jung's researches into transference is his consistent championing of the patient as a person in need of relationship. This applies to the end of the opus, for 'Turn and twist this situation as we may, it always remains an inner and outer conflict' (Jung, 1946, p. 304). So the need for relationship must be considered as basic to all else, though of course there is much else. Jung, therefore, consistently includes the analyst in the psychotherapeutic set up and so pioneered the idea that a person is in essential respects an 'open system'.

However, there is, in his exposition, a 'doctor' who appears to be very much at sea or consistently puzzled by the situation in which he finds himself – he appears to be the exponent of a closed system obsession. He assumes that the patient being 'ill' has come for treatment and that it is his job to provide it by applying a remedy. He himself should not become part of it and deliberately tries to keep himself closed off. This 'medical' approach applied in the early days of psychotherapy and persists even today most clearly in behaviour therapy. It was this type of treatment which Jung criticized, if not always explicitly at least by implication.

As part of Jung's conception stands the importance of the real personality of the analyst that the patient uses to cure himself. It was Jung who was, if not the only, yet the most consistent and forceful pioneer of this seminal concept. In it he displayed his penetrating capacity to grasp and stick to essentials and so open the way for their detailed elaboration.

What more has been learned about the 'real personality of the analyst' and what does it mean in detail when Jung finds it the bridge to reality for the patient? There is much in this brief statement which is shown up if compared with the rôle which the 'doctor' uses. It is at best only a very indirect expression of his real self, while at its worst it can be defensive persona or false self by which he seeks to deceive his patient. Is it going too far to say that the model Jung sets before us is that a therapist should always express an aspect of the self in everything he does with his patient? As a model, an ideal, it seems to me acceptable but not something to be fully achieved, though analysts need not fall far short of it.

I have attempted to apply this model in some detail elsewhere (this volume, Chapter 8) by linking up the concept of technique with the personal and archetypal knowledge of the analyst which form the basis on which communications are made in the course of analytic therapy.

But to return to Jung's exposition, there are parts of it which need further understanding and especially the states of identity in which the therapist can find himself. That any analytic patient takes on a particular meaning and image for his analyst will be easily agreed and it is now axiomatic that the analyst will have to change or develop in some respect if the analysis is to progress; but the idea that a patient's material becomes persistently bewildering to the analyst who becomes enmeshed in the unconscious processes projected on to him and which evoke counter projections that cannot be easily accepted, and I believe the thesis needs clarification.

Jung left behind him a lecture (delivered in 1937) that was published posthumously as 'The realities of practical psychotherapy' (1937). In it he recounts the difficulties he got into with one of his patients. He did not understand her dreams, she became physically ill and he despaired of helping her; he could not understand the structure and significance of the symptoms either and he says: 'The whole case worried me so much that I told the patient there was no sense in her coming to me for treatment' (Jung, 1937, p. 334). However, this case was a special one, for it was she who led Jung to study the Kundalini Yoga.

The confusion of the analyst may, therefore, often be an indication of his working in an area with which he is not familiar and not a condition which should be regarded as more or less inevitable during analysis of transference phenomena. In other words, it can be considered as a feature of analytic research in contrast to the ordinary run of analytic work.

Looked at from this point of view my experience meets Jung's. It was over the delusional transference that I first got into comparable difficulties, but I am bound to say that having done this once I have not done it again, and I cannot believe Jung did so either when treating a case of the kind he describes. I am rather sure that this was due, in my case, to ongoing self analysis alongside becoming familiar with the state of the patient and grasping the essentially infantile components in them. That her transferences – like others of the same kind – contained structural elements of the personality was clear, for archetypal material was often much in evidence. I concluded that the distortion of the synthetic processes could still with advantage be studied in terms of infancy.

Jung's insistence on the error of 'exclusive' interpretation of the sexual roots of transference is relevant in this context because it may have contributed to confusional states. This technique, if it was ever used much, should no longer need attack because nobody thinks that the sexual drives alone lie at the root of mental disorders; so the topic can be re-examined. Jung did not mean – as is sometimes said – that the sexual impulses in the erotic transference should be so ignored that the patient is left anxious, guilty or ashamed without the analyst noticing it; indeed whatever may be inferred from his writings, the information I have gleaned from some of his patients has convinced me that the criticism is without foundation. So what is to be made of his observation – for so it strikes me – that patients whose sexuality is analysed can develop the most terrible resentments and break off the analysis: was it due to a technical blunder? It is evident that when he used the word 'exclusive' he meant that the archetypal transference was not dealt with, but at the same time he does not give any indication of the envy, jealousy and possessiveness which can also be important. If these components of sexuality are not dealt with, and the aggressive and often destructive affects that they release are not interpreted, the patient can indeed become confused and disorientated and break off the analysis in the way Jung describes. In other words, had not Jung been led to these affects only to react against them? I believe this may have been the case.

Jung was, however, correct in a very important respect. It is not sexuality as a physical, orgasmic discharge between two adult people that is the point, but rather the incestuous need for bodily and spiritual intimacy, unrealizable for adult persons in the flesh, because it can only occur between mother and infant.

Jung clearly knew something of all this, for the alchemical texts contain references to the commixture of love and hate (of the elements); these are however conceived as opposites that can be transcended and I have not been able to find that he goes into the more intense forms of negative transference at any length. In 'The psychology of the transference' he does, however, make the clear statement that transference can be either negative or positive, so the principle is recognized but what is meant by negative is left largely to the imagination (Jung, 1946, p. 165).

Jung seems tentative and sometimes almost apologetic in this area of identity between patient and analyst. It almost seems as if he half sided with rationalistic forms of therapy based on the medical model that he criticized. Yet he says in 1935: 'Against these views' – i.e. those of Freud and Adler – 'which clearly rest on time-bound medical assumptions, I have stressed the need for more extensive individualization of the method of treatment and for an irrationalization of its aims – especially the latter, which would ensure the greatest possible freedom from prejudice' (Jung, 1935, p. 26).

If an analyst found himself in the confused state he described with his patient, rational assumptions, which form the basis on which his conscious systems partly rest, would clearly be of little use. However, confusion cannot be conceived or experienced without a conception or experience of order or reason and, if this is still held to as an aim when no longer appropriate, then the rapidly changing contradictory play of unconscious affects displaying opposites will seem like disorder and the analyst clinging to a rational system may be drawn into them to his confusion. Of course, some consistency must be maintained and Jung relied on ethical virtues and consciousness.

Without denying the importance of these values and especially of ethics which, to my mind, he rather too repeatedly invokes, it is important to remember that they can become defensive and lead to overlooking the affective content which underlies them. In other words they can blind the analyst to the counter-transference which the patient is evoking. To prevent their defensive use the ethical requirements can profitably be related to the infant part of the patient evoking maternal love in his analyst – but, it must be added, all its shadow as well. By making investigations from this position much has been learned about the extent to which not only loving care but also anger, irritation, depression, despair and hopelessness can enter into the experience of analysing patients displaying psychotic elements in the self. If the analyst is not overcome by these feelings they can be understood as counter-transference indicators and as such they are natural to any radical analysis. The analytic ethic is not then to sustain the benign elements in this counter-transference – he should be certain of them as the result of his analysis – so much as to understand them along with their shadow and interpret them at a time when the patient can use his communications.

There is still another element that can be added to the sustaining parts of the analysis: the physical reliability of the analyst, his being physically there and providing regular and frequent times for meeting in a place that does not alter, that is warm and sufficiently comfortable. In this way he provides a frame – holding situation – inside which his unconscious can safely find expression – under the guidance of a sophisticated ego – along with that of the patient. The alchemistic analogy with this is the vessel or retort – the metaphor that can be added is that of the mother and infant. It is here that the subject of interview frequency becomes important and this accounts for the reason why Jung reduced meetings between analyst and patient so soon.

I have become convinced that his practice, as he outlines it in 1935, cannot be generalized and may be considered in relation to his own experience. Though his therapeutic practice was modified by psychoanalysis there are strong analogies in his exposition with his own discovery of individuation. Jung, by force of circumstances, was thrown back upon himself and found in myths, of which the alchemical ones were the most important, a kind of 'analyst' whom he could supersede by translating alchemy into psychology. It is most likely, however, that he felt the lack of a real person with whom to work and that his feelings that the value of the individual was endangered by 'medical authority' may well have been one difficulty in his way. In any case he needed somebody who was not available; indeed it is obvious that no analyst or therapist knew at the time, nor perhaps now either, how to help people like him.

I am not at all convinced by Jung's argument that the authority of a person is diminished by his not being readily available; indeed, it may be argued that it is characteristic of people in authority that lack of close personal contact with them makes for unrealistic assessment of their status. It is in any case simply not true that an analyst's authority is enhanced by frequent interviews; on the contrary it is detailed work through which his true authority emerges and which fosters the real relationship between patient and analyst.

Much of my own work has been to elucidate the transference and discover its roots in infancy and childhood in a way that is congruent with Jung's formulations (this volume, Chapter 1). I have already referred to some of it and will take this opportunity to develop my ideas somewhat further. In his early work Jung agreed with Freud on the infantile nature of transference, and he never completely withdrew from this view though he insisted that it was incomplete. However, when he fruitfully followed up its social, historical and religious aspects and used alchemy as an idiom through which to express his ideas, the infantile roots of the patient's experience did become obscured. In my view any analyst needs to know about and be able to detect them. It therefore becomes relevant to consider whether the complex and systematized medium which Jung used was also a vehicle for representing early infantile states. In approaching the subject from this point of view I shall do so in the knowledge that the alchemist's work was much else besides the expression of infantile fantasy.

According to Jung the personal unconscious as experienced in the transference is made up of persons – father, mother, brother, sister and so on. In this area the projections can be interpreted and reduced because there is a person there who can organize and free himself from the past largely through insight. This procedure can be employed when there is a transference neurosis. Further regression may, however, be necessary and it leads to transference psychosis in which the self cannot be assumed: it has to be discovered and given form because self-representation in the ego has not been achieved. Jung's material shows many features of infantile states in this area and his interpretation of the *quaternio* as representing the *prima materia* in which the elements of the self are not integrated is one of them: it represents deintegration of the self resulting in identity of subject and object such as we find in infancy as well as in alchemy. But in regression splitting of the ego takes the place of and masks deintegration. It is the splitting processes on which Jung lays emphasis and he shows that they lead on to states of integration and to the formation of the hermaphrodite – a self symbol. This sequence corresponds to the theory of recurring sequences of deintegration followed by integration which underlie ego formation and growth (Fordham, 1969). Here Jung's remark about the figure referring to the initial state is relevant. It is not really as puzzling as it seems if we refer to the *Mysterium*, for here we learn that alchemists sought union of the *unio mentalis* with the *unus mundus* (the primary state and primary self) as the end product of their work. My own experience of full analysis enshrined in the concept of the value in regression, depends upon reaching, through representations, the initial state of wholeness – the primary self – from which maturation can proceed.

Following this line of thought leads to reassessment of many of the ideas about the infantile components in the self. Jung often writes as if they could be superseded – 'purged' is the word he uses more than once. Of this I am sceptical, but it would take a separate paper to review what Jung meant by 'infantile'. So let me simply state that I believe the whole matter is worthy of further study which I have begun, and in which the wholeness of the child is kept in mind, estimated and related to his primary self and growth potential, very much in the way Jung approaches the problem in his essay, 'The psychology of the child archetype' (Jung, 1940).

In this paper I have made a critical assessment of Jung's work on the transference in the belief that the time is ripe for it. I have shown beyond doubt that Jung's achievement was to provide a basis for our day-to-day work in a rather wide spectrum of psychotherapeutic practices whether analytic or not. Our debt to him could not be repaid unless we show that we have studied his work, used criticism fruitfully, built on what he left for us and discovered aspects of it which were not fully developed and taken these further by carrying on his investigations in the scientific spirit to which he gave his allegiance.

NOTES

1 Jung's lectures on 'The theory of psychoanalysis' were delivered in 1912 (ed.).
2 The first of the *Two Essays*, 'New paths in psychology' was written in 1912, and extensively revised and augmented in 1917, 1926 and 1943. See Jung's Prefaces, *CW* 7. Fordham's references suggest that he has in mind the H.G. and C.F. Baynes translation (Jung, 1928), which contains important material deleted in the 1943 version, and not reprinted in *CW* 7 (ed.).

Chapter 12

Defences of the self (1974)

This chapter is largely descriptive. It defines the 'total defence' exhibited by patients in a transference psychosis. In this everything the analyst says is apparently done away with either by silence, ritualization of the interviews or by explicit verbal and other attacks direct to nullifying the analytic procedure.

EGO DEFENCES

Before starting to study this condition, it may be useful to glance at the history of defence theory, so that the subject may be put in perspective. Defences were originally postulated when patients resisted analytic work. When transference analysis was introduced, the resistance took on a new dimension. Nonetheless they persisted: interpretations – especially those which referred to instinctual and infantile drives – which seemed evident to the analyst were at first denied by the patient. However, it was held that, as long as the analyst did not capitulate, resistances could be overcome so long as time was given for working through: the unconscious content would emerge from the unconscious and become accepted. These findings were based mainly on the analysis of hysterical patients, and they are still relevant to much analysis of the transference neuroses: we still pay attention to repressed contents and endeavour to make them conscious by following and interpreting the patient's defensive use of symbolization, displacement, compensation, conversion, reaction formation, etc., with a view to making conscious what is unconscious.

Since then there has been a development in analytic technique by ego psychologists, particularly in the United States where it is held, to put it all too briefly, that the essential feature of analysis is defence analysis. If that is well conducted then unconscious processes in the id will become conscious in a way that can be satisfactorily assimilated. The technique is subtle and interesting, but if that technique were used without identifying the unconscious process against which the defences are constructed, it would leave the patient with no idea about what his resistances were all about.

As time went on it was discovered that the postulate of other defences of a different kind was recorded. They were observed in the compulsion (obsessional) states and were called 'isolation' and 'undoing'. Here the affective element defended against is conscious, but its significance is not accessible because of its isolation from the rest of the personality.

Finally, there are the more primitive defences against bad objects; splitting, projective identification and idealization directed against part or whole objects. In the case of part objects there is no unconsciousness, but rather more or less violent attempts to attack and do away with the bad object – they can reach a level at which one must speak in terms of annihilation. It is this last group of defence systems upon which I shall focus, for it is in this area that total defences are mobilized.

TRANSFERENCE PSYCHOSIS

I first became interested in transference psychoses when investigating delusional transferences, because I was made aware that the patient never took what was said to him at its face value but reinterpreted it in the light of the projective identification that held sway at any particular time. An alternative way of putting it would be to say that there was no longer an agreed meaning assigned to words upon which ordinary discourse depends.

First, I proceeded on the ordinary basis that it would be enough to name the projection and suggest, even if I could not prove, how it had arisen, in the expectation that the analysis would then proceed. However, since the interpretation itself was submitted to reinterpretation, this did not work and, I found, could be read to mean that the analyst was defending himself against the truth about himself and was trying to force his own anxieties into the patient. In a variation on this theme, in the patient's view, the analyst was using his technique as a shield behind which to hide himself. Thus the transference interpretation was nullified.

Partly as a result of this situation, confusion arises, and it struck me more than once that this became very much worse if common sense was appealed to or if reference was made to reality – then the patient became convinced, as one patient put it, that his analyst had gone mad!

In its more dramatic forms the syndrome can develop so that the interview becomes filled with negative affects and confusion, until the whole of the dialectic seems to break down. The time may be filled with denigrating the analyst's interventions, ending up in loud groans, screams or tears whenever the analyst speaks: the patient seems to use every means at his disposal to prevent the analyst's interventions from becoming meaningful, or alternatively or concurrently a meaning is given to them that is so distorted as to create confusion if not identified. Almost everything is reversed, turned upside down or subtly distorted so that direct communication becomes impossible.

Perverse destructive aims dominate the picture: the attack on what is good and the conversion of good into bad objects and vice versa, the delusion that the analyst in concealing himself and depriving the patient of himself, that he is ill or is himself so pathological and infantile that he needs the patient for his emotional survival; all these can be prominent features of the transference. At the same time the patient's efforts to preserve the delusional true person of the analyst or foster his growth can lead to the construction of a destroyed or perverted world outside the analysis. Parents are denigrated because of the transference situation, and their failings may be rigidly held to have caused the patient's condition. The denigration extends to relatives, siblings and to society, politics and religion.

All this can be understood as an attempt to ward off destructive attacks on the good person of the analyst, and to project the split-off destructive processes into the past, society and the cosmos. Therefore, in the situation on which I am focusing, the attack on the analyst, by dividing him into a bad technical machine and a good hidden part, which it is the aim of the patient to unmask and obtain for himself, is a step forward in therapy even though the terror of the destructive aim is greatly increased.

A correlate of this situation is disturbance in the sense of time. There is no true historical dimension and, as a consequence, past and present are the same. This is the affective state of affairs, though references can be made to the past and be understood during periods when the delusions recede. However, they lack cogency and are treated as academic niceties; and if the historical reference is accepted, it is because it fits the patient's delusional system. When outside its scope, it is denied: the analyst is said to have 'got it wrong' and the memory may be repeated with the necessary emendations.

It is characteristic that any memories of childhood that have been revealed do not alter and expand as analysis of the transference proceeds in any progressive analysis. The content screen memories are not accessible; they remain emotionally isolated from the setting in which they are known to have arisen.

I think there is a true running-together of past and present, and the patient will exploit this with a view to putting maximal emotional pressure on the analyst, aiming to split him up, or wear him out, sometimes going on to reversing the analytic situation so that the analyst 'becomes' the patient. It can be on this basis that reconstructions are treated as an evasion of the analyst's fear of his own infant self.

COUNTER-TRANSFERENCE

The pressure to which the analyst is submitted can produce characteristic effects:

1 That the analyst can be led to participate in the confusion was held to be, if not desirable, at least an inevitable state of affairs.
2 He can be pushed into masochistic acquiescence to become persecuted and guilty at not being able to help his patient, whom he may feel he is robbing, especially if the patient is relatively poor. This can lead to splitting along the lines that the patient is trying to achieve. If his guilt becomes too strong, he may even make attempts to stop the analysis as Jung (1937) reports he once did, characteristically, without success.

3 Feeling frustrated and inadequate in his efforts to help his patient, the analyst can seek to do something that mitigates the situation: he may more or less abandon analysis, submit to the patient's seductions by excessive use of tokens, or allow the patient to take more and more possession of him physically. This can lead to a sexual relation being started. As far as the counter-transference comes in here, sexual acts, usually of a polymorphous kind (Meltzer, 1973), may be introduced to frustrate the patient's efforts to induce a regression. The transference contents are, as I have suggested, directed towards inducing helplessness in the analyst and this can change the patient into a threatening, persecuting beast. Such a regression may be stopped by adolescent sexual activity.

If I lay stress on these effects, it is because they can become indicators of the patient's attempts to split the analyst and force his way into him. If this is not detected he will succeed, and the analyst may collude with the delusion that it has happened. Thus an amalgam of analyst–patient is set up, and it can be very difficult to dissolve: it is a malignant form of counter-transference.

All these states of the analyst avoid helplessness, despair and depression on his part, so he can begin to consider whether it is not these feelings that are the state of the patient contained in himself. It cannot be underlined sufficiently that the patient remorselessly plays on any weak points he may discover in his analyst, the effect being to destroy the mature, nurturing, feeling and creative capacities of the analyst.

TECHNICAL FAULTS

It is interesting to review theories that the psychotic transference is due to faults by the analyst with the counter-transference in mind:

1 The diagnosis was in error; the patient should never have been taken on for analysis.
2 Technique has been faulty and in particular:
   (a) Interpretations have been directed towards the patient's bad objects and treated by the analyst as though they were really good objects. As a result, the analyst becomes the 'devil's advocate'.
   (b) As part and parcel of this faulty procedure, the patient's defences have not been taken sufficiently into account, or even not at all.
   (c) Interpretations of whatever kind have been so excessive as to induce malignant persecution in the patient. It is these that drive him to hopelessness and despair.
   (d) The analyst has made so many wrong interpretations that the patient's trust in him has been undermined.

These faults cannot be excluded; indeed most of them happen from time to time in most analyses and can usually be detected and rectified: the development of ego psychology amongst psychoanalysis has done a good deal to help in avoiding them.

The feature of the syndrome described, which makes the argument about technical faults inadequate, is that the patient does not go away; on the contrary he often contends openly, but more often by implication, that his whole life depends upon the continuation of the analysis and its successful outcome. He so contends, even when he insists, that for a solution to come about the analyst must mature or cure himself first of the illness that he has (in the patient's delusion). Therefore it is hardly likely that the analyst's real faults come into the picture much.

ANALYTIC METHOD

In the literature there is confirmation of the effects that patients have on their analysts and there is a consensus that some change in technique is required. The work of Little (1981), Balint (1968) and Searles (1965) (though the latter's views are set in a more pathological framework) favours changes. In my experience (and I mean just that; it is apart from anybody else's) it has been difficult to sustain my analytic attitude and so it became doubly necessary for me to be sure of my position. 'Technique and counter-transference' (this volume, Chapter 8) was largely an attempt at digesting experiences of pressure from these patients: in conducting his work an analyst needs to keep aware of his inner real feeling of self in relation to the patient. With this clear the patient's demand that you stop being an analyst and become yourself can be shown as part of his delusional system that is being worked on.

Thus, the analytic attitude needs to be maintained, so that it is not desirable for the analyst to try 'being himself' any more than he is already so doing by making confessions or giving information about himself, etc. Nor is it desirable to become excessively passive or guilty at the amount of pain, terror and dread that the patient asserts the analyst causes. It is important that the analyst should control any guilt he may feel about the patient's claim that he causes confusion, is sadistic, cruel and destructive, etc. It is important also to recognize a feature of the pain: it is a sign that the patient is struggling and of his will to live. It is even secretly valued by the patient as such, so it is mistaken to try and take it away from him.

It is most revealing that if the condition starts to resolve, the patient may say how all along he has secretly valued and made use of those interventions of his analyst about which he has been most negative and was relieved by the verbal continuity as a manifestation that the analyst had not, in reality, been damaged. Thus all along there had been a secret ally of the analyst within the patient. This gives me an opportunity to refer to the need for interpretation of the positive aspects in the patient's behaviour: it is easy to overlook them, but it is most important not to do so. It is also important never to treat the patient as though he really is an infant, but to keep whatever contact there remains with the adult part of the self and, if it is not accessible, to continue as if it were. This attitude I have again found is appreciated when and if recovery takes place.

TOKENS

Though tokens may have short-term beneficial consequences I am very dubious of their long-term positive effect: they can prevent analysis of the very situation that needs analysis by focusing the delusion in them. So I conclude that they should not be given in any case when the patient is actively demanding or pleading. When doing so he is conscious of his need and is near acting on his own – the problem here is that it is not the act, but the anxiety associated with it, that needs analysis so that the compulsive impulses can be brought under greater control. However, this is not to deny that the patient, without having been given permission, will from time to time touch, get hold of, hit or bite his analyst and may break or steal objects in the room, so that it is important to have no objects around of much value. I believe, however, that there are occasions when the annihilation turns against the patient so that he becomes so broken up that physical contact initiated by the analyst may be justified – at least I have not found a way round doing so.

INFANTILE ROOTS

I cannot convince myself that a bad start in life will account for the syndrome. Though there is often evidence of one early catastrophe or more, and though that can look as if it has been all important, this cannot be extended to cover the whole picture, and later traumata can be even more important at any particular time. Nevertheless, early disasters such as manifest in disturbed breast-feeding, illness and traumatic hospitalization can be most relevant. A special situation arises if the family is reasonably good for children; it may even be unusually rich and satisfying as the child grows up. I have met this combination of early trauma with subsequent good family life in other cases and it seems to make access to the infantile root in a historical sense particularly difficult. However, there are instances in which it looks as though the birth of a sibling was far more important, perhaps because mother and infant had been excessively close so that, and in consequence, insufficient self-representation had taken place in her child. The excessive projective identification that takes place in these circumstances would provide the conditions for self-representations to be faulty. In consequence the pregnancy of the child's mother is more than usually disturbing to the elder child, and the birth of the younger sibling is severely traumatic. In addition, owing to the closeness of the mother to her elder child, the father cannot fulfil his role of deepening his relation to the elder child: he is treated as alien and so the child's development is further blighted. Thus the scene is set for the accumulation of traumata which build up in disaster after disaster.

I find it impossible to sort out in detail what originated in the infant and what can be put down to the real parents, because in many cases the force of the child's needs impels him to seek out the failures of his parents, and raise them to monstrous proportions and if, later on, it becomes apparent that his family was no worse than others, then it can be the structure of society that is at fault (compare 'The angry brigade'). I therefore fall back on a mixture, and this seems to serve analytic purposes well enough. However, this position presupposes a constitutional component in the self.

The ravages of envy and jealousy are all too apparent as well as the enormous need for projective identification. There is also arrogance and omnipotence which can cover feelings of emptiness, formless terror and dread. All this becomes built into a system of false maturity so that it is extremely difficult to sort out what is secondary regression and what is primary; it is important to do so as far as possible.

As to the confusion, I must repeat that there can be little doubt of one of its aims; it is to maintain an infantile perverted state of mind. It draws on distortion of the body image so that any one zone can be combined, replaced or identified with any other (so-called confusion of zones). The more stable delusional structure is reparative and is to be understood, with Jung, as containing archetypal forms aiming to re-establish relatedness, although seemingly in a malignant form.

A NOTE ON THEORY

Much work has been done in this field by psychoanalysts and I have found that of Klein, Bion, Rosenfeld and Meltzer illuminating. It is clear that all these patients have not developed an adequate self-feeling, and indeed seem to have largely emptied themselves into the analyst. In doing so, they operate powerful defences against the not-self part of him seen by the patient as technique, method, etc. This has led me to think about their condition in terms of the self and its defences against not-self objects, a subject elaborated some years back by Stein (1967, pp. 167ff). I will not enter here into this theoretical suggestion because I intend to keep close to the more important clinical features I have described.

In this paper I have aimed at clarifying a particular syndrome. It is on the basis of the experiences contained in this chapter that I have profound doubts about the procedures adopted by Kohut (1971). He and his associates base their method on the view that the self is so damaged that it has to be repaired through the analyst's capacity for active empathy. I believe that he would have explained my data as due to my lack of empathy and failure to allow adequately for the mirroring and idealizing grandiose transference. That may be, but it became evident that, as I worked on the data, I was able to metabolize the projective identifications better and better; I was also developing my interpretive skills with pleasing results. Thus I think it valuable to continue analysis of the delusional transference, however destructive it may appear.

My work depends upon the view that the self in its ultimate sense is indestructible, since it does not belong to the realm of sensual experience.

However, its deintegrates can become split up and distorted: these can then be expressed (experienced) in projective identification which forms the basis for the delusional transference. In health, the creative and destructive deintegrates of the self are required for growth, so even when we deal with pathology there must be a question as to whether it is empathic, in the deeper sense of the term, to repair the good aspects of the self at the cost of leaving the bad ones untransformed. So it is not enough to act as a reflector (mirror transference), it is necessary to take in (projective identification) and metabolize the material by digestion until it can be returned to the patient in the form of interpretation usable by the patient. In my view the mirror, which has become such an attractive metaphor, is liable to deceptive misuse. For instance, the study of infants indicates that they are greatly puzzled should they see themselves in a real mirror; but if they see their mother's image in it, there is a familiar image and it is easily enjoyed. It is the newness of the experience of seeing themselves in a mirror that can be investigated. I interpret that to mean that in this instance the mother does not mirror the self image and this is something that is strange to the infant.

Chapter 13

Analyst–patient interaction (1975)[1]

I was indeed pleased and gratified at being asked to address your scientific meeting and I want first to express my warm appreciation to your Committee for so doing. After the first flush of pleasure had passed, however, I soon became aware of difficulties. Though there has been a growing and fruitful interchange between some psychoanalysts and some analytical psychologists, there are still differing attitudes and problems of theory and method that do not make communication easy.

The growing convergence in our two disciplines, which is taking place in many ways, has been reflected in theoretical formulations amongst you. I refer to the investigations of Kleinian psychoanalysts and shall do so again later on, but in addition, and more recently from quite a different direction, there have been developments in ego psychology which are moving in a Jungian direction. I refer to the twin concepts of the self and individuation, long used by analytical psychologists, which are being introduced into psychoanalysis.

In view of these developments it would have been possible to give a theoretical paper, but I am not going to do so, partly because this approach only too easily masks or exaggerates convergences and differences. Instead I intend to focus on clinical practice because that is basic. However much we agree or disagree in the abstract, such interchanges are of little worth unless they be referred to the ways in which we handle patients and arrive at our conclusions about them. It is from these conclusions that abstractions and generalizations were originally, and still continue, to be made.

I was encouraged in my decision by realizing that I have gradually been discovering psychoanalysis, not so much as a body of knowledge, but as a method of understanding the communications of patients in day-to-day analytical work. It is my intention to make statements about what I have been doing.

With this in mind I have divided my paper into two parts. Part I will consider some of the ideas and practices which I have developed over the years. Part II will describe, having in mind the theme of your discussions, a case in which there was a good therapeutic result.

PART I

It may not have escaped some of you that it is only in London, and to some extent in Germany, that amongst analytical psychologists much attention is being paid to analyst–patient interaction. The neglect to do so stems from a definable idea which may be stated as follows: seemingly technical problems vanish if any particular analyst develops through self-analysis. For my part I hold that this is sometimes true and that during any therapeutic endeavour the analyst will need to, or be compelled to conduct some self-analysis. To push this fact too far, however, leads to a subjectivism which inhibits development of the patient, and the organization of analyst experience into a form suitable for general or public communication. This inhibition is rationalized as follows: an exposition is thought to run the danger of imposing a false order on an essentially fluid situation. I have criticized that position because I wanted to understand and describe what I did, and this inevitably involved finding abstractions sufficiently close to clinical experience. There were several concepts at hand and the one that seemed basic was the involvement of the analyst. That concept, however, was too vague and so I looked elsewhere and found the term counter-transference as having rather well-defined characteristics. But neither covered what I was looking for: the analyst's positive effective contributions. To include these I provisionally subdivided the term and introduced the idea of a syntonic counter-transference besides the negative one which I called 'illusory'. The conception of syntonic counter-transference thus grew out of understanding the efforts of analytical psychologists differently from heretofore. It was a term describing a significant part of the analyst's experience of his patient, and it meant that in special circumstances an analyst might have to investigate himself so as to find data about his patient. This I thought might explain the disappearance of seemingly technical problems when the analyst develops. The idea of a syntonic counter-transference was also helpful because it meant that there were certain problems about a patient which could only be dealt with by reversing the subjectivism. It meant that some data which were felt by the analyst to be part of himself were not so: they were part of the patient to which he was being syntonic. Independently I had arrived at a position close to that of Paula Heimann. I worked on this proposition until I came to realize that the division I made indicated the operations of the twin processes of projection and introjection in forms which were often undesirable. These undesirable forms might, however, be further analyzed and resolved so that behind them lay processes upon which analytical interventions are based, and which give effectiveness to what would otherwise be an abstract intellectual communication. With this conception it is possible to include the idea of involvement in terms of a series of usually unconscious and rapid projective and introjective transactions which can become dislocated in the ways I had started from – it is a position close to that of Money-Kyrle, Racker *et al.*

It is inevitable to think next about the nature of an interpretation in the light of these reflections. An effective interpretation is a complex communication; it is partly an expression of unconscious processes but depends also on conscious perceptions, reflection, knowledge and past experience of the analyst. In particular it contains an explanation of data in the patient's associations, and a prediction about how what the analyst says will affect the patient. These are all attributes of the ego (as the term is used by analytical psychologists, but which I do not think is far from psychoanalytic usage). So when I say that projection and introjection underlie the formation of an interpretation I do not conclude that it is a sort of inspirational communication unrelated to the patient's defence systems though it includes the element of spontaneity which is, I believe, important.

Consider a single interview. At the start an analyst needs to empty his mind partly to be receptive and to pay attention, but also so as to let the projective and introjective processes come into operation and so initiate a kind of mix up with the patient's conscious and unconscious mental processes. The act of knowing what is the essential content which the patient is bringing to the interview, usually discovered by the analyst and put into the form of an interpretation, takes place some time perhaps after the middle of the interview. This knowing is, in my view, a combination of the processes that I have already outlined. It is brought about by the analyst proceeding in the opposite direction to the patient who starts from what is in his conscious mind first – the analyst on the contrary starts from the unconscious and becomes conscious as the interview proceeds.

Concurrently with these developments I have investigated the relative importance of using a chair or couch. I have accepted the idea, first openly expressed to my knowledge by Pearl King, that the habit of many of my colleagues of treating patient's by sitting them up in a chair facing the analyst interferes with making conscious the patient's transference. I accordingly use the couch in all cases for which I consider analysis suitable, and after trying out various positions, I have settled for sitting beside the patient rather than behind him. This brief statement must suffice though I must add that the way the patient uses this arrangement has become a matter of considerable interest and will be brought forward later in my case presentation.

As my thoughts developed, all of which were checked clinically, the patient's transference became increasingly important, my position about it may be stated as follows: every communication by the patient may be considered as a transference manifestation even if it is not important, and even if it be decided that there is no transference. I recognize that what is meant by a communication to the analyst could be made the subject of a whole paper, for many of a patient's utterances are not addressed to the analyst, but to himself or a part of him.

By transference I do not mean all the patient's verbal activities but those which are only seemingly addressed to the analyst, and only when the patient is using him as another person, or part of a person who is not the analyst in reality. Further, I have come to understand, as psychoanalysts do, that transference phenomena must be regarded as a reliving of the past, and that a whole part of this is the ontogenetic past. In addition there is a social historical element in it all which can be called archetypal. When it is archetypal it is a sign of health, and is not to be understood as a transference neurosis but as part of the ongoing processes operating beneficially so as to further individuation conceived as progressive self-realization. I can use these terms here nowadays because Sandler and others have introduced them into psychoanalysis in a way that is sufficiently like the manner in which I understood them. Further, Winnicott (1960) distinguished true and false self in very much the way Jung conceived the difference between self and persona.

Let me say that besides the transference there are communications by most patients that take sufficiently into account the analyst as he understands himself to be, to consider them as real communications and that enough reality of this kind must be present for analysis to take place. I believe that this corresponds to the notion of a therapeutic alliance – there are patients to whom this state of affairs does not apply.

What I have said could be greatly expanded but I hope I have said enough to show you some of the ways in which I have come to understand more about psychoanalysis. The matters that I have so far detailed, and the way I have stated them, could be considered by my colleagues in London who might agree or disagree in detail, but it would not be beyond their comprehension. I take it that this is about the attitude that you by now will be taking.

PART II

In the treatment of character disorders and borderline narcissistic personalities it has been the practice of analytical psychologists to see patients once or twice a week as soon as possible, especially when archetypal, i.e. myth-like material, in dreams and fantasies, becomes apparent as a result of 'raising the images onto the subjective plane'.

This can lead to quite good results. Its main disadvantage is that the transference cannot be well handled and so personal relations suffer. In its best aspect, however, a sense that the patient's life has a meaning deriving from the elaboration of imagination or myth can be fostered. This conception and practice was important to Jung, and he found that it could be important for others. It derived from his own experience after separating from Freud. When he had finished writing *The Psychology of the Unconscious* (Jung, 1912), he began to investigate his own fantasy and found himself producing imagery having myth-like characteristics. He found that this was so meaningful to him that he continued it intensely for about seven years. It was his technique of self-analysis. Later he formulated what he did as active imagination. It led him to intensify researches into the history of religion and especially into alchemy, in which he found the closest parallels to his own experiences, and to a sense of his own cultural history and his place in modern society.

I now want to present some aspects of a case in which I did not follow classical Jungian technique though I could have done, and in which the influence of psychoanalysis will be apparent. A young woman of 24, when I saw her, had married a man twelve years her senior and had produced four children in quick succession. As a response to her husband's neglect and infidelity she had made a suicidal attempt and been in a mental hospital with a depression from which she made a rapid, but partial recovery. Recently she had relapsed, and when I saw her she was still in hospital but was going home for the weekends – she found it almost impossible to manage her family life for even this brief period. Her psychiatrist was thinking of her relapse in terms of marriage conflicts and sexual deprivation, he was pressing for both partners to receive treatment. It is true that she and her husband lived in an almost perpetual state of crisis. He was engaged in a highly speculative and risky project involving large financial transactions, which now showed signs of succeeding, and now threatened disaster. It was evident also that her husband used religion to contain his strongly compulsive trends; he made excessive and even extravagant demands on her, and he sometimes attacked her with physical violence for alternately being ill and useless, or evil and dangerous. But in spite of this state of affairs both he and his wife did not intend to be pushed into a project to which they could not agree, so I was consulted for a second opinion.

In the first interview my patient was disorganized and frightened. She told me about herself in terms of her mother's death and its psychotic-like manifestations, and about her father's violent behaviour to her during adolescence and childhood. She wanted to get help more than anything else over the management of her children; her inability to cope with them caused her very real distress. Also she referred to nightmares remembered from childhood and other details which, like the rest of her communications, she seemed to force out of herself.

This interview was largely controlled by her previous therapy; she seemed to be telling me what she thought her previous therapist would want her to say, and she made it rather clear that she had objections to it. He was a doctor who thought he knew best what was good for her 'like most doctors'. She repeated more than once, 'they are after all only human'. I told her that she was afraid that I would become a doctor of the same kind as she had encountered before, who would think of her as mad and would compel her to talk in a prescribed way. After interpreting this I asked whether she would come again, and she agreed. The second time was quite different and she gave a good account of the difficulties in her marriage and more about her childhood, and also about her belief that she may have been damaged as a baby because she had been told by her father that her mother had a psychotic breakdown soon after her daughter's birth. My patient also detailed her childhood dreams which contained symbolic myth-like material. At the end of this interview, especially because of the response to interpretations, I recommended analysis and said I would want her to come five times a week. I made this conditional because I thought she was so emotionally labile that it was important to contain her affects within the transference as quickly and as much as possible.

At once her hostile transference manifested itself. She would not lie down on the couch: sometimes she sat cross legged on it, the position she often adopted at home when she sat on the floor; sometimes she sat upright and sometimes she lay half sitting up. Interpretations directed towards eliciting her phobia of doctors – their violence, their supposed obsessions about sex – which I was sure to manifest sooner or later were profitable, but made no change in her behaviour. I did not interpret in detail the sexual fears that her behaviour clearly referred to – this was an early non-verbal communication.

A prominent feature of the early stages of her analysis was her denigration of herself as a woman. Why did she have all those children who stood in the way of her developing her mind and prevented her learning skills that would give her a profession so that she would not need to be dependent upon a husband whom she no longer loved, and whose compulsions were so ridiculous though dangerous? Alongside environmental stresses which were undoubtedly considerable her penis envy was particularly strong as were her destructive attacks on the mother's body; all this lay quite near the surface and could be interpreted.

Once she tried lying down on the couch, immediately she became depressed and silent until near the end of the interview when she announced that she would not do it again and left threatening suicide. This began a period of acting out in which she would take days off from her analysis: at first there was always a reason which depended upon the need for action in the management of her own affairs. She went to look for flats because of a compulsion to break up her marriage, or she went for a job which would make her independent and so on. These acts occurred when she was attacking my interpretation, and indeed any talk, as empty of meaning and purpose. Concurrently she paid particular attention to tones of my voice which she scanned for feelings that I was supposed not to be communicating; she easily came to feel me as a threat, as a person who would force her to become what she was not. Her defences became most impressive and when in full operation left no room for anything but destruction, words in particular became missiles to be warded off and destroyed at all costs. The management of her acting out depended upon the management of this transference situation and it took time. It would have been tempting to interpret on the basis of her infantile conflicts, on the supposed psychotic state of her mother after her birth, but all these would have been lacking in foundation in her transference communications so largely expressed in acts.

In not making speculative interpretations but in confining them to times when words were more appropriate or when some were required, never mind what was actually said, I had in mind her primary need for the analytic framework to be maintained so that she could use it to form her own style of therapy, and to come and go without interference. After some time, how long I cannot be sure, she started telephoning during the time of her absences. There were a variety of reasons given for so doing: to see whether I still existed, to see whether I was waiting for her, to find out whether I had used her time to see somebody else; these progressed to ringing up to tell me beforehand when she was not coming. During this period my patient gave indications that she was making good use of the times in which she was absent: she would detail how she was better able to manage her children, furthermore she developed a method of working through an acute depression which derived from acting her depression in the interview. At home she went to bed for twenty-four hours, locking the door and refusing to have anything to do with her family; at the end of that period she would be viable once more. She would do this because of my existence and the confidence that I would not put her in hospital – it must be added that her husband had, at this period, sufficient confidence in me not to interfere; it was the destructiveness in the depressions that had previously alarmed him and led to disastrous interventions.

I should like to add here a note on her depressions: they had schizoid characteristics in the sense that she felt herself to be falling apart and disintegrating. This had been analyzed sufficiently for her to understand the violence and destructiveness turned against the self which lay behind the feelings of disintegration.

Looking back at this period, during which she was never more absent than present, it seems that it had been more fruitful than I had known at the time. Though it had often been difficult to find a suitable interpretation in any particular interview I had never let an interview end without interpreting something of its content. She had taken this away and had used it as a focus for self-analysis which was going on nearly all the time. In this she moved so quickly that the interviews could, as it were, never quite catch up with where she had got to. All this was not psychotic in a psychiatric sense, though she displayed a manic state with hysterical features.

This patient's development has been impressive. From being alienated from herself and her environment without friends, she gradually developed a rich and resourceful personality. Her relationships improved all round, she not only looked after her family and acted as hostess to her husband's business associates, remained aware of her inner life, almost took control over her husband's violent moods and provided good ideas which helped in his financial crisis. She also started to earn money to eke out the increasingly inadequate financial provision. Another feature of her improvement may be illustrated by the change in her memories and fantasies of her childhood. She came with a story of bad parents: her mother's violence before her death, her madness after her birth and an almost complete absence of memories about her during her childhood. Her father was neglectful, violent and heartless; a man who even now she could not be with for more than twenty minutes. Indeed the only good feature of her childhood was her relation with her brother which broke up at adolescence and was replaced with an adolescent love affair, having many satisfactory features but which ended when her lover went abroad.

As the analysis proceeded all this changed and good memories of her mother emerged. She became a beautiful and gifted woman, appreciative of her daughter as a 'lovely girl'. As to her father, he changed from a terrifying or hateful phantom into a man who she could enjoy and who proved a support in her exceedingly difficult home life and marriage.

This case was therapeutically successful and I would consider the good result due to the formation of positive self-feeling deriving from a level that is non-verbal and needed to be lived as much as interpreted. My technique was analytic throughout and confined to clarification and interpretation of what was going on at those levels at which it was appropriate. I did not interpret the nature of the holding situation that I was providing.

The analysis was not complete and I fully recognize that much of what was not verbally communicated, not revealed and so not interpreted, was of the nature that could have been verbalized, but I think that essentially my patient was touching on pre-verbal levels in the mother–infant pair, and had found the basically healthy self which had gained representation in her infancy, whether her mother had been psychotic or no. It was from this that individuation could proceed.

I now want to look at the methods that I used in the light of classical practices by analytical psychologists when treating a case of this kind. The overall idea would be to mobilize the healthy parts of the patient. At the start she would have been seen frequently but probably not more than four times a week; soon, when there was evidence of archetypal imagery emerging, the interviews would be reduced. To foster the ongoing processes and to prevent supposedly undesirable regression, the patient would have been required to write down her dreams and record in writing any associations that she might have; to support any tendency in her to objectify her material she would have been encouraged to draw, paint or sculpt and so forth. At this stage it would have been the therapist's aim to further an internal dialectic with archetypal elements (identified with mythological parallels) and the conscious ego – a process called 'active imagination'. In all this the analyst would have sat opposite his patient and reacted with a sort of disciplined freedom to the material produced by her.

For many years I pursued this method – its subtlety is not contained in my bald statement – but eventually I have virtually abandoned it or modified it considerably. My reasons for doing so can be stated shortly: it is too formalized and introduces a lot of matter which interferes with the patient developing a relation to his analyst whatever be its nature; in particular it obscures the transference; and can lead to intellectualization of the analytic relationship. An additional reason for my abandoning it derived from my interest in understanding the relation between Jung's findings and their origins in infancy and childhood which I thought it essential to understand if the nature of archetypes was to be grasped.

Having, then, in my case study adopted a strictly analytic attitude I would like to point out that my patient spontaneously adopted a considerable proportion of the behaviours required by the classical method. She showed:

1 Difficulty in using the couch and indeed sat up on it for a lot of the time. By making it available, however, it could be shown to her that she feared it because lying down would make her disintegrate, and also that it would, in fantasy, lead to sexual vulnerability and violation.
2 Interest in her dreams. Though these were first remembered from childhood,

later she dreamed one or two dramatic myth-like dreams. She never wrote them down.

3 Capacity to develop an internal dialectic (an equivalent to active imagination) during her absences.
4 A strong inclination to reduce interviews as soon as possible. This was eventually, after eighteen months, reinforced by shortage of money. I still see her from time to time if there is a crisis at home, though often the crisis is over by the time she comes for the interview.

Thus, though I initiated none of the classical procedures usually associated with the practice of analytical psychotherapy which aim to foster on-going individuating processes, and its correlate self-realization, many of them nonetheless took place. It has interested me that a method one has used for many years can turn out to be unnecessary.

What I have said is but a sketch that has raised a large number of problems. First of all I might have used interpretations designed to make the patient more aware of what she was doing in the hope of diminishing the extensive and sometimes quite dangerous acting out. This would not have been impossible for it was manifestly related on the one hand to her transference fantasies, her present day real life, and to the period in her childhood when she and her brother would disappear from home without giving notice; it was a collaboration felt at the time to originate in a mixture of neglect by their mother, and rebellion against their father whose arbitrary and sometimes violent use of his authority made for hostility from his children. There was, in short, material with which her transference behaviour could have been interpreted. In my view it would, however, have been a violation of her to do so and it was much better to wait until she was ready to arrive at these conclusions herself, focusing on the transference to my interpretations as a whole.

It may be that this patient will return for further analysis and then it may be possible to reconstruct a far more detailed picture of what was going on, but this does not alter the fact that it was not done so at the time: that is the essential point in my conduct of this case.

I started this paper by saying that I had been discovering psychoanalysis in my own way, and I gave a number of instances of how observations and conceptions about parts of analytic practice could be related to the view of analytic practice that I had been developing. I do not think that I would have dared to treat the case in the way I have presented this evening without a knowledge of the approaches to such cases that are being made by psychoanalysts. Whether what I have said contributes anything to psychoanalysis I do not know, but in view of the amount that I have gained from psychoanalysis, I hope that I may, if not contribute to your knowledge, at least raise questions that are worthy of discussion.

NOTE

1 This paper was delivered under the title 'Analyst–Patient Interaction, With Special Reference to Non-Verbal Communication', at a scientific meeting of the British Psycho-analytical Society on 19 March, 1975, chaired by Adam Limentani, with John Klauber as respondant. This was the first occasion in which a Jungian analyst had addressed a scientific meeting of the British Psycho-Analytical Society. See Recording, Archives of the British Psycho-Analytical Society (ed.).

Chapter 14

Discussion of Thomas B. Kirsch, 'The practice of multiple analysis in analytical psychology' (1976)[1]

I am particularly glad that Kirsch should have made a coherent, informative and much needed statement on 'Multiple analyses'. Heretofore only Hillman (1962) has published anything about it.

I have no experience of concurrent multiple analyses, but the theoretical part of Kirsch's paper contains the necessary conceptions for so doing. Why therefore do I not try to send my patients to other analysts when they are in difficulties which stem from sexual and typological problems? The answer can be developed from a statement in Kirsch's paper. He states, 'Hence, one analyst only constellates one aspect of the unconscious.' According to my experience this is false, because the way I and trainees in supervision constellate patients varies from the start of any analysis, and it continues to change as the analysis proceeds. This, as I understand it, is what Jung elaborates in his 'The psychology of the transference' (1946): the whole individuation process can become re-enacted in the transference.

I believe that we have to look for the source of our differences in the area of technique despite Kirsch's disclaimer. I assume that Kirsch follows the usual Jungian practice of seeing patients twice, or possibly three times a week, and that he sits facing them in a chair. I and many analysts in London, on the contrary, prefer to see them four or five times a week and they lie down on a couch with the analyst sitting near their heads. Having tried both positions I conclude that the physical arrangements make a considerable difference. It is much easier for the patient to develop fantasies about the analyst if he is not in full view, and it is much easier for the analyst to work on his counter-transference if necessary.

It would of course be absurd to attribute the differences between us to the relative positions of analyst and patient, and interview frequency. What the analyst says, his other techniques and his style must remain central. Yet the physical positions are significant because the transference only takes marginal account of what an analyst is really like, and this can be masked or missed altogether if the analyst, as a body and a personality, takes up too much of the patient's attention and interest. By using the couch a patient can imagine his analyst as male or female with considerable ease, and typology becomes less significant because the analyst can be imagined as of the same or different type without difficulty. I can be classified as a thinking type and it is true to say that some patients believe I think, but others say I have inspirations (intuitions), others that I am very down to earth (sensation) and others remark that my feelings determine what I say.

However, I can agree in recognizing the relevance of typology, as well as sexual differences to the conduct of therapy, but believe they are less important than Kirsch believes! If, for instance, I am analyzing a feeling type (usually a woman), my thoughts may evoke her *animus* and she will become resistant; the defense may take the form of her saying, 'But I don't feel like that,' whenever I make an interpretation. Yet if this happens quite often it becomes a question of psychopathology, not types, in need of analysis. I also agree with Kirsch when he says that analysis with a similar type is more 'comfortable' than with a counter type, but either way does not interfere essentially with the progress of analyses; one is less, the other more, turbulent.

Having emphasized the importance of technique I will turn to Kirsch's case material. The changes that he describes in his first patient can take place after any good piece of analysis, so they do not *depend* on the second analyst. Case two is more useful in illustrating the differences between our positions, though the description is inadequate to do more than indicate where these differences lie. The patient, Kirsch comments, kept coming to see him though the patient thought that his analyst was not helping him. If the case were mine I would look very carefully and skeptically at such a state of affairs and I would be wondering why the patient keeps on coming at all. I would then notice that the patient *tells* me that he keeps ringing up his previous analyst. At first I would not think that it was due to his positive transference to the first analyst, for if it were I would not expect him to tell me. Because of this I would consider first whether his communication might not contain his positive transference to me which was being concealed from all partners. This would explain why the patient continues and why his 'transference,' which it may well be, but cannot be assumed, does not shift to the third analyst.

All this may seem as if I am in a different camp from Kirsch in that I lay so much emphasis on transference analysis. However, I do so when there is clear suggestive evidence that it may be there. Yet when I turn to the last part of his paper I find that I am closest to the central group in which he locates himself, because I think there are other important matters in a patient's communication which require treatment, and there he notes, or I would.

I do not recognize the third group and can only assume that it is a caricature based on Strachey's paper on mutative interpretations (1934).

Kirsch states that I 'and my followers' do not favor multiple analyses 'because of the danger of transference leakage and resistance.' I assume this idea came from a symposium on training conducted in the *Journal of Analytical Psychology* in 1961 (this volume, Chapter 3) in which I discussed the *dilution*, not leakage of transference which takes place when training begins, and continues, I maintained, until the end. It is of a similar nature to the condition which Kirsch describes in his second case and because of it analysis may continue after training is completed. This I maintained was a fact and so attention should be paid to the management of it. I believe that with increasing understanding, post-training analysis has become less necessary. In my paper I did not consider the two analyst problem at all, and have never done so until now, but as my comments on Kirsch's second case show, it may be that dilution is worthy of consideration. However, I would only so consider it if the first analyst had been colluding with the patient in any of a variety of ways. The one that is most difficult to manage would have been to encourage the patient to continue his therapy with Kirsch, I need not dilate further on that insidious method of interference.

It is true that in London the question of whether a candidate in training goes to one or more analysts does not arise and I think that this may be due to our having developed skills in transference analysis which, as far as I can make out, other groups have not done. Again it may depend upon how the qualities of a Jungian analyst are understood. As they are set out by Kirsch at the start of his paper they present considerable difficulty. I find it hard to understand how it could be that he finds himself intruding on the patient's psychological space (cf. case 1) if he has abandoned all of his preconceptions and techniques and confines himself to a purely dialectical procedure, not unlike Sullivan's conception of the analyst as 'participant observer'. But to list or paraphrase some statements by Jung as Kirsch has done, so as to give a picture of a Jungian analyst, results in unattainable or ambiguous requirements, and one is not much wiser at the end except in understanding the ideals he sets before himself. I do not see how any analyst can in reality abandon all his 'preconceptions' and 'techniques'; I think it unrealistic to believe that 'each Jungian analysis is quite different from any other'; further, the notion of equality in status between analyst and patient is untenable. These matters, though apparently distant from the central issue of his paper, are none the less important because fruitful discussion of a specific procedure can only take place when it is known what an 'analyst' does. To construct an ideal does not tell much about this. Besides Jung, the 'London School' alone has given much attention to this topic and some conclusions of its members have been published in the volume *Technique in Jungian Analysis* (1974). Let me now sketch out a position based on this work.

An analyst's job is to clarify and interpret any material that a patient brings to the sessions. Consequently the subjects of constellation and projection become matter that may or may not require analysis. Kirsch discusses archetypal projections and thinks that they may necessitate another analyst for them to become fully conscious – at least that is how I understand him. In my view this is not an analytic aim because archetypal systems are part and parcel of everyday life; they do not in themselves require analysis. It is only when the protections contain pathological material that analysis is indicated. Then the urgency of the conflict transcends the person of the analyst as I have indicated. If this proposition is true, then one would expect that as the techniques of analysis improve, a second or third analyst would become unnecessary or redundant. Nonetheless it is still true that in any school of dynamic psychology there is a tendency for analysts to go to more than one analyst. It has even been my task to help one psychotherapist to end analysis once and for all, and so free herself from an extraordinary sequence of unfinished analyses. It is my impression that as skills improve one analyst will increasingly prove to be enough and it is my impression that this is taking place in London.

Those who advocate multiple analyses seem to feel that we are closing doors to realization of the *anima*, *animus* and the *self*, to which I can only reply that I have reason to believe that we do not. Kirsch has made a welcome start in clarifying issues, and it may be hoped that the practice of "multiple analyses" will be further developed and described. In estimating some aspects of it critically I hope to have made clear not that it is not necessarily undesirable therapeutically, but that there is an alternative way of benefitting patients. I leave open which is best because I believe in view of the lack of data that we have no way of deciding. I can state that his first case could have developed as he described by using either method. His recent case suggests that the positive transference was not worked through and interpreted, which is why the positive transference to Kirsch was not revealed. It follows that the addition of another analyst would not produce the desired result, and it is possible that the analysis necessary for development of the case was delayed if not prevented altogether.

To conclude I would like to make a distinction between psychoanalysis and psychotherapy because the two are frequently confused and this confusion blurs issues. Kirsch does just this in his paper especially when he refers to a woman patient who '*discusses* her difficulties in mothering or relating to her feminine problems with a woman analyst whereas she *discusses* her problems relating to men and her career issues with her male analyst' (italics mine). *Discussion* is not psychoanalysis. I have shown how failure to analyze material brought by a patient results in the introduction of a second analyst to the probable detriment of the patient. The therapeutic question is important, but not the central issue which may be stated as follows: by and large Jungians of Kirsch's type have mostly abandoned analysis. The London School has not. This is a large subject and cannot be taken up in this short comment. It has been developed in *Technique in Jungian Analysis* (Fordham *et al.*, 1974) and I hope to publish a further volume on this subject so as to elucidate the subject.

NOTE

1 Kirsch gives the rationale for multiple analyses, focusing on concurrent analyses. Due to the individuality of the analyst, the analyst can only constellate an aspect of the unconscious; this is particularly marked in relation to the gender and psychological type of the analyst. It is felt that an analyst of the opposite sex is needed to constellate the *anima* or *animus*, as the case may be, and that working with analysts of differing psychological types allows the same material to be discussed from different perspectives. Kirsch gives two examples from his practice in which he recommended that his patient concurrently see a woman therapist. He concludes by describing its differing use in different Jungian groups, and notes that it is mainly used by orthodox Jungians who focus on the transpersonal aspects of analysis (ed.).

Chapter 15

Analytical psychology and counter-transference (1979)[1]

In this paper I shall approach the subject of counter-transference from the point of view of analytical (Jungian) psychology.[2] Since this differs historically and conceptually from classical psychoanalysis I will begin by explicating Jung's position and then consider how his followers have criticized, modified, and developed his point of view. Jung conceived analytic practice to be a dialectical process between two involved persons. By implication he advocated what has lately been called an open systems viewpoint. A closed system is one with clearly defined limits or boundaries. When this obtains there may be two persons related to each other but functioning as two different entities. In their conversation words have an agreed meaning or, if there are disjunctions in their communications, these can be clarified if necessary by reference to the psychical system of one or the other. Open systems, on the other hand, are those in which boundaries do not have fixed definitions with the result that the two systems interact and change in relation to each other. Difficulties or confusions therefore require a change in *both* psychical systems before validation is possible.

Developments in psychoanalysis appear to have led psychoanalysts close to conceptions being worked on by analytical psychologists, particularly in London. I have used the work of psychoanalysts extensively and I recognize that many of my propositions were considered before I thought of them. However, since this article is about analytical psychology I shall not refer to their specific publications but will content myself by making a general acknowledgement to the following: Bion, Heimann, Klauber, Langs, Little, Meltzer, Money-Kyrle, Racker, Searles and Winnicott (see Langs, 1976, for a complete review).

Jung has laid great stress on the patient's individuality. He believed that every analysis differed in essential respects from any other. He stated, 'Psychotherapy and analysis are as varied as are human individuals. I treat every patient as individually as possible, because the solution to the problem is always an individual one. . . . A solution which would be out of the question for me may be just the right one for somebody else' (Jung, 1962, p. 130). Therefore he placed less emphasis on method than he did on interaction. In later years he even adopted a sort of non-method. Of this he commented, 'Naturally a doctor must be familiar with so-called methods. But he must guard against falling into any specific routine approach. In general one must guard against theoretical assumptions. Today they may be valid, tomorrow it may be the turn of other assumptions.' And: 'In my analyses . . . I am unsystematic very much by intention,' and, 'We need a different language for every patient' (Jung, 1962, p. 131).

These remarks were Jung's last statements on psychotherapy, but their spirit had for many years influenced the development of analytic psychotherapy. In my view they were to its detriment. I believe the study of the analytic situation was seriously delayed because there did not seem to be any point in describing what happened with one patient since it would not apply to others. Thus Jung's statements lent themselves to an abhorrence of a general theory of technique since it could only foster a misunderstanding and be used as an intellectualized defence against the patient as an individual.

However, if Jung's expositions are studied in context, a different picture emerges. While Jung was consistently suspicious of theoretical abstractions it did not prevent his developing a number of theories: the theory of types, of archetypes and the collective unconscious are typical. He was, moreover, a master in their application as a study of his analyses of dreams shows. The Tavistock Lectures (Jung, 1968) revealed his method of amplifying symbolic dream material. This procedure, which Jung used when studying alchemy, aims at elucidating symbols by placing them in their historical and cultural contexts. The method derives from the notion that there is always a penumbra of mystery around symbolic data and it is desirable to make that as explicit as possible while preserving the context of the imagery. In view of these brief reflections, Jung's final statements cannot be taken as denying the value of theoretical guidelines for psychotherapy, but as suggesting that the treatment of the patient is an art.[3]

The development of Jung's conception of the analytic situation[4] may be said to have started when he emphasized the need for the analysis of the analyst. He thought that it was the influence of the analyst as a person that was the decisive therapeutic factor, a conception that had been formulated in the deceptively obvious idea that no analyst can help his patient to progress farther than he has gotten himself (Freud, 1910).[5] In line with this position Jung held that transference could often be the result of interaction between analyst and patient (Jung, 1946). He conceived that though transference was ubiquitous, found in personal and social living, it was intensified in the analytic setting as a reaction to the analyst's behavior. The real attitudes and personality of the analyst played a significant part in the form and intensity of transference. When the analyst was incapable of empathizing with his patient an intense transferential reaction would develop, representing his patient's effort to close the gap. Jung also believed it could represent an effort by a patient to adapt to an analyst who, endowed with the qualities of a parent, could now act as a bridge so the patient could move from his regressed state back to reality.

A more relevant conception to my thesis is that Jung recognized the analyst's capacity to introject his patient's psychopathology and become confused or disoriented. He wrote, for instance (Jung, 1946, pp. 175–76),

> The doctor by voluntarily and consciously taking over the psychic sufferings of the patient, exposes himself to the overpowering contents of the unconscious and hence also to their inductive action. . . . The patient by bringing an activated unconscious content to bear upon the doctor, constellates the corresponding unconscious material in him. . . . Doctor and patient thus find themselves in a relationship founded on mutual unconsciousness . . .; [and] the unconscious infection brings with it a therapeutic possibility – which should not be underestimated – of the illness being transferred to the doctor.

All these ideas are related to the theory of archetypes which suggests that there is a common substrate to all human beings. It is conceivable that the archetypes reveal virtually no difference between one person and another. It is this archetypal activity that sensitizes analysts to their absorbing and taking over aspects of their patients.[6]

In Jung's writings there are a number of other observations which imply his interactive approach:

1 He believed that a patient's resistances could be thought of as not only intrapsychic but related also to the therapist's conflicts (Jung, 1951, p. 115, and also Lambert, 1976).
2 He implied that a patient might be ahead of the analyst in understanding and lead the therapist into appropriate functioning. During his lifetime he delivered (Jung, 1937), but never published, a paper describing how he had become depressed at his inability to understand what was going on, with his patient becoming more and more ill. He offered to refer the patient to someone else. To his astonishment she said she thought everything was fine, and added that it did not matter at all if Jung did not understand her dreams. Jung continued the treatment.
3 He made it clear that in his relations with his patients he would from time to time express strong emotions openly, and that he did so because he thought they were needed by the patient (Jung, 1937, p. 139).

In his writing Jung hardly mentioned counter-transference though he seemed to refer to it often in its current sense. In addition to his idea of the analyst absorbing the psychopathology of his patient, he thought the analyst was just as much in analysis as the patient. If the patient was to change or transform himself, the analyst must be prepared to do so, too, and to have previously experienced the essential nature of this process in his own analysis.[7]

Analytical psychologists, influenced by Jung's dialectical 'method,' have noted some of its inherent dangers. The open interactional approach, it was believed, led to intrusiveness by the analyst. It was weak in just the area in which classical psychoanalysis was strong: the development, analysis and resolution of the transference neurosis. It was one thing for Jung to be 'unsystematic by intention' but his open systems attitude was very difficult to apply satisfactorily. Furthermore, when divorced, as it often was, from his recommendation that methods were needed, it led to undisciplined responses by analysts with insufficient knowledge and experience, especially with respect to the transference neurosis and counter-transference.

It was further argued that to develop a generalized description of how analysts behaved need not mean that anything was necessarily imposed on the patient.[8] The individual nature of the analytic situation could be preserved by attention to what a patient said and understanding by the analyst of the patient's participation could be facilitated by his own analysis. The concept of counter-transference is useful in this regard since it relates to the apparent subjectiveness in Jung's ideas and helps in distinguishing between their valid and invalid aspects (this volume, Chapter 1). Counter-transference theory has been developed by classical psychoanalysts based on different assumptions about the analytic situation from those proposed by Jung. The earliest classical view was that an analyst could develop illusions about the patient due to residues of the analyst's infantile neurosis or to disturbances in the analyst's personal life, which have no relevance to the patient. These data were to be treated by the analyst just as he treated his patient's transference. That is, they must be analyzed and mastered intrapsychically. The difficulty with this viewpoint for analytical psychologists arises from the theoretical formulation about the data. To classical psychoanalysts, it is all related to the notion that transference and counter-transference originate in the unconsciousness of separate persons with firm boundaries, that is, not as open systems interacting with each other.

Though it is convenient to think of transference and counter-transference illusions emanating by projections or displacements from essentially closed systems, to Jungians there can be, at the same time, unconscious interactions. The contrast between the open and closed systems models, each of which appear to have relevance, does not necessarily mean that they are antithetical. The differences can be related to stages in analysis or even to the requirements of different patients.

Analytical psychologists have worked extensively with borderline cases, and with some psychotics. Also, one of Jung's special contributions had been to encourage the treatment of persons in the second half of life. With older patients he did engage in a form of therapy which included considerable personal interaction and more or less frank education (Fordham, 1978b, Henderson, 1975).[9]

With severe as well as with the less disturbed, the analyst's affective reactions to the patient may contain some validity. Elsewhere (this volume, Chapter 1) I have suggested that as a result of some patients' effects on their analysts, the latter tended to introject their patients' unconscious fantasies or archaic objects. Consequently, I surmised, that the analyst is in a position to further study his patients within himself.[10] This impact of patients on analysts was originally labelled *syntonic counter-transference* (this volume, Chapter 1). Unlike counter-transference illusions, which should be mastered and resolved by the analyst, syntonic counter-transference provides constructive information about patients. The concept of the syntonic counter-transference was derived from Jung's observation that an analyst could introject his patient's psychopathology and the idea that this could have therapeutic potential. Accordingly an analyst might find himself behaving in ways that were out of line with what he knew of himself, but syntonic with what he knew of his patient. Among Jungians, Moody (1955) was the first to make the observation which indicated that this kind of response by an analyst might have a significant influence on the progress of analytic therapy. Plaut (1956) studied the influence of a patient upon him which showed that he (the analyst) might, as he put it, 'incarnate an archetypal image' and worked through that situation with the patient (see Langs, 1976 in this regard).

Later I came to think that something of the same nature might be contained in counter-transference illusions. This idea was developed in a paper by Kraemer (1958). He described the case of a depressed patient who was treated by a therapist who in turn came to him for analysis because the therapy was at an impasse. Kraemer's patient had developed a counter-transference love for the patient. She actually inhibited her patient from doing the analytic work because she had dreamed about him in a positive light. She insisted on expressing her positive feelings to the patient despite his strong objections. Such behavior obviously needed analysis and the therapist knew it. Yet it soon was realized that some depressed patients tend to evoke loving feelings in their analysts, and it was conceivable that the therapist's feelings could have been used to advance the patient's treatment, if the analyst's compulsion had not been in the way.

These two forms of counter-transference are rooted in projective and/or introjective processes, although other defense systems also enter into their formation.[11] For example, the analyst may identify with the content of his introjection and then inadvertently play out a rôle for his patient, which is actually a powerful way of perpetuating his patient's neurosis. Or the analyst will crudely or subtly force his patient to comply with his projection. These are deviations from the therapeutic process but are only destructive when they become inflexible, remain unconscious, and are not used as sources of information on which to build interpretations or interventions.[12]

The question remains as to how counter-transference data can be utilized, since 'technique' has been criticized by analytical psychologists as a disguised defense, which wards off the patient's natural effort at establishing a relationship with the analyst. Whether erroneous or not (and I believe that it is mistaken), this is tantamount to asserting that technique itself constitutes an impersonal and sustained counter-transference. Jung never went so far (this volume, Chapter 8). His criticisms of technique rested mainly on the need to preserve a patient's individuality. That must never be glossed over by those methods of interpretation that come to depend upon the analyst's authority. Jung rejected the assumption of irrational authority by analysts, asserting that the analyst should consider himself just as much in analysis as his patient. As an expression of this egalitarian attitude, he and the patient would sit in chairs facing each other. Of course, a person comes to another for help on the assumption that the other person has the expertise needed to be helpful. This inevitably gives the analyst authority which is demonstrated by his capacity to understand the patient and provide conditions under which the patient can resolve or modify his conflicts.[13] Thus authority in itself is inevitable, but it must be rational.

In this context a counter-transference illusion may have one useful characteristic: it demonstrates the fallibility of the analyst. Though optimally it does not last for long, it does seem to place the analyst on the same level as the patient. In addition it reminds the analyst of his tendencies to become irrationally involved. When counter-transference does interfere with an analytic attitude and technique, the analyst must struggle to find some resolution. These occurrences can be quite subtle. Minor manifestations of counter-transference illusions may seem unimportant. Some may derive from the analyst's life outside the analysis, so that the analyst will inevitably go through periods of stress which in turn influence his work. Overtly he may proceed consistently, but with an underlying mood change his participation will be colored. Sometimes this is unnoticed. With others the effect is repressed. And with others it may be observed and reflected upon without being communicated. It will, however, influence the course of patients' associations. I do not call this counter-transference proper, in the sense that it is a reaction to a patient. However, if a patient consistently induces a specific mood in the analyst then it is counter-transference, and it must be understood, interpreted and brought into consciousness. I mention this because they are human attributes. They are to be expected. Otherwise they can be the springboard for serious and pathological counter-transference reactions.

Another criticism of technique centers around the tendency for it to become divorced from an analyst's affects, especially his love and hate (and their derivatives) for his patient. If an analyst believes that being loving, tolerant, kind, understanding, and long-suffering is enough for the relationship he is mistaken. Yet that attitude can be supported by arguing that his patient's transference behavior is only to be expected because of his developmental history.[14] Having understood the genesis of the transference the analyst interprets and then waits for the working-through process to complete itself.[15] Unfortunately, all this can conceal contempt for the patient. If, however, the patient is not cooperative, it may result in the analyst reinforcing the patient's detachment by increasingly splitting so that the patient becomes isolated and frustrated, in reality. This is liable to occur usually with the more severe character disorders, the narcissistic neuroses, and the borderline cases. These patients will attack the analytic frame as a whole (Fordham, 1978b) and try, in a delusional way, to engage in a 'human' relationship. Since the analytic frame is threatened, the analyst may decide that the patient has developed a negative therapeutic reaction and conclude, erroneously, that the patient is untreatable. Then he either terminates the patient's treatment or clings to technical clichés long after they have proven fruitless.[16] Such consequences do not, however, invalidate the need for a well defined analytic method. They do suggest that descriptions of such a method are incomplete because they have yet to pay sufficient attention to the affective states that analysts go through during its use.

At one time the *syntonic counter-transference* was seen as providing a clue to the patient in that it defined a condition from which an analyst could gain information about the patient without the patient's awareness, giving greater access to the patient's affective state. It was soon learned, however, that in order to accomplish this the introjection had to be reprojected, for only then could it be perceived as part of the patient. A *counter-transference illusion* led to the converse conclusion. Before any positive content could be defined the projection had to be withdrawn and assimilated. Thus, the concepts of projection and introjection came to be viewed in a different perspective. Could it not be then that in any analysis there is a sequence of projections, introjections, and identifications that provide affective information complementing the conscious use of the analyst's skills (this volume, Chapter 8)?[17]

Take the interview itself. When a patient comes into the room how does an analyst behave? Does he immediately know about the state of his patient? I think not. He tends to wait till the patient tells him what is in his mind. But this does not answer the question: what is the analyst's state of mind in the interim? While it will vary from patient to patient, it has occurred to me that a helpful attitude for the analyst is to empty his mind of what he has learned about the patient on other occasions. What happens if the analyst does this? The patient is approached by the analyst on each occasion as if they had never met before. Having emptied his mind he waits to see what happens. He lets his observations, thoughts and fantasies develop in relation to his patient till they link up with material from past sessions which he recalls spontaneously, and without effort, his own constructions, his interpretations, etc.[18]

CLINICAL EXAMPLE

A patient, over 60 years, gets up from her chair when I come into the waiting room. She looks bright, with eyes sparkling like a little girl. I feel annoyed at something hungry about her and think that she wants to be met with a hug and a kiss. It seems inappropriate and I don't want to do either. She lies down on the couch and says nothing. I feel a growing frustration and become aware that it is I who am hungry. She is not going to feed me with associations and I reach for my pipe. Then she starts talking and I put my pipe down, and am able to listen comfortably as the interview proceeds.

These incidents and reflections would not have become conscious had I not emptied my mind. This patient had been in analysis for some time and I actually knew quite well what this was about. I could have documented each of her actions. She was a somewhat narcissistic personality and easily felt angry if her virtues were not appreciated. I knew enough about her childhood to know why she had regressed when she came to session and could have interpreted it without difficulty. But if I had done that none of the affective content of the meeting would have been felt and my underlying irritation would have been missed. Also, my projective identification, and the way it was withdrawn to discover my own hunger, would have been lost sight of. Finally, I might very well not have noted that she started to talk out of competition with my pipe. My technique had additional aims to the ones considered here. These were: (a) to individualize the meeting with my patient; and (b) to proceed in a sequence from unconsciousness to consciousness.

The details would have come through directly, I believe, in timing my interventions and small indications such as movements or tones of voice. I might even have made an interpretive reconstruction later on when an occasion arose, and done so tactlessly. In short, instead of resolving my own state of mind I would have developed a concealed counter-transference.[19]

THE ANALYST'S ERRORS

Many errors by an analyst are, with good reason, laid to counter-transference. But in order to make judgements about errors it is necessary to know when an intervention is correct and when it is not. Indeed to work with any degree of refinement on counter-transference requires some criteria for judgment.

There are some criteria derived from the patient's response and these are important (Wisdom, 1967). But initially they stem from the analyst and these are more relevant to the thesis of this paper. How is the analyst certain that an intervention is relevant and needs to be made? He listens and arrives at a hypothesis of the unconscious content of his patient's communications – the projective and introjective identifications playing an essential part in stimulating it. Though the idea is tentative at this stage it stimulates interest in what is going on. As the analyst continues to listen his idea may have to be discarded as faulty. If it is confirmed he reaches the conviction that it is relevant. Then he may communicate it to the patient. When the analyst has done so he listens again to what use, if any, the patient makes of this contribution.[20] A useful interpretation will refer to what is unconscious in the patient. In that sense it may be relevant but incomplete. Therefore, it will not be accepted immediately. Indeed, it may be energetically rejected and only afterwards stimulate reflection or change in the patient's associations. Interventions are best thought of as a part of a dialectical interchange.[21]

Apart from flagrant errors, counter-transference is indicated if the dialectical process is interfered with, and especially if (1) the analyst finds difficulty in listening dispassionately to his patient's response so that he cannot estimate whether it is being digested, accepted, or rejected; (2) when he becomes aware that he is failing to pick up those indications that his patient may give that the intervention has been appropriate or not; and (3) when he misses when the patient begins to guide him to a better formulation, or discovers it too late.

DEVIATIONS FROM THE ANALYTIC ATTITUDE

There are a good many instances in the literature where analysts have expressed their affects forcefully and I have discussed some of these elsewhere (Fordham, 1978b). They are all non-analytic and, as responses to the patient's transference, may be classified as counter-transference. They are usually aggressive and seem to be common with patients who are borderline, have psychotic traits, or are frankly psychotic. Often they take place when the patient threatens the analyst's posture and self-definition either by consistently acting out or by frustrating the analytic process.

Some of these responses seem to be related to establishing the frame of analysis. Jung (1937) gave a dramatic example of an obsessional woman who had the habit of slapping her doctors in the face. When she threatened to hit Jung, he related: '"Very well, you are a lady. You hit first – ladies first! But then I hit back!" And I meant it. She fell back deflated before my eyes. "No one has ever said that to me before!" she protested. From that moment on therapy began to succeed.' An example given by Giovacchini (1977) illustrates this as well. His psychotic patient's delusions at first involved Giovacchini in protective actions, but to no effect, and his patient eventually ended up in jail. In the course of the subsequent treatment Giovacchini told his patient that he would absolutely 'not get involved again and if [the patient] found himself in trouble, he would have to depend on his own resources.'

Little (1957) illustrated what she called 'R' – the analyst's total response – in the case of a patient who told repetitive stories about children. Little told her that she was 'as tired of them as [the patient] was of the children's behavior. The patient "did not know" and went on into another story. I said, "I meant that; I'm not listening to any more of them."'

No doubt many of these are states of the analyst which will not be repeated. Giovacchini (1977) infers as much when he describes another patient who made excessive demands upon him. He became furious and told him so. 'I felt that I had over-reached. . . . But I did not become further distressed and the patient has not made any further demands of me. Undoubtedly he will, but I now believe I can reinforce the condition I set up without becoming upset' (p. 438).[22]

PATIENT A.[23]

Mrs A. developed a delusional transference and did everything she could to break down my analytic posture. This was clearly expressed by her question, 'Can't you stop being an analyst and become a person?' It was followed with great ingenuity and vigor. My reaction tended to be passive, to suspend my analytic efforts and sometimes to retreat masochistically. Occasionally I found myself projectively identifying with my patient: the analytic method had no validity at all and I started looking at myself through her eyes.

In the face of her apparently negative therapeutic reaction, I reflected guiltily about what had gone wrong. Had my diagnosis been at fault, and should I never have taken on this patient? Had my technique been too inadequate? Had my interpretations been wrong too often or badly directed? Had I failed to analyze defenses adequately? Had interpretations been too numerous so as to drive the patient to hopelessness and despair? And so on (see Chapter 12). During this period of self scrutiny I felt very much more like a patient than an analyst. And the patient reinforced this by making attempts to analyze my state. Occasionally she was right. She believed, for instance, that my infantile traumata had emerged, but she consoled herself with the thought that I would eventually mature into a state in which I would be able to be of help to her. Despite what appeared to be a predominantly sterile, even destructive process, she showed no signs of wanting to terminate. The lengthy process that my patient and I went through did produce a satisfactory therapeutic result although I had to initiate its ending. The analysis was not as complete as I might have wished. During it I learned how to sustain my analytic stance much better with such patients so that when comparable situations arise, I am no longer inclined to react the same way.[24]

PATIENT B.[25]

Mrs B. was concerned about her tendency to see penises everywhere. She apparently suffered from mild hallucinations, not to be thought of as clinically psychotic but making her concerned lest she be on the edge of psychosis.[26] In this context she told me a dream in which there were long objects on a couch. She was uncertain as to whether they were feces or penises. The dream had occurred many years ago and she told me that she had taken it to her previous analyst and together they had agreed to call them 'fecal penises'. Some days later I had occasion to remind her of this incident. She adamantly asserted that she had told me nothing of the kind, that I had 'gone mad'[27] and that the incident was a figment of my 'fertile mind'. In various contexts similar situations had arisen before when the patient, in addition to her denial, asserted that I had confused her with somebody else. On this occasion she inferred that I was in need of analysis indicating that she would be ready and glad to undertake the necessary work. Like Mrs A., she implied that only when that had been completed could her own analysis proceed.

On previous occasions I had bypassed this quandary, unable to find a way of resolving it. Here it presented itself again. This time I emphasized that there was a difference of opinion which, distressingly, did not seem possible to resolve, and I made no further attempt to do so. She made an attempt to object but the interview ground to a halt, giving me time for reflection. I did not give serious thought to the possibility that she was correct (as I had done at length with Mrs A.). I was at a loss until I became convinced that an intervention was required. I told her that I thought the idea or feeling of a penis as fecal was relevant and I would tell her why I thought so, emphasizing the word "I" to indicate that it was offered to her as my idea and not necessarily one which she need agree to as relevant to her. It might, in short, be treated as part of my bit of 'madness'. There had been a number of times in her life from childhood onwards when she had been frightened or repelled by penises as disgusting, or otherwise undesirable objects, and I summarized them at some length. After considerable reflection and further objection she came to agree that what I said felt true, but that her intellect kept producing arguments against such a mad proposition.

What were the elements in the interchange which are relevant to this discussion? There was the period after my patient's assertion that I was having an illusion about her which must have felt more to her like one of her 'hallucinations'. During this time I did not know what to do and was forced back on myself as with the counter-transference to Mrs A. Here was food for thought, but it was indigestible. Introjective identifications were contained in this and hence some uncertainty about whether she was correct. Looking back, it is clear that I had also identified with my patient's attitude in a projective way and this made it possible for me to respect and empathize with her contention and temporarily identify with it. Though these affective processes tended to make for a feeling of confusion, I was still able to reflect. The conviction that I had to intervene actively was not accompanied by the knowledge of what I was going to say. Indeed, I was still under the influence of my counter-transference when I started to speak. When I began to talk, however, I found it surprisingly easy to develop my theme in such a way, as it turned out, that my patient could understand its sense so that a shift in her transference took place. If, as on previous occasions, I had not been able to respond adequately then there would be no doubt that I had developed a counter-transference which had interfered with the progress of the analysis. But what of the rest? The affects roused by my patient are the consequence of her attack and they counter it. There was introjection, temporary confusion, and after that the intervention came out of me, reflectively, but also as a spontaneous interaction. I had a certain feeling of surprise and satisfaction. It would be possible to consider all this is part of a syntonic counter-transference and to conceptualize it in terms of my reprojecting the introjected content with the intervention. This even might account for the spontaneity of my communication. But is the term counter-transference necessary? It was an interaction in which projection, introjection, and identifications took part. Between these two clinical experiences I conducted a good deal of self-analysis. This paid off in my personal and social life. Since this occurred in relation to a patient it also facilitated the therapy.[28] There were also other contributing activities: discussion with colleagues, writing papers (this volume, Chapters 8 and 12), and reading the literature, thereby discovering that my experience was not unique. I ended up by developing a new hypothesis about defenses of the self (this volume, Chapter 12). I had apparently engaged, more or less under compulsion, on a research project. Such a project was, to a large extent, personal at first and required significant changes in my affective states – a 'transformation' as Jung would have put it. This seems to me an essential ingredient in all analytic research, and here counter-transference entered into it. Once completed, I needed to discover whether it was a contribution of the body of psychoanalytic knowledge. Writing this paper is an attempt to find out.

Additional consequences of this research were that I reevaluated some patients' need for statements about the analyst's own affective states and also gained further insight into the notion of an analyst as a child.[29]

A CONCLUDING STATEMENT

Looking back at the development of the concept of counter-transference it can be seen to have gone through various phases. First it covered a set of undesirable data arising from the analyst to be controlled, analyzed, and resolved by him. It fitted in with the aspiration of analysts who hoped to achieve objectivity so as to know correctly what went on intrapsychically in their patients. Their own psychological states were to be thought of as essentially irrelevant. Not much attention was paid to Freud's (1910) view that the analyst uses his unconscious as an organ of perception, nor to Jung's emphasis on the importance of the analyst's personal influence. Next, the term was expanded to cover the analyst's intrapsychic states. This had an important consequence: the analyst's personality, not only his psychopathology, could now be brought under review. In the light of this approach the analytic situation came under close scrutiny and thus led to a far more detailed description of what goes on between analyst and patient. There is the holding capacity of the analyst, as well as his capacity for projective and introjective identification with his patient. This is necessary for arriving at sufficient comprehension as to the processes going on in the patient, and between the analyst and his patient. A further study of how to validate the analyst's interventions led to understanding that a patient might collaborate over mistakes, guide the analyst to a correct or a better formulation, and facilitate the analysis of the analyst.

It seems to me that these issues can all be brought under one heading, the analytic dialectic, and that they lead toward a view of the analytic situation as two open systems interacting.[30] In the course of the development of the theory, the terms transference and counter-transference have been expanded and generalized. Thus an analyst's appropriate feelings and affects about his patient have been included so that the original concepts to which the terms refer are in danger of losing meaning. Now the whole analytic situation is to be thought of as a mass of illusions, delusions, displacements, projections, and introjections. I would suggest that, apart from an analyst's appropriate reactions, his transitory projections and displacements cease to be called counter-transferences since they represent the analyst acting on and reacting to his patient. These actions may contain false perceptions, fantasies, illusions, or even delusions, but these can be contained by the analyst till they are resolved and utilized to extract appropriate interventions. It is when the interacting systems become obstructed that a special label is needed and, to my mind, it is then that the term counter-transference is appropriate.

I have suggested that rigidity be used as a criteria to indicate counter-transference, but I must qualify this. There are areas in analysis where there is rational rigidity: for example, the frame of analysis into which projections are made needs to remain stable till termination. In addition, there is a need for the analyst's stable style.[31]

I believe the theory of counter-transference has performed its main function. It has had the most desirable effect of taking analysts out of their ivory towers, making it possible for them to compare notes on what they actually do during analytic psychotherapy.[32] The pathological reactions of the analyst, comparable to the patient's transference, may be called counter-transference. I would call the rest part of the interactional dialectic.[33, 34]

NOTES

1 A manuscript of a talk presented to the Society of Analytical Psychology entitled 'Counter-transference and interaction' exists, which is a variant of this paper. As Fordham regards 'Analytical psychology and counter-transference' as a pivotal paper that crucially revises his earlier work and sets forth a new agenda for clinical research, some of the significant additions in 'Counter-transference and interaction' have been reproduced below, together with some of the significant additions from the revised version of this paper, retitled 'Counter-transference' in *Explorations into the Self* (Fordham M., 1985). The latter are indicated by the postfix (1985) (ed.).

2 In this paper I shall consider the status of counter-transference and suggest that the time has been reached when the scope of the term can be reduced. I shall start by asserting that Jung's method was interactional and will summarize sufficient of his pronouncements to define what I mean. Next I shall consider ideas on counter-transference as developed in this Society and their relation to technique and the transitory affective states of the analysts to be described as interaction rather than counter-transference.

3 Like any artist he had acquired a thorough grasp of his method whilst recognizing that it could only be valid when used in creative work with his patients.

4 I have analyzed Jung's position in a number of essays starting in 1957. Since then others have appeared in 1969 and 1974 and I have collated them in a forthcoming volume (Fordham 1978).

5 I have never been happy with the statement because it seems to depreciate the capacity of analysts to learn from their patients both in an emotional and mental sense. I think it likely that in any good analysis the analyst's psychic life is enriched, and if he does not understand his patient, he can act as a container while his patient works on seemingly incomprehensible matter. In line with this position, Jung held that transference could often be the result of interaction between analyst and patient. He thought that transference, though ubiquitous in everyday life, is intensified in the analytic setting in reaction to the analyst's behavior. The real attitudes and personality of the analyst play a significant part in the form and intensity of transference. Furthermore, he held that when the analyst is incapable of empathizing with his patient, an intense transference develops, representing the patient's effort to close the gap. Jung further believed that transference can also represent an effort by a patient to adapt to an analyst who, endowed with the qualities of a parent, can act as a bridge so the patient can move from a regressed state back to reality (1985).

6 These states of identity between analyst and patient are liable to occur because of archetypal activity. It would follow that, because of this condition, emphasis on a patient's individuality, in non-neurotic cases, would facilitate assimilation of the common substrate, throw differences between patient and therapist into relief thus counteracting the states of identity.

7 I have argued previously in favor of developing a theory of analytic practice and that such a theory would facilitate interaction rather than imposing a system of ideas on the patient. The individual nature of the analytic situation can be preserved by careful attention to the patient's communications; understanding by the analyst of the patient's participation can be facilitated by the former's own analysis and his capacity for transformation (1985).

8 . . . nor that the construction of such a picture need be disadvantageous; it might after all lead to guidelines which would be of value in training as well for practicing analysts.

9 It might, therefore, be expected that he would develop an open systems theory but he never did so in detail nor did he generalize what he had to say, holding that different cases required different forms of treatment and so varying behavior by therapists. It may be held, however, that though caution is necessary lest differences be overlooked, the more disturbed patients reveal, clearly, aspects of those that are less disturbed. Consequently, in some respects, the one may shed light on the other. Thus when a closed systems approach seems relevant, interactions between patient and analyst might also be present but overlooked: it may not be noticed that, even in a counter-transference illusion, there may be affects of the analyst which could be relevant and valid. To put it differently: in neurotic patients, with well enough established self-organization, interactions take place but are not relevant to the treatment. On the contrary, in borderline cases interaction becomes much more significant and the closed systems view can even get in the way and can be inappropriately maintained. In both cases the analyst's reaction to his patient could contain some validity. With the idea that this was so, a development in the idea of the counter-transference became possible.

10 It was not enough, however, to apply this information without waiting for confirmation: their conclusions would usually have to be kept to themselves for a considerable time till the necessary data emerged from patients – only then would communication be possible.

11 . . . especially identificatory actions.

12 At first it seemed surprising to consider technique in relation to counter-transference. Technique is the use of skills by the analyst to his own satisfaction and the benefit of his patient. Provided a patient achieves enough capacity to communicate his thoughts, feelings and observations, an analyst can sustain his analytic attitude (cf. Fordham, 1978b), use his experience, his knowledge and interpret his patient's material. So how can counter-transference enter into the subject at all? I have already indicated that the use of techniques was criticized by Jung and other analytical psychologists as a disguised defense constructed to ward off the patient's efforts to establish a relationship to his analyst.

13 These capacities are indeed an important basis for the patient developing a transference.

14 An alternative is to refer the 'projection' to archetypal sources, and again it has nothing to do with either the patient nor the analyst as persons (1985).

15 . . . even though it may work quite well for those areas of analysis in which the analyst is not stirred up much by his patient.

16 I suspect that it is this that gave rise to the anathematization of technique in Jungian circles. Such consequences suggest that descriptions of method are incomplete in that they fail to pay sufficient attention to the affective states that the analyst goes through during the application of a technique. I am impressed with Bion's description of transformation in 'O' and transformations in 'K.' When using techniques the analyst is looking for transformations in O, but that would mean divesting himself of memory and desire. These would be expressing themselves as preconceptions about the therapy and the patient and not knowing what could or what ought to be done or thought (1985).

17 It is not easy to demonstrate this state of affairs, especially as analysts generally focus their free floating attention on the patient and not on themselves. Trainees and students show counter-transference deviations and from time to time these lead on to a useful line of approach to their patients. But this may not apply to trained analysts and so I thought that a common practice among analysts might be refined and examined more closely.

18 Thus a series of changes (transformations) takes place in the analyst. Bion has given a sophisticated account of the processes I have described. It is highly complex and I will only extract one segment of it. Once (the 'ultimate') O has been reached it will lead first to transformations leading in the direction of K (K being knowledge resulting from sensual experience). I translate this formula as the desirability of starting from the self at first without characteristics, but later developing characteristics through processes of deintegration. Bion's assertion that this involves faith in its scientific (not religious) sense is cogent, as is also his formula that O–K involves transformations in O (leading to symbolization of the self as I understand it) (1985).

19 The fantasy of an analyst as a child. It will be noticed that following this procedure I put myself in the hands of my patient: I am absolutely dependent upon her (metaphorically speaking) feeding me with associations. I can do little or nothing without them. If there are no associations it is not quite starvation because there will be non-verbal communications from which I may be able to feed. The dependence of an analyst is liable to be overlooked, yet it is a state that may need recognition, especially when a patient notices it, builds on it and expands this state of affairs into a delusion that his analyst actually is a child in his whole relation to him. In that situation it is valuable to know just where that state of affairs applies.

20 This formulation raises the question of whether an intervention can be called correct or incorrect and whether, if it be so called, it has contributed anything to what the patient does not already know.

21 Only within limits can their correctness be estimated.

22 In other words as an analyst, Giovacchini had matured so that such reactions are not to be taken in only a negative light. Many of the affective states in the analyst need analysis, they are true counter-transferences that refer to him only and not to the patient, but they are not necessarily to be left as only faults in technique because they may be the seeding ground for new formulations and so constitute a basis for learning.

23 It is sometimes the case that a patient focuses a development in his analyst.

24 I am no longer inclined to sink into a masochistic state, nor have I been the victim of excessive projective identification. In the meantime I have constructed a theory to account for the patient's behavior (this volume, Chapter 12). Thus I hold that the states occur in patients whose self is active in defending itself against the delusion of being threatened. The defense is overtly negative but it is really part of the ground for creating a more satisfactory self feeling.

25 To illustrate how the result of work with this and other patients as well led to developments in technique, I will offer a single interview in which a bit of delusional transference appeared and was dealt with. It contains matter to be compared with that of the first patient, Mrs A. This example is an amalgam made up from a number of sufficiently similar cases.

26 She had made several open attempts to find out whether mine was erect or not, sometimes by peering at where it would be behind my trousers. She had previously told me that, many years back, when having intercourse she liked it best after male orgasm. Then the penis, lying in her vagina, felt like a large warm comfortable fecal mass.

27 . . . or that my brain cells were in decay owing to my age.

28 Nowadays, I ensure as far as I can that I have only one or two such cases like this at a time.

29 I eventually found that these discoveries had application to daily and more ordinary analyses.

30 . . . without invalidating the closed systems notion as a practical approximation.

31 The result of these features is that the analysis becomes set along non-verbal paths which never change so long as they represent the analyst's true self. The vicissitudes of counter-transference theory are of considerable interest and stimulate reflections as

to the place of theory in analytical psychology. It will be remembered that Jung was ambivalent here. Whatever faults it developed it has made it possible for analysts to relax the rather too stringent and so unrealistic standards they set up for themselves. The ideal could be applied to a restricted class of patient; with the rest it was patently impossible to sustain them. Even when we come to review the restricted class a number of behaviors not easy to detect are, though excluded, nonetheless there – may be the detriment to both analyst and patient.

32 This achievement has been invaluable even if the analyst's response to his patient is better classed a part of the therapeutic interaction with his patient. It is no criticism of a theory if its nature changes with the requirements of analysts whilst it is acting as a stimulus. It appears as if the theory of counter-transference has performed its main function and we can now return to a more restricted use of the term. The conception of the analytic process as a dialectical interaction stands.

33 Having said this I would not have it overlooked that every action of an analyst may take on characteristics of counter-transference.

34 Many years ago now Jung defined such a 'stage of transformation.' I find that any analytic encounter with a patient involves transformation, whether it takes place in a single interview or whether it takes time over weeks or months. When it fails for too long, then one can speak of a counter-transference in its deeper sense. To facilitate transformations, the analyst's capacity to reach the self is important. Bion's formula that the analyst divest himself of memory and desire means that he starts from a state at which there is no past and no desire for change, especially desire to change a patient in a social or intrapsychic direction. He can then receive the patient's impact and start to transform that. Hopefully he will arrive at a state when he can digest the patient's material and feed it back to him in a way that facilitates the transformative processes in the patient. Counter-transference occurs when the analyst's transformation fails to take place (1985).

Chapter 16

Contribution to symposium 'How do I assess progress in supervision?' (1982)

I would like to contribute to the present Symposium by making some remarks about the supervision of students in their handling of cases taken in the child analytic training, London.

I have previously stated my position with relation to supervision as a whole (this volume, Chapter 3), and a re-reading of that paper does not make me want to alter the essential argument: supervision, in contrast to analysis, should be directed towards the student's performance with his case and not to the student's affective internal world. I have now some further comments to make as to the result of knowledge gained about students, their differing styles of analysis, and how these help in defining the directions in which improvement in their analytic skills might be made.

In view of the various usages of the word analysis I would draw the reader's attention to previous of my writings on the subject (this volume, Chapter 3), and summarise these by stating that analysis is essentially an attitude of mind which sorts out complex structures with a view to gaining insight into the operation of their more simple components.

The reflections that I shall present are derived from the supervision of child analyses which require a formal setting or framework in which the student sees the child frequently, four or five times a week. The room contains a sink and available water, two chairs, a table, a couch with a rug and cushions. Toys are kept in a cupboard outside the treatment rooms and are those selected by the child with others that the analyst may wish to add. Before the session begins, analyst and child go to the cupboard, the analyst unlocks it and the child takes the toys if he wants them – he usually does. The toys represent a gift by the analyst to the child, and the child can do anything he likes with them, including taking them home or adding to them as he sees fit.

This arrangement maximises the interactional nature of the analytic process and, hopefully, minimises the child's capacity to escape into acting out types of play. It has not always been possible to achieve these standards.

Under these conditions the student brings the supervisor his, or her, detailed account of what has gone on in the interview. As might be expected the accounts vary greatly, not only because of the differences in children who are being treated, but also because they reveal the basic styles of the student. Here are two contrasting examples.

The first case is of a boy who had an intellectual inhibition. As evidence accumulated it became rather clear to me that the disorder was due to castration anxiety displaced upwards. The trainee recognised the relevance of my observation, and tried to put it to the boy in her own way. As might have been expected, her patient did not enthusiastically acclaim this insight but became resistant, and the student, noticing that, did not press forward her interpretations. I should explain here that I had left a good deal to the student, avoiding spelling out the interpretation I would have given. Thus I had not said: 'Look, this child is so uncommunicative because he wants to seduce you, but is too afraid of the consequences should he try it on.'

The student went on with her analysis, working sensitively and carefully with the material he produced so that her patient gradually relaxed and became more open with her. Eventually he started attempts at seduction: he became interested in the contents of her room and, in particular, in a cupboard which represented the student's body. He also wanted her to play games with him. The student went along with that but, I thought, extricated herself in time. I understood that the castration anxiety had mitigated through the analyst's careful and sensitive relationship with her patient. Though this analysis was skilful, it was rather passive, and, as her supervisor, I missed penetrative insights into the unconscious processes at work – she tended to wait till they emerged and they did not always do so.

Now to consider a contrasting student. Again the patient was a boy. The student was much more robust and rooted in her body; she soon gave evidence of great capacity for containment.

The boy came each time with an account of the journeys that he had made: he came by London Underground and went well out of his way to get to the clinic. He recorded the stations that he had been to or through, and described his fascination with the train coming out of the tunnel into the station; he would lean over the platform's edge as far as he dared, to see how far down the tunnel he could detect the oncoming train.

The interviews became stuck on these repetitive accounts, so I asked the student what she would say to the boy if neither I nor anybody else could know what she had said. Her reply was somewhat as follows: she thought that his 'geographical' study indicated a sexual interest in her (the student's) body and especially an interest in her genital (the tube) and its contents (represented by the train); he seemed to be asking: would she allow him to look into her genitals and the penis inside it? I asked, 'Why not say that?' thereby implying tacit approval of her doing so. I do not remember in detail what she said to the child, but it was in substance what she said to me. From being petrified the analysis became alive – the immediate effect was impressive, and that, in my view, was because she had the capacity to contain the emotional content of the words so that they were neither an attack on the child's consciousness nor a provocation.

It is my contention that during supervision a supervisor should not evaluate or judge the student's capacities, but facilitate the development of what is available. He may evaluate them afterwards, and will need to do so when the student applies for acceptance as an associate member of the Society of Analytical Psychology. Nor is he there to teach in a formal sense, though he may have to from time to time. Thus I did not give either student a theoretical framework into which to fit their observations – that is the function of seminars – I rather tried to convey my experience in the context of the student's emotional and intellectual capacities. To consider how each might improve involves evaluating their work, and that I will now proceed to do.

Comparing the two examples indicates lines along which development of the students' analytical capacities might go: student 1 needs to increase her capacity for containing and transforming the patient's sexual and aggressive impulses and phantasies. Student 2 could do that, but she needs to pay more attention to the surface data, at which student 1 is adept. Student 2 goes behind or under the surface and gets the analysis going in an intimate interactive fashion, but the surface defensive operations get brushed aside and cause trouble later. The appreciation of the surface can begin by studying with more care the way her patient reacts to her interventions.

My intention in considering these two students is to suggest that lines of development can best be defined from comparative experience rather than from abstract standards. Theory cannot be altogether left out and it is there as a shadow monitoring the interchanges between student and patient on the one hand, student and supervisor on the other. This statement raises questions about the places of abstraction in analytic practice and, also, the ambiguous meaning of experience – after all theory is experience of a kind. I hope, however, my description has been sufficiently clear for it to be understood without further discourse or definition.

Chapter 17

How I do analysis (1988)[1]

The question about what analysts do is recurrent and is curious. There is a large literature on the subject: Freud described in his case studies how he treated his patients and Jung tried much the same in his essays contained in Volume 16 of the *Collected Works*. There has since developed a large literature on the subject, especially from those who have deviated or have developed the supposedly recognized techniques.

That the question arises in the mind of the lay public is not surprising but that it arises in analysts themselves, and not only some young ones in training, is curious. They have all submitted to a personal analysis and presumably received some instruction on the subject of how to treat patients analytically.

It arose at the Society of Analytical Psychology in London in the 1940s but latterly the question has ceased to be asked. That Society was in the forefront of Jungian societies and institutes in both analyzing the transference and in training students by asking them to take cases under supervision. Concurrently, papers were written on technique and method by Society members. That policy has not always been pursued by other societies and institutes. It is my impression that only by undergoing supervision with an analyst that poses the question of how he proceeds can one get a good impression of what he actually does and for that the London Society provided opportunity.

Apart from these inconclusive reflections, the question of what an analyst does has two facets: (1) There are methods that can be acquired from training analysis and supervision, plus reading and seminars. These can be described and are available in the literature. Some may have to be discarded as useless to any particular candidate; (2) There are irregularities which can be described but which are difficult to generalize, though once an irregularity has been detected it may prove fruitful and can later become generalized to become part of a revision of method. It may not do that, however.

Here is an example that I would not like to generalize: I see a male patient at eight o'clock in the morning twice a week and once at eight o'clock in the evening after dinner at which I have drunk wine. I am regularly more talkative in the evenings than in the morning interviews. That my patient notices and decides that 'You are an after-dinner man.' Of course it might be interesting to investigate the effects of an analyst's eating and drinking habits in relation to his analytic work but I would not recommend my behavior as a matter for general practice. My intention here is to introduce the idea that the life of an analyst outside his work influences what he does in his practice.

There have been several stable features of my life as an analytical psychotherapist which need to be stated before saying what I do when seeing a patient. In the first place I have always had a supervisor in my wife, Frieda Fordham, and can scarcely imagine how an analyst gets on without somebody to talk to about his patients, especially those who cause him distress or puzzle him. I talk about patients in seminars, of course, and in other discussion groups and, although that is also helpful, it is not in the same intimate and 'hot' way. Then there is writing: I do not often write notes, only when something has struck me as important and then only after interviews, but writing in a generalized way is also necessary and is an obligation so that others may know what I am doing at any particular time.

All these activities help to heal myself: analytic practice involves introjecting parts of various people and it may not be possible to find the means of digesting and projecting these parts back into the patients. That is particularly difficult when there is much projective identification. When that predominates, my identity may become threatened, boundaries become insecure, and I may be put in the position of 'fighting for my life'. That discovery, which I recorded in Defenses of the Self (this volume, Chapter 12) opened the doors for me to the treatment of patients as a whole, and seeing it as a precarious operation for any analyst who opens himself to patients so as to individualize his analytic endeavors.

I find I usually have a special interest I am pursuing at any one time. At present I have that in a patient who spends his time denigrating 'analysis'; what you say is said to have no effect or is made the subject of ridicule, even if what you say is recognized as correct – then you are met with the defiant 'so what?' I have also written about this and listed the counter-transference responses which such behavior is liable to evoke. So it is a long-term interest as well. Now it is different from what happened originally, because I am no longer vulnerable to such patients – I have learned from them.

That brings me to the point of saying how difficult it is to describe what one is doing with patients because of the changes that are taking place, for the shape of any analysis is made as much by the patient as the analyst. That is in line with Jung's idea that the analyst is as much in the analysis as the patient, though I do not agree that he needs analysis in the same way as the patient; what he needs is supervision, including that provided by his patients.

With the same class of patient, I may make an interpretation which is new to me though I have come near to it before. A specific patient, as part of his view of analysis, stated: 'I do not understand a word you are saying.' To that I made the following interpretation, which I have never made before: 'I don't think that matters but it is important that you continue to believe I know what it is all about even if you do not.' I follow this up with an amplification; saying that what he experiences is like that of a baby to whom it is important that his mother talks to him though he cannot possibly understand the words. Here I had for the first time incorporated the memory of an observation on mother–infant interaction. That development can be reflected upon as part of a technique for detecting very infantile manifestations easily dressed up in argumentation.

I think that these remarks go in very well with Jung's claim to being unsystematic by intention. Indeed I now try to do just that within the analytic frame. My effort to be unsystematic can also be gleaned from the attempt I make to meet a patient at each interview as if I had never seen him before. I empty my mind, as far as I can, of thought, memories and understanding. That makes it difficult to pursue a policy from interview to interview though a continuity in the analytic process may emerge – it arises as it were from between myself and my patient. Proceeding thus gives space for the patient who can bring to the fore the state of affairs which predominates in his mind in the present, i.e. today.

To further describe what I do as an analyst and therapist it may be helpful if I look back and survey what I have done and how I changed. These retrospective reflections highlight the skills I have acquired and used, digested and discarded or gone beyond, as it seems to me.

Early on, I observed children and did whatever I could. I was taught passive technique in which one did almost nothing. Then I heard about Melanie Klein and tried talking to child patients about their play as much as she did but fumblingly, as I now know. Much of that has stuck; much has been digested and altered as experience grew.

In adult analysis, I did my best to persuade patients to write down and work on their dreams as I had discovered how to do in my two analyses. I also wanted them to make pictures and paint, which a few could do but most could not or if they did their productions were not especially revealing.

During this first period I tried to apply methods and develop technique – Jung had said that it was required. I read what was available and found psychoanalysts much more explicit than my Jungian colleagues. Feeling at a loss with patients that neither dreamed nor painted, I listened much more carefully and was greatly helped in discovering more about how to listen in Theodore Reik's book, *Listening with the Third Ear* (1949). I consider this change in technique has been invaluable for I discovered much better how to listen to what a patient did not say as well as what he did say. I was, however, being 'unsystematic' – not, as Jung says, 'by intention,' but out of ignorance and confusion.

I then attacked the problem of transference with renewed vigour. I had noted that, in my view, my first analysis ended because the transference was not analyzed, nor was I supported in working on it; my second analysis ended on an enacted counter-transference. When I had developed sufficient skill and, I may say, had learned from my patients, I wrote the paper on transference which, to my great delight, was highly praised by Jung.

In that paper, I introduced the term syntonic counter-transference. At the time, analysts in London were asking the question: 'What do analysts really do?' It was often met with a silence which was justified and enshrined in the alchemical notion of the enclosed vessel which must be kept sealed lest the spirit escape. In London, supervision of students' cases was carried out and that did not have any bad effect on the analyses; indeed, the reverse seemed true. It might be that analysts' reticence was somehow due to the lack of a framework within which to talk about the patient's effect on them. If that effect could be made respectable, it might help – it was as primitive as that.

The idea of a syntonic counter-transference was derived from the discussions amongst colleagues and the hints that Jung had given: for instance, about induced psychosis in therapists treating psychotic patients and having dreams about them which were as relevant to the patients as to the therapist.

The next step was to try and interest analysts in technique, which, I believe, had been wrongly understood. I used to – and still do – have quite acrimonious arguments with Jo Wheelwright who, when he talked about his ingenious use of type theory, seemed to me the arch-exponent of technique whilst declaiming against it! Analysts, especially beginners, need to learn a technique and to digest it as much as is possible, throwing out what they can't use. So, I wrote 'Technique and counter-transference' (this volume, Chapter 8), which included a further development in that I used the concepts of projective and introjective identification to include unconscious interactions between analyst and patient.

The paper also indicated changing views on transference and counter-transference which occupied me more and more so that I came to realize that the unconscious processes involved were the equivalent of a dream or an active imagination. I therefore paid much less attention to night-time dreams, though I continued to be pleased if patients brought one along. I liked it best if it elucidated the transference and it usually did.

As I have already inferred, as a patient I had found painting pictures, dreaming, remembered mostly only if I wrote them down, holding 'internal' conversations with 'inner figures' all too easy and so I began by expecting patients all to do as I had done. Some could, but most could not and then I discovered transference analysis; it was the instrument that went far to solve the problem.

It took me a very long time to understand that, in many if not all of these transferences, the patients were trying to get me to analyze their childhood. That was galling because I wanted these transferences to develop as Jung had described them but they did not. Progress only became possible if their infantile nature was worked on. I got no help from Jungian analysts in this discovery and it was inferred – and I was occasionally told – that I was too Freudian.

Though I had read much Freud, it was not from him that I gained most help but from the writings of Melanie Klein, which were invaluable. My work with children was greatly helped, not so much by her theories as by the way she talked to her cases. I tried to use her methods and found that I could come into much closer contact with children even with my very fumbling efforts. In any case, I worked best in the inner world of children and here Klein was producing an extra dimension: she was the first psychoanalyst that entered into their inner life from a different vertex to Jung but many of her findings were analogous and some of her theories were identical. So I began to understand more and more about children and that helped with my adult patients. The essential nature of many, perhaps all transferences became increasingly apparent and I had the means of dealing with them. Only in the last few years did I include infancy with any confidence, thanks to the collaboration of Gianna Henry from Tavistock Clinic in London.

Much of what I do is reductive analysis and I am reproached for it. I can now say, having divested it of its plethora of reproaches, that it is beautiful and productive. So I am not abashed by derogatory comments about it. I believe that my conclusion is due to a differing meaning that attaches to the term: I have come to realize that the analysis of childhood, of infantile sexuality and violence, includes and assimilates aspects of patients which have been neglected by Jungian analysts and a good many others that I have known with interests in developmental lines and spiritual life. That made them unable to work in the area of sexuality and childhood at all adequately – they manifestly preferred dreams and fantasy so that their work became often seriously disembodied. That statement may suggest a reaction formation on my part but I do not think that the word 'beautiful' is to be explained and dismissed in that way because I am looking not for causes but for additional meanings of the person's 'inner world'. It is a completion which prevents fantasy from becoming fantastic, and in this way, idealizing processes are placed in their right proportion.

LISTENING AND LEARNING FROM PATIENTS

Listening to patients has to be acquired, but the idea and method of so doing was greatly facilitated by Jung's admonition not to know beforehand. Having scientific interests, I was struck when I read that Claude Bernard wrote that when he went into his laboratory he left his theories outside with his overcoat. An additional and more recent support for my ideas came from Bion who recommended that an analyst divest himself of memory, desire and understanding. I currently express my attitude to students as follows: I tell them that it is true that I and they are there to acquire knowledge but that generalizations have to be left outside the interview room and locked up in a 'filing-cabinet.' I do not deny that sometimes the knowledge in my filing-cabinet (and probably theirs also) gets out – that can be productive but too often it is used defensively: one feels safe at last because the interpretation is familiar, it is a 'stock interpretation.' When I do that, I suspect that I have stopped listening. If you listen, there is much less likelihood that your interventions will be 'stock' but will have that element of originality, spontaneity, and surprise which indicates not only listening but learning.

THE USE OF MYTHS

Though I have spent much time reading myths and enjoying them, and though I used to use them in analytic interviews, I now scarcely ever do so. A powerful element in this change has been that I gradually discovered, mostly from my own experience, how to create interpretations about the inner world. These were quite often mythical in nature and are in a sense original creations in as much as they grow out of my reflections on what a patient tells me – they often have no relation to reality and are mainly concerned with the interrelation between inner objects.

I will invent an intervention of this kind; it is like one that I have given but have somewhat idealized it for the sake of clarity. Suppose a patient has a mass of fragmentary thoughts in his head which he can't use and he complains that he gets nothing from his analyst. I will interpret as follows: he feels helpless like a baby when there is no breast. The absent breast is felt, owing to his hunger, to be a bad breast inside him and he tries to convert that into thoughts which fragment because they get attacked as representations of the bad breast. I would probably not say any more but subsequently I add that the bad breast became violent at the attempted transformation and squirted sperm-thoughts into his mind, thereby disorganizing what was being arranged by creating too many.

I will now refer to my filing-cabinet: (1) The aspiring element makes me think of Prometheus (my patient is a forethinker with gifts he can not realize). (2) The trickster archetype. Much of this is contained in my interpretations. (3) From Alchemy, a quotation: 'What is below is like what is above, that the miracle of the one thing may be accomplished.' (4) Bion: no breast equals a bad breast inside. One way of evacuating this is to create thoughts which mitigate pain. (5) Bion: attacks on linkage of thoughts. (6) The Kundalini Yoga.

From this list of headings which were immediate associations, I could now add many more so that it seems perhaps inappropriate even to make it. I only do so because I want to illustrate why I do not bring that material directly into the analysis. Nevertheless, all that and much more has, I think, to be digested before I could make the interpretations (somewhat idealized) that I did.

NOTE

1 This piece was a contribution to a volume *Jungian Analysts: Their Visions and Vulnerabilities* (Spiegelman, 1988), in which the contributors were asked to describe how they do analysis. The papers were responded to by Marvin Spiegelman and Joe McNair (eds).

Chapter 18

Fordham's rejoinder to Spiegelman's comments (1988)[1]

I want first to thank Spiegelman for his appreciative comments of my sketchy essay; it is condensed and could lead to unnecessary confusion, some of which I will try to dispel now.

1 I believe that I could make out a case for mutuality and the conjunctio lying near the centre of my analyses. That was suggested, I think, in a paper called 'Technique and counter-transference,' although I did not there use either term. I would not implement my experience in the way Spiegelman illustrates his – one must allow, however, for variations in the styles and idioms of expression from analyst to analyst. A clear difference between Spiegelman and myself is that I do not give raw emotional responses, when I have one, which is not often, but transform them into an interpretation.

2 As to the truth of an interpretation: I assume that the aim of any analysis is to arrive at the truth and so any interpretation I give is intended to serve that end.

My interpretation given at the end of my paper is liable to create more incredulity than is necessary because the context is omitted. I will add some of that: my patient had been in analysis for over ten years – nine years with another analyst. Other attempts to understand his communication had signally failed. In addition, I have not made it clear that months of work together was directed more specifically to try and understand what it was all about. Neither are recorded because I do not know how to compress it into reasonable space, nor is my memory good enough to record sufficient detail. I will, however, mention a feature of our work which was influential: once out of my room, interpretations became useful and he could benefit from many of them. The presence or absence of my body was therefore important. In addition, we had found that interpretive reconstructions about infancy in other contexts were meaningful whereas others were not.

3 The psychoanalytic attitude and method: a difficult question to answer, largely because psychoanalysts are too often bogies to criticize and not psychoanalysts as they are. I have, however, written more at length about how I conceive the analytic attitude and I fancy that some psychoanalysts would not

disagree much. I cannot decide whether Spiegelman wants to be 'brought down' or not! [Spiegelman: to the body, yes! Psychoanalytically, no!]

4 There are some phrases that grate. I am not happy with the idea that I 'do' childhood. I analyze patients and when data arise that require the understanding I have gained, and that is not only about childhood and infancy, I use it. I cannot agree that I have come up with an archetype. I have gained knowledge about development. I would regard my original work under the heading of a historical study. In that study, archetypes emerge but there is more to history than archetypes.

Conclusion: I am not at all sure how much Spiegelman and I disagree essentially – I suspect not much. The difference is more in the matter of how our rather different special knowledge is implemented. I hope neither of us thinks there is only one way to analyze patients and I would like to point out that I am not uninterested in religion whilst I hope he is not uninterested in childhood and infancy.

NOTE

1 Spiegelman claimed that Fordham's interpretation was based on a myth of mother–infant interaction, and that other myths could be used. He describes his own myth as being that of the "conjunctio" and mutuality, which is based on the analyst disclosing his/her own states, and hence interpreting in a participatory way, rather than from an exterior position. Spiegelman writes that his own bridge was to various religions rather than psychoanalysis, and his embodiment came through Reichian therapy (ed.).

Chapter 19

The supposed limits of interpretation (1991)

INTRODUCTION

My point of departure for this paper is the assertion that interpretations become of no use when primitive emotional states emerge, as Spiegelman (see Chapters 17 and 18) and Schwartz-Salant (1989) maintain. This, it is said, takes place in borderline or psychotic cases, or in relatively normal subjects who have reached archetypal layers of the mind. Then a change of tactics is indicated. It is a proposition reminiscent of Jung's own practice where he changed from reductive analysis to the hermeneutic, synthetic method via an interpretation on the subjective plane, and is probably derived from it without being identical.

I shall maintain that such an essential feature of analytic practice need not be abandoned just because an impasse has been arrived at, but that the nature, meaning, and effect of the interpretations being used need examining carefully.

The assertions have a psychotherapeutic ring and I will, therefore, differentiate a therapist from an analyst as follows: a therapist has a therapeutic goal controlling his activities, which may be anything from the removal of symptoms to an alteration of character in a desirable direction, such as fostering greater adaptation, increasing consciousness, and so forth. An analyst, though not indifferent to 'improvements' in his patient, is primarily concerned to define, in the simplest terms possible, the patient's state of mind in relation to himself. He does his best not to have goals for his patient but, by sustaining his analytic attitude, he lets the patient define his own goals. I consider the method of Spiegelman and Schwartz-Salant to be psychotherapeutic, without, as is sometimes done, implying that this is a derogatory thought. After all, Jung's papers in Volume 16 of the *Collected Works* are all, with the exception of the 'Psychology of the transference', concerned with psychotherapy (Jung, 1946).

I must mention, as it is not made clear by these authors, what is meant by an interpretation. I shall assume that for them it aims at conveying knowledge about material produced by the patient with which the analyst is familiar. From that vantage point, the analyst might have said: 'The interpretations that I know about seem to have ceased to have any effect and I am unable to conceive any other one that is effective.' Then it would be possible to study the material which the analyst could not interpret effectively in order to see whether some other interpretation might have produced a desirable result – a procedure adopted by Rosenfeld (1988) in his book *Impasse and Interpretation*, with which I am in substantial agreement. But when that does not seem possible, the statement 'interpretations are of no use' would then be final, beyond dispute, almost as if some undesirable object (presumably the method of interpretation) has at last been got rid of. Now the analyst could turn into a therapist and break the impasse by telling the patient about how he feels: for instance, he may confess that he is sexually aroused, though he will not act on his impulse, or that the material produced by the patient terrifies him.

The procedure is said to be good because the therapist can now be 'open' to the patient, though that does not appear in fact to be the case; indeed it is quite the reverse, since the analyst intrudes his own undigested emotions and feelings. It also suggests that interpretations represent some kind of closure, a *claustrum* in which analyst and patient were in danger of becoming trapped.

In his paper on sexual acting out, Schwartz-Salant (1984) discusses Mary, a schizoid personality. After four years of analysis he 'recognised her deep spiritual connection' (p. 15). Somewhat surprisingly she was then able to be frankly angry with him. Two months later there followed a revelation that 'my brother always put me down, always humiliated me'. Schwartz-Salant 'felt a new kind of clarity; I intuitively understood how her ego split. There is a union between one part of her ego and the spirit; the two of them are in a distant connection, far from the here and now. Then there is another union, also split off, between another part of her ego and her brother who represents an inner persecuting force' (p. 15). Note the abstractness of the interpretation, presumably made in that form so as not to offend her 'deep spiritual connection', though what the patient describes is a state of affairs during development which is concerned with establishing sexual identity.

After further work 'trying to sort out projections and reality' (p. 16), with presumably a good deal of mutual expression about how analyst and patient experienced each other, the nub of the matter emerges:

> At this point something unusual happened. I was aware of the incestuous link she had with her brother. I experienced an erotic energy field between us. She also experienced it. As we both felt this energy, which seemed like something between us, my consciousness lowered a bit and, just as in active imagination, I saw a shimmering image, which partook of both of us, move upwards from where it was near the ground. I told her this. She said, "Yes, I also see it, but I am afraid of it." I continued to share what I saw and experienced, I saw the image between us as white; she saw it as a kind of fluid which had a center. She said that she knew that if she descended into her body it would be too intense, that she was afraid. She stated that she now felt I was her friend, that it felt like an I–Thou relationship, and that she had never had such an experience before with anyone. She told me that she was afraid and felt herself slipping away. I responded that she needed only to embody more, only to come

down into her body. A feeling of timelessness pervaded; I did not know if one minute or twenty had passed.

(p. 16)

An account of impressive changes follows and an extensive amplification from the *Rosarium Philosophorum* as interpreted by Jung in his 'Psychology of the Transference' (Jung, 1946). Schwartz-Salant also introduces the concepts of liminality (to indicate the very concrete nature of the material), *communitas* (meaning the sense of community in relationships), and the subtle body (an amalgam of body and spirit), in addition to the main focus on the *conjunctio*. Later, he notes again his patient's need to come down into her body and states that, 'Reductive analysis was not called for at this time' (p. 23). I would maintain that was just what she did need, that is, as part of the work necessary when reclaiming the body as an essential source of spiritual experience. Schwartz-Salant describes a complex situation made more so by his confession, presumably in the interests of *communitas*, and justified by the idea that archetypal layers, that is, the common basis of human experience, had been reached.

I propose now to sketch out how it might have been possible to help Mary to become more embodied, especially as Schwartz-Salant considers it desirable. I assume that, since he is working in the field of incest, sexual congress could take place only if analyst and patient split so as to render the taboo ineffective. As we learn that it did not take place and the check on it was conscious, it would have been possible to begin thinking about the material presented in an embodied way, noting that the only mention of the body was 'the pull to engage in sexual intercourse'. Apart from that the account is essentially disembodied by both of them, so I will attempt to embody it in a fanciful way. First of all it appears that Schwartz-Salant is excited by the patient's breast, the white object which ascends. This is confirmed by his extensive regression with disturbances in his time sense and consequent disorientation, that is, to a period before time and space are finally established in the infant mind. On the other hand, Mary experiences a fluid which has a centre, that is, vaginal excitement with a penis inside, followed by a sense of friendly union, then fear and drifting away. Is not that because her genital excitement had not been recognised and she had had an orgasm (the 'drifting away')?

I do not want to depreciate the therapeutic value of Schwartz-Salant's procedure nor the extensive discussions on alchemical and anthropological data which follow. They are interesting, but if he wants to help his patient to become more embodied I think he misses an opportunity for so doing because of them. All he can do is to give Mary a generalised injunction to come down into her body. Such injunctions tend to foster repression by being taken as, at best, a reproach and, at worst, a condemnation of her present state. Such a proposition is not impossible in the case of Mary, for we learn that she experienced Schwartz-Salant as a '"kind of judge, a Hades type of judge". She explained that when she inwardly begins to feel young and has the experience of her inner child I [Schwartz-Salant] am critical of this child, especially when she presents problems with relationships' (p. 16).

A simpler form of acting on an identification is given by Spiegelman (this volume, Chapter 18). Considering those patients who complain that the analyst's interventions are no use and give him nothing, he states that he might say to such a patient: 'As you say that I give you nothing, I feel as if I were a mother with empty breasts, and feel hurt and guilty. No matter how I try I cannot satisfy you. How does my reaction affect you?' He considers that this way of proceeding 'is participatory rather than from the "outside"'.

It is considerations such as these that stimulated me to define more clearly not so much what an interpretation consists of, though that is important, but how it can be arrived at in a way that is essentially participatory, how it fosters *communitas*, and involves a conjunction through the action of projective identification.

First of all it is necessary to attempt a more detailed definition of an interpretation and distinguish it from other interventions by analysts or therapists. As regards the interventions of a therapist it is much easier to say what it is not. For instance, it is not an interpretation if he asks a question, or if he asks a patient to say more about a subject, or confronts a patient with something he has said, or voices some inconclusive ruminations. If he introduces psychological terms such as shadow, animus, anima, with reference to a figure in a dream or a fantasy, that only names or locates an object. There is another form of communication which is translating, and naming can be a part of that. This form of communication is near to, but still is not an interpretation. For instance, symbols can be translated as follows: the sun or a lion can be translated as the father; or the sea as the great mother with her babies and penises inside her. In the case of Mary I translated the white object as the breast, and Mary's 'kind of fluid which had a centre' as her excited genital with a penis inside. Finally amplification, the evocation of parallels from various sources but especially from ethnology, provides material which can make interpretation easier. So what can be classed as an interpretation? Since I have discussed the subject of interpretations at length elsewhere (Fordham, 1978), I shall give only a short definition which will be sufficient for my purposes: an interpretation is composed of that part of the patient's unconscious digested and thought about by the analyst. The result is then communicated to the patient in such a way as to give meaning to the patient's material. To do this it must have a clear structure and contain a verb. It can be short or long, clumsy, beautiful, poetic, and the tones of voice can make it musical.

Next I want to consider how an interpretation which includes participation and primitive concrete layers of the mind (liminality) can be arrived at. When supervising students I urge them to do their best to lock up in a metaphorical filing cabinet all that they have learned during seminars, or read about in books, and approach the patient as if they knew nothing about him and had never seen him before, at the same time emptying their minds of all psychodynamic processes. They should attempt to do this every time they meet their patients. It is a rigorous requirement but can be increasingly achieved: many students know what I mean and even though they cannot succeed, they recognise the value of the attitude and so cultivate it. That is a practice which makes real openness to their patients possible. It is not a new idea, but it corresponds to Freud's free floating attention, Jung's admonition not to know beforehand, and Bion's idea that a psychoanalyst needs to divest himself of knowledge, memory, and desire. The object of this attitude is to ascertain the patient's mental and emotional state on any particular day; not what he has been like before nor what he may be like tomorrow. I would emphasise that it also puts the therapist in a position to be affected mentally and emotionally by his patient.

I have previously drawn attention to the unconscious effect of the patient upon the analyst and the need for the analyst to trust his own response to it for it is there that the process of digestion begins. The idea of projective identification gives greater precision to the underlying ingestion by the analyst. The process takes place in both analyst and patient, or, as it might better be described, both in them and between them. It is possible to experience only its effects and so its nature cannot at first be known. It is nonetheless the main and most intimate participation between the couple that takes place in any interview. Out of it an interpretation is distilled and then its effect will be noted and studied.

EXAMPLE ONE: DETECTING A PROJECTIVE IDENTIFICATION

A good-looking woman, beautifully dressed, who has been away for about a month, sits down and tells me what has been happening to her. She has been having good times with her family and friends, she has also been travelling in Europe and many people have commented upon what a good state of body and mind she was in. That had often been true, but behind the scenes were her fears and terrors which she kept only partly at bay with pills. Gradually this good account of herself changes and she retails how terrible her state is now – a lone woman in her late forties returning to her luxury flat in London with nobody to share it with her, no body to find lying beside her when she wakes in the morning. She has no lover to live with, no husband, no children, and no work that absorbs her interest. I privately reflect that if she is in a relatively good state with her friends and family why does she come back from abroad to her lonely life in England? I begin to think of explanations of various kinds but discard them as 'filing-cabinet' matter. The urgency of the 'terrible state' increases and I begin to experience something similar. When it becomes urgent, and to mitigate the tension, I find something to say, especially as the interview is drawing to a close. It is out of that urgency that I interpret as follows. I tell her that she has come to see me in the hope that I will experience her 'terrible state' emotionally. She does not yet feel that I do so but believes that, unless I do, there is no hope of my taking her fears away or transforming them. . . . Only if I am truly upset is there any hope. It is an interpretation that focuses only on the transference and does not include an explanation of how her need came about.

I can now refer to my filing-cabinet. I find references to the toilet breast (in psychic reality the infant did evacuate its excreta into the breast). I have references to the mother's beauty. She is said to be particularly beautiful and a much loved woman. She needed to have a happy family and could not tolerate the thought that her daughter's childhood was anything but happy. Once when my patient suggested that such was not the case, her mother was so upset that her father told his daughter not to say such things because her mother could not bear it. I can now hazard a further conjecture: that it would be impossible for that kind of mother to allow her baby such an experience, the baby who would consequently be left with the terror that she might poison and even destroy the breast, consequently, the infant had to conceal her urgent fantasy and split it off from the good parts of the self. That would account for why, in the present, her terrors are sometimes greatly enhanced when on her own for, to her infant self, absence means death of her loved parents and lovers and terror of her nameless self.

During the interview I could infer that I had such ideas at the back of my mind, but I would reject them because the patient did not give any indication that a more complete understanding was possible – she made only one reference to her mother in passing and that was to say she was becoming difficult in her old age.

The interpretation was thus a partial one, to which the patient responded by leaving the interview on her own initiative without trying to prolong it as she often does. The interpretation does not refer to the verbal content of her communications but to an unconscious content (a projective identification) which was operative in our relationship and was dominating the situation. Under such conditions the 'filing-cabinet' material would have been an intrusion though I anticipate that on another occasion the patient will produce material which will make something like it appropriate.

EXAMPLE TWO: THE USELESSNESS OF INTERPRETATIONS

I will now consider a case of a middle-aged man for whom the uselessness of interpretations was a prominent feature during several years of treatment. When he came to me, after a previous analysis that had lasted nine years, he soon started to mount his attack on analysis with such assertions as: 'I've had nine years of useless analysis, what is the use of analysis? It has not done me any good!' He seemed determined to undermine all my efforts to enlighten him by making general statements such as these. Later he became more specific: 'What is the use of that?' was one style, or, 'I do not understand what you are talking about!' was another, each theme being elaborated in various ways. Why then did he come with great regularity?

One day this same patient came into the room. He did not look in my direction but settled into the chair and said nothing. He looked half suspicious and half miserable. This procedure had often been repeated before and I had drawn his attention to what looked like a ritual and related it to the fact that I regularly filled my pipe at the same time; but no progress had been made except that it was related to his silence and to the idea that he needed me to start off the interview, even if he did not understand what I meant or even if my intervention was felt to be of no use.

After this I pursued my method of not knowing. Soon an infant observation came into my mind. A certain baby, from soon after birth, persistently whined and grizzled. In most other respects his relation to his mother seemed satisfactory. Feeding and nappy changes were well negotiated but the mother never talked to her baby. One day she handed him over to the observer and the infant whined and grizzled as usual till the observer started talking to him – and the whining and grizzling stopped. The mother, usually an observant and sensitive woman, noted what had happened and started talking to her baby; the whining behaviour disappeared though he could not have understood his mother's words. I tried a similar technique with my patient, reflecting that the important thing might be to talk never mind whether he understood. Then I remembered that my patient often said he did not understand what I said and that encouraged me. I regard this memory of mine as an amplification which led on to an interpretation as we shall see. The amplification was not communicated to the patient.

On this occasion I noticed that he soon began casting sidelong glances at me, so I told him that he wanted surreptitiously to look into my mind to try and discover what was in it today. He polished his glasses so I said that he did not feel sure that he was seeing correctly and wanted to be certain. He put on his glasses and looked out of the window at the garden, to which I responded by saying that he felt I was in not too bad a state but he preferred to look at something reliably pleasant. I got the impression that what I said did not cut too much ice with him, which is what I might have expected, so I told him that I was talking mostly to his infant self who could not be expected to make sense of my words while his rational self thought it was rubbish anyway. If I talked, however, I suggested, it temporarily relieved his pain and so enabled him to mobilise more mature parts of himself. The interview then became alive because a way had been found for more detailed interchanges centring round his sense of futility and of not understanding what I said; what had previously been vexing was now balanced by my special interest in the state of affairs before me.

If I saw him as an infant, why did I not talk baby language as a mother does? To do that, however, would have been a grave mistake. I had before me an adult man and was seeking to enlist his help in digesting the pain felt by another (infant) member of his inner world. It should be noted that I used my memory of the infant–mother observation only as a private amplification and did not identify myself with either the mother, as Spiegelman did, or with the infant, as Kohut appears to do, but used the memory to give significance to a number of observations. It will also be noted that I mobilised memories from past interviews to support my position, which seems contrary to my idea of the contents of my 'filing-cabinet'. But this is valuable and desirable once the emotional climate of the interview has been established.

Though work had been done on his sense of futility and impotence, more work was needed to enable him to discover that an adult part of himself (his father) had understood but denigrated what I said. The patient continued to express doubt about interpretations. It was later that I discovered how important it was that I talked and still later that, though he did not understand, it was essential for him to feel that I did talk to his baby self. Gradually he moved on to acknowledge the correctness of what I said. That was, however, a more polite way of disposing of me, though it did lead him on to respond and to make use of interpretations. None the less, it was necessary to emphasise firmly and persistently the deception in his apparent acquiescence till he gradually moved on to think about what I said and make use of it.

I was sure that this persistent negative transference was not the whole picture and he gave evidence of this by his regular attendance and the fact that he was never more than a few minutes late: furthermore, in a grudging way he came to admit that the interviews were not a complete waste of time. For instance, he acknowledged that he felt better for 'three-quarters of an hour' after meeting me and that I could also make him feel worse. Furthermore, his over-general assessment of our relationship was not in accord with my observations: it was possible to trace the effect of what I had said perhaps the next day, perhaps a week or a month afterwards.

DISCUSSION

In 1974 I proposed the idea that this kind of absolute defence was a defence of the self, in the sense of Jung's conception, and concluded that it was important for the analyst, or psychotherapist, not to be deterred but to maintain his analytic attitude, thus remaining consistent and in that sense reliable (this volume, Chapter 12). The case I used to illustrate, or I should rather say the case that became the source of, my thesis induced a painful hypochondriacal and delusional counter-transference which I succeeded in containing sufficiently. Nowadays that does not happen and I am more and more certain that my procedure is correct, for in this way the patient's conflict and pain is confronted and his battle to find space for his real self to obtain and develop a form is not given up. Why the change has taken place may be of interest: on the one hand, there is my personal development and, on the other, because of it I have become better at listening while my capacity to create interpretations out of material produced in an interview has increased. Concurrently, I have become more aware of how projective identification works. Thus I think I have found a way of extending the analytic process as far as I am concerned. Other analysts know this very well. I say this with the reservation that amongst psychoanalysts Kohut does not seem to have discovered it and that some psychoanalysts, following Freud, do not consider psychotic processes analysable.

What is the place of memories and explanations in all this? I do not regard either of them as central. During the period when my patient was denigrating interpretations it was known to both of us that his father used to relate his developing thoughts about stories he was writing to his son without any regard to his son's ideas – it was simply an extended monologue. The father, I was told, never appreciated any of his son's achievements; they were considerable, but were remorselessly criticised as worthless. It is tempting to identify with the son but I reserve judgement about the truth of this 'memory'. However, this memory had orientating value and suggested that he was, in his own way, doing to me what his father had done to him. That interpretation was made and rejected: 'All right so what!' Of course, a great deal about his past came to light, especially about his mother, a predominantly depressed woman with diabetes and periodic 'fits', either diabetic comas or concurrent epilepsy. Complex consequences of her recurrent state of mind and body were evident, but my patient felt that, though she knew how to look after his body, she could not respond to his mind. Thus his defence of the self was made even more essential since both parents in their different ways gave what he felt was either no recognition or inadequate recognition to what he was really like. By inference the archetype he struggled with was the androgyne – an important figure in Schwartz-Salant's discussion.

His daily life in its deplorable aspects was a regular feature of my patient's discourse. It is not, however, that part of his analysis to which I am drawing attention, but rather to a particular segment of it which, on a superficial assessment, seems to indicate that interpretations are useless and that some other procedure is called for. That is what I rebut because if the analyst decides to describe in personal terms the effect the patient is having on him then he risks identifying himself with his patient's delusion based on projective identification. It is that which needs to be worked on and the value within it discovered. In my patient's case it was an attempt to make a space in which his unconscious inner world could express itself, and through which he could find his true self.

Chapter 20

Rejoinder to Nathan Schwartz-Salant (1991)

It is gratifying to know that my essay on interpretation has produced such a rich response, but I find the result in Schwartz-Salant's case surprising in many respects. For instance, some of the things I say I do I am told that I do not do, and I have views that I cannot recognise as mine.

It was in 1947 that I postulated a primary self, a mystery without characteristics, a creative absence from which characteristics arose by the development of two opposite processes: deintegration and integration. It is true that this postulate was related to infancy but in the sense that infancy is the period in which patterns of behaviour, feelings, emotions, and thoughts are being built up to persist throughout life. It was in relation to that conception that I adopted Jung's notion of not knowing beforehand so as to make a space between analyst and patient for something to emerge between them. So I agree with the 'necessity for an essentially unknowable or transcendent dimension within the analytic endeavour, a dimension that can and needs to be experienced within a human relationship' (Schwartz-Salant, 1991, p. 347). Now, it appears, I do not recognise that, I do not empty my mind of knowledge, memory, and desire, and seem to know nothing about the imaginal realm or the sense of space between analyst and patient in which that realm emerges nor do I penetrate into the 'psychotic' layers of mind, and so on. Now I may not know enough about it but I have, up to now, certainly considered that all these areas of experience, including not knowing, and the essentially interactional field in analysis or psychotherapy, were those which I have, over the years, studied with particular attention.

With such a formidable indictment I can only assume that Schwartz-Salant is mentally constructing a model of an analyst who is a scientist in the grip of Cartesian methods of thought, because that gives him a jumping-off ground to expound on his own views and practices. I am somewhat confirmed in this because many of the features he describes and the criticisms he develops are those that I myself have been wont to make. Later, when he discusses my woman patient, his fanciful diatribe – I can only call it that – provides more evidence to make me think that I am on the right track. So I do not believe he is doing more than use me as an embodiment of that person.

It is true that I find his method of communication unnecessarily complicated and scholastic, and that one has to plough through too many quotations from various rather familiar sources. I am sure that the 'wisdom of the past', which Jung studied in such an illuminating way, is important, and I am not ignorant of what he did, but I do not get any indication that Schwartz-Salant's patient derived much value from it. I know, however, that amplification features prominently in much Jungian therapy and Schwartz-Salant may have assumed that it is so well known that no mention of it is necessary. I do believe, however, that it is important to know what he thinks its value is. As it stands it seems that he uses it to digest his experience with his patient.

Now it is experience with patients on which I have laid especial emphasis and not the application of models. I consider that Klein made a great leap forward in psychoanalysis but I do not think her idea of the paranoid-schizoid and depressive positions is more than an ideal construct. The two conditions do sometimes appear in clinical practice, but mostly they do not occur in pure culture but in partial or mixed states. Also, Winnicott's notions about the space between the mother and infant leaving room for transitional objects and transitional phenomena cannot be substantiated as a general phenomenon. I say this to show that I do not adhere to the model Klein built up: it is her discoveries and method that I value. It was, correspondingly, Winnicott's clinical acumen that I admired. Nonetheless it is known that I did much to introduce Klein, Winnicott, Bion, and others by showing how in many respects their findings were tantalisingly like Jung's. So I was called a Kleinian and told that the clinical method I espoused was due to my English empiricism; but I have a great respect for scientific empiricism and in this I am in line with Jung's claim to make use of its disciplines.

The main gist of Schwartz-Salant's argument, and of his useful descriptions of his experience, seems to be that there is an area where something more than rational thought is found: it is non-verbal and imaginal, and I do not doubt that.

I was further interested in his reference to the subtle body because I have speculated that the experience of small infants in relation to their own and their mothers' bodies, and to their insides, could shed light on that realm of experience.

It will not be surprising to your readers if I say that I do not get much out of Schwartz-Salant's essay, though I am glad to read that he has a much less rigid view of interpretations than the one I had come across among some Jungians. Our skill in this field has grown considerably and can, I believe, develop further since it is a valuable, but not the only, instrument for movement from O to K. That transformation, often and perhaps always, grows out of the space between analyst and patient.

At the same time I know that some patients, as a matter of survival, need to lead one from their false knowledge (–K?) in the direction of O. It is these patients that I suggest that Schwartz-Salant is studying.

Chapter 21

On not knowing beforehand (1993)

The subject of this discussion is derived from a phrase in Jung's essay on the transference. There he writes: 'Inseparable from the *persona* is the doctor's routine and his trick of knowing everything beforehand, which is one of the favourite props of the well-versed practitioner and of all infallible authority.' That, Jung contends, is impossible when it comes to psychotherapy because, sooner or later in any deep analysis, 'Doctor and patient . . . find themselves in a relationship founded on mutual unconsciousness' (Jung, 1946, p. 176).

That was written in 1946, as part of a criticism of using medical procedures in the conduct of psychotherapy. At that time was he finding it difficult to describe his stage of transformation which turned out to be a sort of non-method.

It was not that he found methods and techniques inapplicable, for he claimed to conduct psychotherapy according to the methods of Freudian or Adlerian psychology in suitable cases. He presumably used his theory of types to arrive at a decision; it will be remembered that he had classed Freud as an extravert and Adler as an introvert. But neither of these authorities had described adequately what he himself had evolved. It was not until 1961 that he made a step forward. He formulated his practice by the statement: 'I am unsystematic very much by intention' (Jung, 1962, p. 131) – that was said in the context of placing the individual at the centre of his practice; he continues: 'To my mind, in dealing with individuals, only individual understanding will do. We need a different language for every patient. In one analysis I can be heard talking the Adlerian dialect, in another the Freudian' (ibid.). His own dialect was not mentioned directly but it would seem to be a story-telling method imbued with his great knowledge of the symbolism inherent in myths. So it does not appear that he has divested himself of method as much as he sometimes claimed.

Jung also laid great stress on the importance of the analyst being involved personally with his patient, for he says that 'in any thoroughgoing analysis the whole personality of both patient and doctor is called into play' (ibid., p. 132). Yet in his first presentation of how the archetypes and individuation appeared in clinical practice he shows himself as a passive observer: 'I had', he writes, 'the privilege of being the only witness during the process of severance [of the transference]' (Jung, 1928, p. 134). It was a development based on archetypal processes, and it was not he that brought it about.

I have so far presented a paradox in Jung's psychotherapeutic practice, picking out some features of it which have particular interest for me. Without, I believe, being inaccurate, I have not included the width of his approach, nor his addition of his synthetic, hermeneutic method requiring an extensive knowledge of myth, legend, and religion. These developments were not analytic, but synthetic and transformative. Nonetheless he also claimed to conduct psychoanalyses he was greatly influenced by Freud, so I will now consider some significant indications that Freud left us and which I want to pick out.

In his paper, 'Notes upon a case of obsessional neurosis' (The rat man), we read: 'The true technique of psychoanalysis requires the physician to suppress his curiosity and leave the patient complete freedom in choosing the order in which topics shall succeed each other during the treatment. At the fourth session, accordingly, I received the patient with the question: "And how do you intend to proceed today?"' (Freud, 1909, p. 174). I believe Jung would not have disagreed with that. And what about the therapist being involved with the patient? That came into Freud's cognizance as the counter-transference especially, but it is also quite clear that his analytic procedure is also an involvement of a technical kind, implying a higher degree of objectivity than appears in Jung's practices, and markedly so in some of his followers.

Of course objectivity is important, but at one time it led, whether in fact or fantasy I can never be sure, to a picture of an analyst being only a projection screen, hardly intervening at all in the free flow of associations. If that be psychoanalysis, Freud did not practice it! Indeed in his early work he was quite directive, providing a brief outline on the nature of psychoanalysis or the nature of the unconscious. On one occasion he provided food for a patient who was hungry, and so on (his raising a fund for the Wolf Man does not come strictly into this category, for the patient was no longer a patient and had returned from Russia impoverished). But I think it is relevant and shows that Freud was human and not just a disembodied scientist without emotional involvement.

Jungians like to think of Jung's behaviour as contrasting strongly with the suppression of emotion and it can lead them into expressions which interfere with the development of the treatment – at least in my view. Some of them anathematize techniques in any form, including Joseph Wheelwright who was extraordinarily adept in applying type theory in his practice – according to my understanding he was the exponent of a technique, so I must conclude that the subject could become largely verbal.

It was in 1969 that I addressed the subject of technique in some detail and came to the conclusion that there were two interrelated communications going on between patient and analyst: the one was conscious, the other unconscious. The conscious communication came from the analyst's prior knowledge and experience; this could be developed into a method of treatment which could be applied across the board to a class of cases. Such appears to have been the case when Jung treated cases according to Freudian or Adlerian principles, and of course much psychotherapy is conducted in an analogous fashion. The other was more subtle and depended on the projective identifications that went on unconsciously between analyst and patient. That formulation was a step on the way to revising the notion of a syntonic counter-transference in which the analyst would find within himself alien matter which referred to the patient and only marginally to him. When detected, the introjection could become a means of gaining information. The revision in my essay was to make the process two-sided: the analyst could gain information about the patient through projective identification and so could the patient. That made my formulation nearer to Jung's contention that the analyst is as much in the analysis as the patient; I could not agree, however, that the involvement was symmetrical: through his own personal analysis, his training and subsequent experience, the therapist is in a better position than the patient to appreciate what is going on, while the matter to be dealt with comes almost entirely from the patient who is consequently more absorbed in himself.

In all this I was attempting to recognize the actions of method and non-method. Projective identification, because it is an unconscious activity, could not be regarded as a method – so it is in this part of the interaction that analyst and patient are both involved. Is there, however, a method of using the information it provides? That is what I cannot decide, but it is certainly not a technique in the sense that is currently used; it is rather a process that goes on when the therapist is digesting the projective identification. It is not easy to describe what I mean by 'digesting the projection' because the process is essentially unconscious, though some sense of influence can be discerned, just as one can sense a change in body feeling after eating food. At this point it is desirable to trust one's unconscious and wait further developments, rather than fall back on technical, i.e. conscious, knowledge. It is out of that emergent experience that a communication by the analyst, relevant to the patient, can develop, because it relates immediately to the patient's emotional experience. In making this hypothesis I was asserting that analyst and patient were always in some sense involved in 'mutual unconsciousness', though not, I think, in the radical sense that Jung meant it. That would occur less regularly.

That was about as far as I had got in 1969. Since then I have studied 'not knowing beforehand' as a way of investigating mutual projective identifications. I focused on single interviews. I considered what might happen if, each time I met a patient, I tried to perceive him as if I had never seen him before and had no knowledge of him; attempting to do this would mean that I would have to develop an attitude of, as Bion puts it, eschewing knowledge, memory, and desire. It might be relatively easy or it might be difficult. When the attitude can easily be sustained there is nothing that can be said about it. It is when the difficulty is greater that understanding can be increased.

So let us consider a case where I managed to sustain this attitude sufficiently but had to be very much on the alert to do so. A distinguished-looking young woman came to my consulting-room door that is made of glass. She tapped on the door, entered and lay down comfortably on the couch, looking at me with pleasant eyes. In order to be seen, I did not sit right behind her. Her look was friendly and affectionate.

That event was pleasing and I was surprised since it had not taken place before (intrusion of a memory), which I knew to be true (a piece of knowledge), and I wanted to enjoy the experience of her being like that (intrusion of desire). I had therefore memories, knowledge, and desires and these had to be eschewed if I was to proceed according to my procedure of 'not knowing beforehand'. I succeeded in blocking off all that material but I had to be very alert to do so, for I could soon have had enough material to make quite a number of interpretations and so could have relieved myself of the effort involved in not knowing. My point is that if I had started intervening I would have shaped the interview myself instead of leaving the patient to do so. It turned out that none of my memories, knowledge, or desires were relevant to the shape of the interview as she developed it.

There are a number of questions arising from this description. First of all you may say: well, is that not what we all do? In that case all that I have done is to put into words a general procedure – a piece of what may be called microanalysis hardly worth mentioning. Yet, if you proceed thus, I consider that you must have learned to do so. That was so in my case at least, and I think it is so for others. I introduce the idea to students as follows: when you meet your patient, each time I want you to imagine that you have a mental filing-cabinet; in it you have records of all that you have learned from seminars, from other discussions and from previous experiences. Be careful to lock up its contents so that they are not available for use, and approach your patient as though you had never met him before. Now it is very rare for a candidate to implement such an idea, so I usually add that I have outlined an ideal to be approximated to. I believe that many students want to have a blueprint of how to behave and what to say to the patient (usually what interpretation to make), so that they can develop a therapeutic strategy which they can know beforehand and apply. If they can do this, then they may feel that they are getting what they came to training for and are spared the often quite severe bewilderment that the not knowing behaviour, which I am advocating, can evoke. The desire for a blueprint or model with which to work is not illegitimate, but that should develop on each occasion out of the relation to the patient on any particular day, and not out of the filing-cabinet material: as Jung put it, the therapist needs a new theory for every patient. In my ideal construction I wanted to extend that to each interview – the new theory being expressed in one or more interpretations.

I will not pursue these thoughts further, but turn to the next question: what happens to the material I have dismissed, and does it not influence my attitude to the patient unconsciously? In the case of the patient I have cited, as far as I could ascertain, it did not influence the way the interview progressed, but I thought afterwards about what would have come into my mind: I had wanted to comment on my experience, and that might have then led me to tell her I thought that she was glad to come because her previous interview had gone so well and had increased her capacity to love and trust me, or that she had found herself able to manage some situation better than before, attributing that to the valuable interview the previous day. Thus I might have built up an interpretation. There are two points about this: first of all, my filing-cabinet material had not been repressed but had gone into a space in my mind; secondly, it was accessible for me to work on later and find that I had a wish to interpret which, in my judgement, would have been intrusive.

Now it is evident that my formula about not knowing beforehand does not mean that during my interview I get to know enough about a patient to make a needed interpretation without drawing on previous experience and knowledge. I am not an especially passive analyst but the memories, knowledge, and desires that, so to speak, arrive are geared to the present and, by not knowing at the start, I can more easily listen with the third ear, as Theodor Reik so beautifully expressed it, to what is unconscious and not being expressed. It is that form of listening that gives access to the unconscious processes going on during the interview and provides material to which memory and knowledge can be applied.

Now I will turn to another example. A middle-aged man came in and lay on the couch. He lay still and said nothing. The silence continued for about forty-five minutes, until the interview was drawing to a close. During this period I had begun to experience a sense that the silence was numinous, i.e. highly significant, so just before he left I told him that his silence had been important because it was the best means he had for conveying his experience to me. He was, I think, surprised and went out giving me a suspicious sidelong glance. Looking backwards, it seems that after that interview silences ceased to be problematic to both of us.

Now I knew a great deal about this patient, more than about the first case, and silences had taken place before. We had discovered that he often did not speak because there were so many thoughts racing through his mind that he could not decide which of them to begin with, or by the time he had fixed on one he had forgotten it because another had taken its place. Then there were the more usual reasons, such as that his thoughts were too fragmentary or not worth communicating, or too personal and embarrassing, etc. I had discovered that sometimes, if I said something – it did not seem to matter what – he could begin to talk. These features had all been worked on with varying results and some silences could be related to pre-verbal mental states. I have mentioned this previous knowledge because none of it came into the interview and if it had started to do so I would, I believe, have eradicated it. It is clear that I arrived at a bit of knowledge, but memory did not enter into its formulation; it remains to consider desire. Towards the end of the interview I felt a certain inner pressure that I would not have relieved if I had not found a way of dispelling it; it was then that my knowledge could become conscious and be communicated. Thus a desire grew up during the interview.

It is now apparent that not knowing beforehand can be considered as a starting point, so that memories, knowledge, and desires will develop in the therapist during any particular interview. I would emphasize that they develop and are not imposed. That raises the interesting question of why a therapist intervenes at all. We like to think we do so in the interest of the patient, to help him overcome a resistance which is no longer serviceable, and so enable him to become conscious of unconscious experience of one sort or another. In this way we hope to enrich the person's life by clearing away the debris from the past and opening up new possibilities for the future. That leaves out of account any desire other than to benefit the patient, but I think that the need to intervene can be of a different order: it can arise from the urgent need of the analyst to expel from himself an almost intolerable experience. Let me give an example which will probably be familiar to you: A well-dressed woman, looking slightly haggard, began at once to say that her life was intolerable. She hated her work, she hated London, she did not sleep well, in the morning she woke up terrified, could not get out of bed without taking pills and then she could hardly eat anything. She had ceased to look after her rather beautiful flat, she had lost her lover and could not bear living alone and so on. I listened attentively but could not feel any compassion for her. Indeed, I found the way she went on nearly intolerable. There was no gap in the diatribe till late in the session when I disgorged the following statement: 'You are needing to force me to feel as you do because if I do not then there is no hope.' She left a minute or two early and I felt relieved. I was able to analyze this situation again in some detail afterwards and I mention it, as I have said, because I think my understanding grew out of my own desire to disgorge the venom which I could not digest satisfactorily. It is an extreme example but I believe that, in less extreme ways, it is quite common. It is notable that analysts vary considerably in the amount they communicate, and in their accounts there is often no indication of how the patient responded. John Wisdom once wrote a paper on the subject, because he gained the impression that it was enough for the interpretation to have been made. He developed very exacting criteria for telling whether the interpretation had produced the desired effect or not.

Then there are some observations from the supervision of analysts and trainees. When candidates start taking cases for analysis, they want to be good trainees and make interpretations – and, often with more or less trepidation, they start to do so. As supervisor I think some are useful, others are odd, while a few strike one as probably injurious. I am tempted to suggest alternatives but it may be important not to criticize and I am frequently surprised at how much benefit the patients derive, children, particularly, get along quite well. So I have concluded that many analysts need to put a certain amount of their own need into their interventions – they have certain desires which need a varying amount of satisfaction and patients can be quite tolerant of it. Thus some interpretations are made because of the analyst's need to do so. That does not apply only to trainees.

I do not mean that if an analyst has a desire he should always dismiss it. For instance, I had a patient who was regressing and it alarmed me. I therefore enquired about her real day-to-day life. The result was a very competent and well organized account. It all came in a most reassuring way and my anxiety was allayed. That led on to considering the way she communicated. I need not go into the details, but it came out that she had a way, if she knew what was wanted, of pressing a mental button and then what was required poured out of her almost automatically. Subsequently I enquired about this, and she related how, when a child, she did not talk in social situations, for she had been criticized and attacked for it. She later learned to talk as she did to me. I informed her that she seemed to respond in this way to my real anxiety, as must also have been the case when she was a child – her silences having made the adults anxious. I want to point out that the whole structure of the interview was determined by my anxious concern. This is wrong if considered in the light of my ideal, which includes the idea that the form of an interview should be constructed by the patient. Divesting oneself of knowledge, memory, and desire aims to make a space in which that can happen, but I have my reservations.

It will now be quite evident that, though an analyst may divest himself of memory, desire, and knowledge at the start, filing-cabinet material will be used, but only that which is tailored to the material in hand. Sometimes, however, he may make an interpretation quite quickly so that he may doubt whether he may not have known beforehand.

A middle-aged man came in and lay down on the couch. There was a short silence. Then, 'There is nothing to say; it is all the same as before,' he remarks. I reply, 'We both know that is an attack on analysis,' a pause follows, and then I add: 'But you did collaborate in saying what was in your mind.' There was no verbal confirmation or otherwise, but he seemed more comfortable and the interview developed satisfactorily. It appears that the interpretation contains a memory concealed in the statement 'we both know'. Yet I had engaged the ambivalence of his mood today, and one might also include the many occasions when he had begun the interview in this way.

I do not wish to enter further into the many problems which holding up the ideal of not knowing beforehand raises, for they do not invalidate the basic intention: to build up the interview out of the unconscious interchange between patient and analyst, so that as little as possible is imposed by the analyst.

I will now consider contrasting interviews with a patient.

INTERVIEW 1

A woman entered looking pale and wan. She put two envelopes on the desk and lay down. I knew that these were cash payments, and I had noticed the two envelopes before: one had contained £20 notes, the other £50. I had been struck by this and, unlike my usual behaviour, enquired about the envelopes and their contents, mentioning the differing notes in each envelope. I should mention here that I liked being paid in cash, because it reduced the number of times I had to go to the bank. The patient broke down in tears, and said 'Why am I always misunderstood?' She curled up on the couch, but sitting up. She repeated the words several times, weeping and rocking her body about in great distress. Now I knew about such regressions and attempted to bring her out of it by insisting that she had felt misunderstood because of my enquiry. After much work she said it was not the differing notes that were important, but separating the money paid by her from that which her father contributed. I reached for the envelopes: each contained £50 notes, one lot new and the other lot old and dirty notes. I acknowledged my factual error. She said she had carefully collected the clean money during the month but acknowledged that I had not really misunderstood, though she thought I was fishing for infantile behaviour. After that she lay down, but no serious analytic work was possible in that interview.

INTERVIEW 2

The next interview was all about work and how she hated working under compulsion. She had to complete a report in two weeks. There was quite interesting further material which I eventually interpreted, using largely, but not entirely, my filing-cabinet.

INTERVIEW 3

She started by saying that, while motoring up to London, the penny had dropped about my interpretation and she poured out many relevant memories from her childhood.

My point in retailing these interviews is to show, first, how knowing beforehand can obstruct the analytic work (interview 1) so that an interview becomes absorbed in repairing the damage, and, second, that filing-cabinet material can be used profitably once it can be related to the here and now. But ideally one aims to relate to the patient without reference to the filing-cabinet, and, having understood the content of the interview, relate it to earlier states, etc., recorded in the filing-cabinet. In practice this ideal can often be reached.

I can now relinquish the metaphor of the filing-cabinet, which is unlike real filing-cabinets in that it is quite permeable, is receiving messages from the patient all the time, and is learning from the projective identifications made, digesting them and providing material for interpretation. In my exposition I have used a metaphor, for the sake of simplicity, in making a point which I regard as important but I do not overlook the complexity of analyst–patient interaction (cf. Fordham, previous writings but especially 1969 and this volume, Chapter 15).

SUMMARY

This paper starts from recommendations of Freud and Jung on the desirable attitudes of analysts to their patients, and especially openmindedness which I have named 'not knowing beforehand'. I use the metaphor of a filing-cabinet to illustrate how to empty one's mind and, so to speak, lock up one's knowledge, memory, and desires in that filing-cabinet. That gives space for the patient to structure his interview. I illustrate how knowing beforehand can disrupt an interview and how 'filing-cabinet material' will get used when tailored to the interview structure. The metaphor is used for the sake of simplicity. It does not include the complexity of the analytical dialectic.

Sources

Chapter 1 'Notes on the transference', in Fordham, M., *New Developments in Analytical Psychology*, 1957. Reprinted in M. Fordham, R. Gordon, J. Hubback and K. Lambert (eds), *Technique in Jungian Analysis*, 1974.

Chapter 2 'Counter-transference', *British Journal of Medical Psychology*, 33, 1, 1960. Reprinted in M. Fordham, R. Gordon, J. Hubback and K. Lambert (eds), *Technique in Jungian Analysis*, 1974.

Chapter 3 'Suggestions towards a theory of supervision', in Symposium on Training, *Journal of Analytical Psychology*, 6, 2, 1961.

Chapter 3 'Reply to Dr Edinger', in Symposium on Training, *Journal of Analytical Psychology*, 6, 2, 1961.

Chapter 5 'Comment on James Hillman's papers', in Symposium on Training, *Journal of Analytical Psychology*, 7, 1, 1962.

Chapter 6 'Problems of a training analyst', previously unpublished paper presented to the Society of Analytical Psychology.

Chapter 7 'Reflections on training analysis', in J. Wheelwright (ed.), *The Analytic Process: Aims, Analysis, Training*, 1968. Reprinted in *Journal of Analytical Psychology*, 15, 1, 1970.

Chapter 8 'Technique and countertransference', *Journal of Analytical Psychology*, 14, 2, 1969. Reprinted in M. Fordham, R. Gordon, J. Hubback and K. Lambert (eds), *Technique in Jungian Analysis*, 1974.

Chapter 9 'Reply to Plaut's "Comment"', *Journal of Analytical Psychology*, 15, 2, 1970. Reprinted in M. Fordham, R. Gordon, J. Hubback and K. Lambert (eds), *Technique in Jungian Analysis*, 1974.

Chapter 10 'The interrelation between the patient and the therapist', *Journal of Analytical Psychology*, 17, 2, 1972.

Chapter 11 'Jung's concept of the transference', *Journal of Analytical Psychology*, 19, 1, 1974.

Chapter 12 'Defences of the self', *Journal of Analytical Psychology*, 19, 2, 1974. Revised in Fordham, M., *Explorations into the Self*, 1985. The revised version is reproduced here.

Chapter 13 'Analyst–patient interaction', presented to the British Psycho-analytical Society, 19 March, 1975. Previously unpublished.

Chapter 14 'Discussion of Thomas B. Kirsch, "The practice of multiple analysis in analytical psychology"', *Contemporary Psychoanalysis*, 12, 2, 1976.

Chapter 15 'Analytical psychology and countertransference', in *Contemporary Psychoanalysis*, 15, 4, 1979. Also in L. Epstein and A.H. Feiner (eds) *Counter-transference: The Therapist's Contribution to Treatment*, 1979.

Chapter 16 'Contribution to Symposium "How do I assess progress in supervision?"', *Journal of Analytical Psychology*, 27, 2, 1982.
Chapter 17 'How I do analysis', in *Jungian Analysts: Their Visions and Vulnerabilities*, J. Spiegelman (ed.), 1988.
Chapter 18 'Fordham's Rejoinder to Spiegelman', in *Jungian Analysts: Their Visions and Vulnerabilities*, J. Spiegelman (ed.), 1988.
Chapter 19 'The supposed limits of interpretation', *Journal of Analytical Psychology*, 36, 2, 1991.
Chapter 20 'Rejoinder to Nathan Schwartz-Salant', *Journal of Analytical Psychology*, 36, 1991.
Chapter 21 'On not knowing beforehand', *Journal of Analytical Psychology*, 38, 1993.

Bibliography

All books published in London, unless otherwise stated.

Adler, G. (1955) 'On the archetypal content of transference', in *Report of the International Congress of Psychotherapy, Zürich 1954*, Basle/New York: Klager.
—— (1961) *The Living Symbol*, Routledge.
Anon. (1963) 'Report of the 2nd International Congress of Analytical Psychology', *Journal of Analytical Psychology*, 8, 2.
Balint, M. (1968) *The Basic Fault*, Tavistock (Routledge, 1989).
Bash, K. W. (1962) 'Training and psychopathology', *Journal of Analytical Psychology*, 7, 2.
Baynes, H. G. (1950) 'Freud versus Jung', in *Analytical Psychology and the English Mind*, Methuen.
—— (1955) *The Mythology of the Soul*, Routledge.
Bion, W. R. (1955) 'The language of a schizophrenic', in *New Directions in Psychoanalysis*, Klein, Hyman and Money-Kyrle (eds), Tavistock, Maresfield Library (Karnac, 1985).
Davidson, D. (1966) 'Transference as a form of active imagination', *Journal of Analytical Psychology* 11, 2.
—— (1986) 'The child analytic training, 1960–1985: the first quarter century', *Journal of Analytical Psychology*, 31, 3.
Edinger, E. F. (1961) 'Comment', *Journal of Analytical Psychology*, 6, 2.
Ellenberger, H. F. (1970) *The Discovery of the Unconscious*, New York: Basic Books.
Emch, M. (1955) 'The social context of supervision', *International Journal of Psychoanalysis*, 36, 4 and 5.
Fairbairn, W. R. D. (1952) *Psychoanalytic Studies of the Personality*, Tavistock (Routledge, 1990).
Federn, P. F. (1953) *Ego Psychology and the Psychoses*, Imago. (Maresfield Library: Karnac, 1977).
Fenichel, O. (1945) *The Psychoanalytic Theory of Neurosis*, Routledge & Kegan Paul (Routledge, 1990).
Fordham, F. (1969) 'Some views on individuation', *Journal of Analytical Psychology*, 14, 1.
Fordham, M. (1954) 'Chairman's address, AGM, Society of Analytical Psychology', unpublished.
—— (1956) 'Active imagination and imaginative activity', *Journal of Analytical Psychology*, 1, 2.
—— (1957) *New Developments in Analytical Psychology*, Routledge & Kegan Paul.
—— (1957a) 'The origins of the ego in childhood', in *New Developments in Analytical Psychology*, Fordham, Routledge & Kegan Paul.

—— (1957b) 'Note on the significance of archetypes for the transference in childhood', in *New Developments in Analytical Psychology*, Routledge & Kegan Paul.
—— (1958) *The Objective Psyche*, Routledge & Kegan Paul.
—— (1961) 'C. G. Jung, Obituary', *British Journal of Medical Psychology*, 34, 3/4.
—— (1964) 'The ego and self in analytic practice', *Journal of Psychology* (Lahore), 1, 1.
—— (1965) 'The importance of analysing childhood for the assimilation of the shadow', *Journal of Analytical Psychology*, 10, 1.
—— (1968) 'Review of Henderson, J. L. *Thresholds of Initiation*', *Journal of Analytical Psychology*, 13, 2.
—— (1968a) 'Individuation in childhood', in *The Reality of the Psyche*, J. Wheelwright, (ed.), New York: Putnams.
—— (1969) *Children as Individuals*, Hodder & Stoughton.
—— (1975) 'Memories and thoughts about C. G. Jung', *Journal of Analytical Psychology* 20, 2.
—— (1976) *The Self and Autism*, Library of Analytical Psychology Vol. 3, Heinemann.
—— (1978) *Jungian Psychotherapy*, Chicester: John Wiley (Maresfield Library: Karnac, 1986).
—— (1978a) 'A discursive review of Robert Langs, *The Therapeutic Interaction*', *Journal of Analytical Psychology*, 23, 2.
—— (1978b) 'Some idiosyncratic behaviour of therapists', *Journal of Analytical Psychology*, 23, 2.
—— (1979) 'Analytical psychology in England', *Journal of Analytical Psychology*, 24, 4.
—— (1985) *Explorations into the Self*, Library of Analytical Psychology, Vol. 7, Academic Press.
—— (1989) 'Some historical reflections', *Journal of Analytical Psychology*, 34, 3.
—— (1990) 'The Jung–Klein hybrid', unpublished.
—— (1993) *The Making of an Analyst*, Free Associations.
—— Gordon, R., Hubback, J. and Lambert, K. (eds) (1974) *Technique in Jungian Analysis*, Library of Analytical Psychology, Vol. 2,Heinemann (Karnac, 1989).
Freud, S. (1909) 'Notes upon a case of obsessional neurosis', Vol. 10 in *The Standard Edition of the Complete Psychological Works of Sigmund Freud*, James Strachey (ed.), 24 vols, Hogarth (1953–73).
—— (1910) 'The future prospect of psychoanalytic therapy', in *SE*, Vol. 11.
—— (1918) 'Lines of advance in psycho-analytic therapy', in *SE*, Vol. 17.
—— (1918a) 'From the history of an infantile neurosis', in *SE*, Vol. 17.
—— (1920) 'Beyond the pleasure principle', in *SE*, Vol. 18.
Giovacchini, P. L. (1977) 'The impact of delusion and the delusion of impact', in *Contemporary Psychoanalysis*, 13.
Greenacre, P. (1968) 'The psychoanalytic process, transference and acting out', *International Journal of Psycho-analysis*, 49, 2–3.
Greenson, R. R. (1967) *The Technique and Practice of Psychoanalysis*, Hogarth.
Harding, E. (1963) 'A critical appreciation of Jackson's "Symbol formation and the delusional transference"', *Journal of Analytical Psychology*, 8, 2.
—— (1965) *The Parental Image*, New York: Putnam.
Heimann, P. (1950) 'On counter-transference', *International Journal of Psycho-analysis*, 31, 1.
—— (1960) 'Counter-transference II', *British Journal of Medical Psychology*, 33, 1.
Henderson, J. L. (1955) 'Resolution of the transference in the light of C. G. Jung's psychology', in *Report of the International Congress of Psychotherapy, Zürich, 1954*, Basle/New York: Klager.
—— (1967) *Thresholds of Initiation*, Middletown: Wesleyan U.P.
—— (1975) 'C. G. Jung: A reminiscent picture of his method', *Journal of Analytical Psychology*, 20, 2.

Hillman, J. (1962) 'Training and the C. G. Jung Institute, Zürich', *Journal of Analytical Psychology*, 7, 1.

—— (1962a) 'A note on multiple analysis and emotional climate at training institutes', *Journal of Analytical Psychology*, 7, 1.

Hillman, J., Plaut, A. and Fordham, M. (1962) 'Symposium on training, Part two', *Journal of Analytical Psychology*, 7, 1.

Hubback, J. (1966) 'VII sermones ad mortuos', *Journal of Analytical Psychology*, 11, 2.

—— (1982) 'Editorial introduction to symposium "How do I assess progress in Supervision?"', *Journal of Analytical Psychology*, 27, 2.

Jacobi, J. (1951) *Psychology of C. G. Jung*, Routledge & Kegan Paul.

—— (1967) *The Way of Individuation*, Hodder & Stoughton.

Jung, C. G. (1912) *Wandlungen und symbole der libido*, trans. by Beatrice Hinkle as *The Psychology of the Unconscious*, Moffat Yard, (1916).

—— (1913) 'The theory of psychoanalysis', Vol. 4 in *Collected Works of C. G. Jung*, 20 volumes with supplementary volumes, H. Read, M. Fordham, G. Adler and W. McGuire (eds), R. F. C. Hull, trans., Routledge & Kegan Paul.

—— (1914) 'Some crucial points in psycho-analysis: the Jung–Löy correspondence', *CW*, Vol. 4.

—— (1916/1928) *Two essays on analytical psychology*, *CW*, Vol. 7.

—— (1917) 'The psychology of the unconscious', in *CW*, Vol. 7.

—— (1921) 'The therapeutic value of abreaction', in *CW*, Vol. 16.

—— (1928) 'The relation of the ego to the unconscious', in *Two Essays on Analytical Psychology*, trans. H. G. and C. F. Baynes, Balliere, Tindall & Cox; revised in *CW*, Vol. 7.

—— (1930) 'Introduction to Kranefeldt's *Secret ways of the Mind*', in *CW*, Vol. 4.

—— (1931) 'The aims of psychotherapy', in *CW*, Vol. 16.

—— (1931a) 'Problems of modern psychotherapy', in *CW*, Vol. 16.

—— (1931b) 'The stages of life', in *CW*, Vol. 8.

—— (1935) 'The principles of practical psychotherapy', in *CW*, Vol. 16.

—— (1935a) 'What is psychotherapy?', in *CW*, Vol. 16.

—— (1936) *Dream Symbols of the Individuation Process*, seminar held at Bailey Island, Maine, USA, September 20–25. Mimeographed notes.

—— (1937) 'The realities of practical psychotherapy', in *CW*, Vol. 16.

—— (1938) 'Foreword to the 3rd edition of Frances Wickes' *Inner World of Childhood*', in *CW*, Vol. 17.

—— (1940) 'The psychology of the child archetype', in *CW*, Vol. 9, pt. 1.

—— (1943) 'Psychotherapy and a philosophy of life', in *CW*, Vol. 16.

—— (1944) *Psychology and Alchemy*, *CW*, Vol. 12.

—— (1946) 'The psychology of the transference', in *CW*, Vol. 16.

—— (1951) 'Fundamental questions of psychotherapy', in *CW*, Vol. 16.

—— (1952) 'Answer to Job', in *CW*, Vol. 11.

—— (1954) *The Practice of Psychotherapy*, *CW*, Vol. 16.

—— (1959) *Aion*, *CW*, Vol. 9, pt. 2.

—— (1955–6) *Mysterium Coniunctionis*, *CW*, Vol. 14.

—— (1963) *Memories, Dreams, Reflections*, Aniela Jaffé (ed.), Routledge & Kegan Paul.

—— (1968) *Analytical Psychology: Its theory and practice*, Routledge & Kegan Paul. As 'The Tavistock Lectures' in *CW*, Vol. 18.

—— (1987) *Seminare: Kindertraume*, L. Jung and M. Meyer-Grass (eds), *Gesammelte Werke, Suppl.-Bd.*

Jung and Löy (1914) 'Some crucial points in psychoanalysis', in *CW*, Vol. 4.

Kerenyi, C. (1960) *Asklepios: Archetypal Image of the Physician's Existence*, trans. R. Manheim, Thames & Hudson.

Kirsch, H. (1961) 'An analyst's dilemma', in *Current Trends in Analytical Psychology*, G. Adler (ed.), Tavistock.

Kirsch, T. (1976) 'The practice of multiple analysis in analytical psychology', *Contemporary Psychoanalysis*, 23, 2.

Kohut, H. (1971) *The Analysis of the Self*, New York: International Universities Press.

Kraemer, W. P. (1958) 'The dangers of unrecognized countertransference', *Journal of Analytical Psychology*, 3, 1.

Lambert, K. (1976) 'Resistance and counter-resistance', *Journal of Analytical Psychology*, 21, 2.

Langs, R. (1976) *The Therapeutic Interaction*, Vols 1, 2, New York: Jason Aronson.

Lindner, R. (1955) *The Fifty Minute Hour*, New York: Reinhardt (Free Associations, 1986).

Little, M. (1951) 'Counter-transference and the patient's response to it', *International Journal of Psycho-analysis*, 32.

—— (1957) '"R", the analyst's total response to his patient's needs', *International Journal of Psycho-analysis*, 38, 3/4.

—— (1960) 'Countertransference V', *British Journal of Medical Psychology*, 33, 1.

—— (1981) 'Transference neurosis and transference psychosis', New York: Jason Aronson (Free Associations, 1986).

Marshak, M. D. (1964) 'The significance of the patient in the training of analysts', *Journal of Analytical Psychology*, 9, 1.

Meier, C. A. (1959) 'Projection, transference and subject–object relation', *Journal of Analytical Psychology*, 4, 1.

—— (1968) *Ancient Incubation and Modern Psychotherapy*, trans. M. Curtis, Evanston: Northwestern University Press. (Revised as *Healing, Dream and Ritual*, Daimon, 1989.)

Meltzer, D. (1973) *Sexual States of Mind*, Ballinluig: Clunie Press.

Milner, M. (1969) *The Hands of the Living God*, Hogarth (Virago, 1988).

Money-Kyrle, R. (1956) 'Normal countertransference and some of its deviations', *International Journal of Psycho-analysis*, 37, 4/5.

Moody, R. (1955) 'The relation of the personal and transpersonal elements in the transference', in *Report of the International Congress of Psychotherapy, Zürich 1954*, Basle/New York: Klager.

—— (1955a) 'On the function of countertransference', *Journal of Analytical Psychology*, 1, 1.

Newton, K. (1961) 'Personal reflections on training', *Journal of Analytical Psychology*, 6, 2.

Plaut, A. B. (1955) 'Research into transference phenomena', in *Report of the International Congress of Psychotherapy, Zürich, 1954*, Basle/New York: Klager.

—— (1956) 'The transference in analytical psychology', *British Journal of Medical Psychology*, 29, 1.

—— (1961) 'A dynamic outline of the training situation', *Journal of Analytical Psychology*, 6, 2.

—— (1962) 'Training and psychopathology', *Journal of Analytical Psychology*, 7, 2.

—— (1966) 'Reflections about not being able to imagine', *Journal of Analytical Psychology*, 11, 2.

—— (1970) 'Comment: on not incarnating the archetype', *Journal of Analytical Psychology*, 29, 1.

Racker, H. (1968) *Transference and Countertransference*, Hogarth (Maresfield Library: Karnac, 1988).

Reik, T. (1949) *Listening with the Third Ear: The Inner Experience of a Psychoanalyst*, New York: Farrar, Straus.

Rosen, V. (1961) 'The relevance of style', *International Journal of Psycho-analysis*, 42, 4–5.

Rosenfeld, H. A. (1965) *Psychotic States: A Psychoanalytic Approach*, Hogarth (Maresfield Library: Karnac, 1990).

—— (1988) *Impasse and Interpretation*, Routledge.

Samuels, A. (1989) 'Fred Plaut in conversation with Andrew Samuels', *Journal of Analytical Psychology*, 34, 2.

Schwartz-Salant, N. (1984) 'Archetypal factors underlying sexual acting-out in the transference/countertransference process', *Chiron: A Review of Jungian Analysis.*

—— (1989) *The Borderline Personality*, Wilmette: Chiron Publications.

—— (1991) 'Vision, interpretation and the interactive field', *Journal of Analytical Psychology*, 36, 3.

Scott, W. C. M. (1949) 'The "body scheme" in psychotherapy', *British Journal of Medical Psychology*, 22, 3/4.

Searles, H. (1959) 'The effort to drive the other person crazy – an element in the aetiology and psychotherapy of schizophrenia', *British Journal of Medical Psychology*, 32, 1.

—— (1965) *Collected Papers on Schizophrenia and Related Subjects*, Hogarth (Maresfield Library: Karnac, 1986.

Spiegelman, J. (ed.) (1988) *Jungian Analysts: Their Visions and Vulnerabilities*, Phoenix: Falcon Press.

Stein, L. (1955) 'Loathsome women', *Journal of Analytical Psychology*, 1, 1.

—— (1955a) 'The terminology of transference', in *Report of the International Congress of Psychotherapy, Zürich 1954*, Basle/New York: Klager.

—— (1967) 'Introducing not-self', *Journal of Analytical Psychology*, 12, 2.

Stone, H. (1964) 'Reflections of an ex-trainee on his training', Journal of Analytical Psychology, 9, 1.

Strachey, J. (1934) 'The nature of the therapeutic action of psycho-analysis', *International Journal of Psycho-analysis*, 15.

Strauss, R. (1960) 'Countertransference IV', *British Journal of Medical Psychology*, 33, 1.

—— (1964) 'The archetype of separation', in *The Archetype*, Basle/New York, Klager.

Whitmont, E. (1957) 'Magic and the psychology of compulsive states', *Journal of Analytical Psychology*, 2, 1.

Wickes, F. C. (1959) *The Inner World of Man*, New York/Toronto: Farrar & Reinhardt.

Winnicott, D. W. (1947) 'Hate in the countertransference', in *Collected Papers*, Tavistock (1958).

—— (1960) 'Ego distortions in terms of true and false self', in *Maturational Processes and the Facilitating Environment*, Hogarth.

—— (1960a) 'Countertransference III', *British Journal of Medical Psychology*, 33, 1.

Wisdom, J. O. (1967) 'Testing an interpretation within a session', *International Journal of Psycho-analysis*, 48, 1.

Index

abaissement 124
acting out 22–3, 37, 60, 152, 155
active imagination 2, 19, 20, 21, 24, 27, 28–9, 34, 85, 87, 108, 120, 123, 150, 154, 155, 183
'actual situation/present' 25–6, 38, 88
Adler, Gerhard 12, 20, 21, 22, 28, 29, 85
Adler, Hella 6
Adlerian psychology 14, 135, 199, 201
affects 46, 47, 92, 96, 121, 135, 141, 164, 166, 168–72, 188
alchemical analogy of interaction 85, 88, 90, 95
alchemical element in 'The psychology of the transference' 14, 29, 123, 124–32
alchemical myths/texts 135, 136–7, 185
alchemy 17, 150
amplification 2, 3, 39–40, 85, 87, 89, 90, 162, 181–2, 190, 191, 194, 198
analysis 16, 50, 177; as dialectical process 5, 36, 40, 70, 71, 89, 91, 96, 105, 109, 161, 172 (*see also* interaction); open/closed system in 133, 161, 164, 172; relation to everyday life 18–19
analyst: as a child 171, 175n19; as container/frame 136, 173n5, 178; authority 165; change as result of interviews 5, 16, 39, 42, 111, 171, 175n18, 176n34; creative illness/psychic infection 43, 113, 130, 163 (*see also* introjection, of patient's psychopathology); deviations from analytic attitude 168–70; embodying archetypal image 39 (*see also* incarnating); errors 142–3, 168–9; involvement in analysis 5, 13, 90, 96, 183, 201; necessity for analysis 116, 162, 181; part played by personality 6, 12–13, 16, 17, 40, 41, 43, 49, 82, 86, 93, 116, 118, 123, 133, 162, 172, 199; personal confessions by 33–4; physical reliability 136; qualities 159; self-analysis 148, 150; significance of sex of 40, 158, 160; states of identity 133–4; style 95, 108, 109n1, 172; typology 157–8, 160n1; *see also* affects; counter-transference; interaction
analytic interview 16–17, 38, 85, 149, 167; non-verbal communication 152, 154, 175n19; not knowing beforehand 39, 167, 168, 182, 184, 191–2, 194, 197, 199–207; physical setting 13, 24, 121, 149, 154, 157; time and frequency 17, 19, 26, 122–3, 136, 155, 157; time and frequency of training interview 63, 75
anima 43, 44, 74, 75, 130, 131
animus 43, 44, 74, 75, 107, 130, 131, 132
archetypal counter-transference, illusory 33
archetypal ideas 3, 17, 26
archetypal imagery 23, 24, 28, 74, 120, 154
archetypal projections 24, 36–7, 39, 53, 159
archetypal transference 2, 15, 20–1, 25, 112, 119, 120, 122, 123, 124, 134, 149–50; in training 53
archetypes, archetypal forms 9, 13, 15, 17, 35, 41, 43, 71, 74, 106, 109, 145, 150, 154, 185, 187, 196, 199–202; theory of 162, 163

Balint, M. 143
Bash, K.W. 73, 77

Baynes, C.F. 138n2
Baynes, H.G. 3–4, 12, 13, 40, 85, 138n2
behaviour therapy 133
Bernard, Claude 184
Bion, W.R. 102, 122, 145, 161, 175n18, 176n34, 184, 185, 192, 198, 201
British Psychoanalytic Society 118

case material: Fordham and use of 3–4, 80; Fordham's 31–3, 44–5, 46, 47, 99–101, 150–4, 168, 169–71, 192–6, 201–3, 204–6
castration anxiety, case of 178
child analysis 9, 15, 182, 183–4; dreams 2–3; training in 9–10, 177–9
childhood 9, 10, 74, 75, 182, 187; individuation in 15, 75, 91; *see also* infants
childhood, analysis of 3, 136, 183, 184; in training analysis 74–5, 77–80; *see also* infantile states
Children as Individuals (Fordham) 91
Christianity, Jung's use of 123, 130
collective/individual, Jung and 88–90
collective unconscious 162
collectivism 88, 130
communitas 190, 191
compensation, theory of 14
concurrent analyses *see* multiple analysis
confession, Jung and 116, 123
confusion of zones 145
conjunctio 43, 44, 131, 186, 187n1, 190, 191
consciousness 88; *see also* ego; perceptions
contiguous boundary concepts 43
counter-transference 6, 16, 30–48, 112, 135, 136, 148, 157, 161–76, 182, 183; case 99–101, 168; and defences of self 141–2; Jung and 30, 31, 41–2, 95, 109, 130, 163; and technique 95–101, 103, 104–5, 165; in training analysis 70, 71, 79, 82; use and definition of term 11, 30-1, 41, 172–3
counter-transference, delusional 195
counter-transference, positive 108–9
counter-transference, supervisor's 53
counter-transference, trainee's 52, 54, 92
counter-transference illusions 25, 31–5, 41, 44–6, 82, 97, 98, 103, 148, 164, 165, 167, 174n9
counter-transference neurosis 104
counter-transference syntony *see* syntonic counter-transference
crossed projections 99

Davidson, Dorothy 10, 108
defences 21, 23, 24, 69, 139–40, 152; analyst's 25, 133; of self 133, 139–46, 172, 175n24, 181, 195, 196
defensive psychosis 72
deintegration 36, 93, 137, 146, 197
delusional counter-transference 195
delusional transference 69, 82, 101, 103, 104, 108, 132, 134, 140, 145, 146, 175n25
dependent transference 24–6, 27, 28; *see also under* infantile states
depressions, case involving 150–3
distillation 95, 108, 109
dream analysis 19, 20, 21, 44, 85, 87, 89, 120, 122, 123, 154–5, 162, 182, 183
dreams 34, 102, 124; theory of 88

Edinger, E.F. 73; Fordham's reply to his comment on supervision and training 57–8
ego 24, 43, 44, 71, 74; analyst's 33–4, 47–8, 93; splitting of *see* splitting
ego defences 24, 139–40
ego development 15, 35, 137; of analyst 93; in children 15, 36; self and 26, 36, 137
ego functioning, technique as manifestation of 106
ego/non-ego 120
ego psychology 139, 143, 147
Ellenberger, H.F. 113
Emch, Minna 51, 60
emotions *see* affects; primitive emotional states
energy, psychic *see* libido
erotic transference 115, 116, 117, 118, 121, 134
ethics in analysis, Jung and 135–6

Fairbairn, W.R.D. 23
false self 92, 133
fantasy 19, 20, 21, 22, 102
Federn, P.F. 104
Fenichel, O. 22
Fifth International Psychoanalytic Congress 117
fixation points 25, 26
Fordham, Frieda 6, 75, 91, 181
Fordham, Michael 12, 26, 50, 75, 85, 89, 91, 97, 109, 110, 137, 159, 160, 164,